Thirteen Years of School

What Students Really Think

Lisa Scherff

ScarecrowEducation
Lanham, Maryland • Toronto • Oxford
2005

KH

Published in the United States of America
by ScarecrowEducation
An imprint of The Rowman & Littlefield Publishing Group, Inc.
4501 Forbes Boulevard, Suite 200, Lanham, Maryland 20706
www.scaroweducation.com

PO Box 317
Oxford
OX2 9RU, UK

British Library Cataloguing in Publication Information Available

Library of Congress Cataloging-in-Publication Data

Scherff, Lisa, 1968–
  Thirteen years of school : what students really think / Lisa Scherff.
    p. cm.
  Includes bibliographical references and index.
  ISBN 1-57886-200-0 (pbk. : alk. paper)
  1. High school students—United States—Attitudes. 2. High school students' writings,
American. I. Title.

LA229.S312 2005
373.18'0973—dc22

2004021560

♾™ The paper used in this publication meets the minimum requirements of
American National Standard for Information Sciences—Permanence of
Paper for Printed Library Materials, ANSI/NISO Z39.48-1992.
Manufactured in the United States of America.

9/19/06

For my former students at Estero and Rickards High Schools because . . .

"As adults, we must really be interested in what
the students' 'answers' are" (Sizer & Sizer, 2003, p. 145).

For my parents, who let me learn the power of words.

For Ted Hipple, mentor and friend.

Photo by Bonnie Grosse

School

It's for the hip-hop, the funk
For the prep for the punk
For the young and the old
The shy and the bold
For the strong and the weak
For the out-spoken and the meek
For the gay and the straight
The love and the hate
It's for the laughter and tears
For the joy throughout the years
For the night and the day
The stop and the play
For the mudstains on the carpet
For the booze we were caught with
For the treats and the tricks
The songs and their lyrics
The strings and the picks
The drums and the sticks
For the rockers, the jocks
The criminals and cops
For the tired and the sleepy
For math and PE
For the torn up and broken
The many, the token
It's for peaceful and dramatic
Serious and sarcastic
For the victim and the easy target
Where you can be judged, you can be outsmarted
A place that is overwhelming, where there is plenty to do
A place to be welcome, a place to be you.
—April Hood, Aptos, CA, 9th grade

Contents

Photo by LeeAnn Jerome

Preface

Schools exist for children, but children are often seen as the school's clients, as its powerless people. (Sizer & Sizer, 2003, p. 142)

Stories are the best way to portray realities. (Palmer, 2003, p. 68)

This year's high school seniors were born in or around 1986, the year I graduated from high school. Because of what I experienced in those 4 years, I decided to become a teacher. My model was Mrs. Harris, my eleventh-grade English teacher, because she cared about us and what she taught, treated us with respect, and made learning fun. However, upon entering the profession in 1996, I became acutely aware of issues I rarely faced, or was too naive to face, when I was in high school. Many of my students thought school was a waste of time, teachers did not care, class work was trivial, administrative methods were unfair, and that they were set up by "the system" to either succeed or fail. Sadly, I agreed with some of them.

Although almost all colleagues, and others I met while teaching, were caring, dedicated, and talented professionals, a few were "waiting to retire" while they spent their time at school; others were underprepared in their teaching area (or teaching out of field); several were antagonistic toward and distrustful of their students; a couple did the minimal requirements of the job (or what union guidelines outlined); and then there were those just plain angry at the world. Sometimes we had the necessary resources to teach; other times we did not. Some classrooms had air-conditioning in the summer; others were stifling. Most often, the school was clean; at other times trash lined the halls and graffiti covered the walls. We were bombarded with mandates and decrees from those on the outside, a majority of whom had not spent any considerable amount of time in school since they themselves graduated, telling us how and what to teach and what the consequences would be if not done to their satisfaction. Because of all this, I wonder to what extent, positively or negatively, we impacted our students.

Recommendations for improving America's schools arrive from all arenas and spectators—business leaders, politicians, standardized test developers, retirees, community members, school faculty and administrators, college and university personnel, and parents. Some argue for a longer school year and/or day. Others want workplace skills promoted in schools. Suggestions for more technology, direct instruction, and test preparation workshops appear from various groups. Although some, even many, of these proposals are sound and offered with good intentions, few, if any, are given or implemented with student input. Yet, students are the players in the myriad programs, some haphazardly put into place (and quickly removed and replaced when not successful), designed to increase achievement. What would students say about their schools, curriculum, and teachers if given the chance? A chance without repercussions? In the current era of accountability and the demise of "good education," the answers to these questions are more than pertinent.

In researching for my dissertation I surveyed nearly 4,000 high school students in Florida regarding the work they completed in their English classes during the school year. Although the results were remarkable in themselves, it was the 60-plus pages of written comments that were a landmark. What I realized was that students had strong opinions about what went on in schools (and I only asked them about English classes): lack of and misappropriation of fiscal resources, condition of the schools, teacher quality, standardized tests, unequal distribution of resources among academic tracks, and curricular matters. That led me to the idea for this book.

I find, like Pope (2001), that while there are a plethora of studies concerning students' achievement, behavior, culture, and dropout rates, very little information comes from students' own point of view. We have not questioned students enough about their experiences—especially students from a wide range of backgrounds, geographic locations, and grade levels. Yet, we decree when to go to school, at what point students are considered proficient, their worthiness to attend postsecondary institutions, and whether or not they are eligible to earn a standard diploma.

I recently came upon a book on my shelf called *Schools That Learn*, which has a perfect analogy regarding students and schools: "Students are the only players who see all sides of the nested systems of education, yet they are typically the people who have the least influence on its design . . . we see students not just as passive recipients of knowledge, but as cocreators of knowledge and participants in the evolution of the school" (Senge, 2000, pp. 12–13).

This book is an attempt to better address students' concerns and suggestions for maintaining and improving schools. Over a year, students from across the country, in grades K–12, were given the opportunity to submit stories, letters, editorials, and art representing their viewpoints. Using the Internet I searched state by state and school by school asking teachers for help with this project. I also posted queries on student-sponsored websites. Flyers were posted in classrooms around the country. By January 2004, I had my first set of submissions. Each week brought another batch until I had nearly 700 writings by March 2004.

What follows in this book are samples, representative of what many students had to say. To protect the students, only first names and locations are cited (unless students and parents specifically asked me to provide full names). To further preserve anonymity, only the first letter of schools' names is provided and individual teachers are not identified. In an attempt to maintain student voices as much as possible I did not change their words, nor did I correct their grammar or spelling. In some cases, portions of their submissions were omitted to keep the book from getting too lengthy. Unless a grade level is specifically noted, writings in this book express the views of high school students.

~

Acknowledgments

This book would not be possible without the help of the many teachers from around the country who agreed to let their students write for me. With busy schedules and pressure to prepare for state tests, they created time for students to voice their opinions.

I am also eternally grateful to Audra Peterson, a former colleague at Rickards High School in Tallahassee, Florida, who volunteered to read initial chapters. Her valuable comments and suggestions saved me time and headaches during revisions.

But, above all, I thank the students for their honest, insightful, and touching accounts of how school has affected them. I wish you all the best of luck and I hope your dreams come true.

Photo by Jose Elias

~

Introduction

The student is the one person who sees all the classes, the stress at home, the multiple conflicting messages from media and the total environments. Kids know when the overall workload is too big or small, when the stress level is too high or the level of respect too low. But they have not power or standing in the system. Their opinions are discounted. They are, after all, just kids—in a system run by adults supposedly for their benefit. I have come to believe that the real hope for deep and enduring processes of evolution in schools lies with students. They have a deep passion for making schools work. They are connected to the future in ways that no adult is. They have imagination and ways of seeing things that have not yet been reshaped by the formal education process. And they are crying out wanting to be involved, to become more responsible for their environment. (Senge, 2000, p. 58)

Two decades ago American was given a warning: "Our nation is at risk. Our once unchallenged preeminence in commerce, industry, science, and technological innovation is being overtaken by competitors throughout the world. . . . We report to the American people that while we take justifiable pride in what our schools and colleges have historically accomplished and contributed to the United States and the well-being of its people, the educational foundations of our society are presently being eroded by a rising tide of mediocrity that threatens our very future as a Nation and a people" (U.S. Department of Education, 1983, p. 5). As in the 1980s with *A Nation at Risk* and America 2000, and in the 1990s with Goals 2000, we are in the middle of a major reform effort aimed at fixing the performance of our schools (Eisner, 2003). Some critics announce that students lag behind those in other countries in mathematics and science, aren't prepared for the workforce, take fewer advanced courses, and have lower SAT scores than their counterparts 20 years ago.

However, data tell a different story about the state of U.S. education. For example, the percentage of students wanting more than just a high school diploma rose from 73% in 1980 to 90% in 1990 (NCES, 1998). The number of students going immediately to college also grew, from around 45% in 1982 to roughly 62% in 1992 (U.S. Department of Commerce, as cited in Smith, 1995). By 1992, public high school graduates earned an average of 2.6 more course units than those in 1982, most of those in academic areas. Likewise, students were taking a greater number of and more difficult courses. In 1982, only 48% of secondary students took geometry, compared to 70% in 1992. In science, only 10% of graduates in 1982 took biology, chemistry, and physics; in 1992, that number grew to 22% (Smith, 1995). Since 1984, the percentage of students taking advanced placement (AP) examinations has more than doubled. In addition, the number of students taking the SAT over the 10-year period grew from 33% to 41% and scores did not decrease (Smith, 1995).

These encouraging findings occurred despite some troubling statistics. In the 2001–2002 school year 46,969 schools were declared as Title I eligible, meaning they were in high poverty areas and, typically, had low achievement levels. Thirty-seven percent of our nation's students were eligible for free or reduced lunches (the high was 59.1% in Louisiana). Mirroring national crime trends, between 1989 and 1995 the "street gang" presence at public schools grew from 15% to 28% (NCES, 1998).

The Politics of Education

Most, if not all, critical decisions about K–12 education are being made by those "outside" the system, like politicians. The problem is that state policymakers are, in the majority of cases, both geographically and psychologically distanced from the schools, which makes it difficult for them to be responsive to actual needs (Marshall, 1988). Most Americans listen to "outside" groups when forming beliefs about school-aged children. A recent survey by Child Trends, for example, found that nearly 75% of Americans reported that their views were guided by the media. Moreover, most in the survey held more negative viewpoints regarding children than were actually true (Guzman, Lippman, Moore, & O'Hare, 2003).

In the mid-1980s, researchers identified 18 groups that policy actors declared as influential to educational policymaking. At the top of the list were individual members of the legislature and at the bottom were producers of educational materials (Mitchell, Wirt, & Marshall, 1986). A disturbing fact is that students were nowhere on the list. McLaren (2003) writes of the flurry of accountability schemes, management pedagogies, and rationalized curricula now flooding the schools, yet there is silence regarding students; many times schools do not allow them to acknowledge their individual and collective voices. Policymakers, working in their own unique organizational cultures, are both geographically and psychologically distanced from schools, making it difficult for them to be reactive to tangible needs. The consequences are often badly chosen, nonimplemented, and incompatible policies and practices (Marshall, 1988). Yet, they, like other "outsiders," are quick to point out the failings of educational systems, two of the most common being a lack of rigor and low student achievement. Interestingly, these attacks come from those who were "educated in the days when the only required courses were driver's ed and home economics" (Ohanian, 1999, p. 22).

Why Listen to Students?

Why should we begin to examine students' viewpoints? As Sizer and Sizer (1999) note, "Schools exist for children, but children are often seen as the school's clients, as its powerless people. They are told that they are in school not because of what they know but because of what they don't know" (p. 20). Susan Ohanian (1999) writes of the disconnect between politicians and students: "It is typical of an education bureaucrat to assume that students . . . must be behind in something called basic skills. . . . Schools can't improve themselves if they ignore the students. It seems such a simple matter to ask our students what they really dislike about school and talk about what we might do to change it" (pp. 20, 23).

There are added reasons to listen to students' opinions such as school improvement and academic achievement, which are interrelated factors. Numerous studies (see, for example, Doyle, 1977; Winne & Marx, 1980; Wittrock, 1986) have documented the importance of students' beliefs and perceptions, linking them with teacher effects on learning, the development of teaching theories, and an analysis of how instruction is put into practice, all of which have potential to improve outcomes. Thus, gathering, reading, and presenting student voices from all backgrounds, schools, and locations are integral to improving educational experiences.

This book is unique in terms of its research pool: first person anecdotes from K–12 students from across the country. To get a real sense of what America's students thought about their educational experiences I went to them and asked for help. Using the Internet, I spent weeks e-mailing teachers at elementary, middle, and high schools outlining the goals of this project. The response was incredible. By the end of January 2004, I had received over 150 stories, and they kept coming on a weekly basis. By the end of April, I tallied over 800 submissions.

Through the chapters in this book I hope to accomplish what Ornstein (2003) notes as important: "The focus of . . . research should be on the learner, not the teacher; on the feelings and attitudes of the student, not on knowledge and information; and on the long-term development and growth of the students, not on short-term objectives or specific teacher tasks" (2003, p. 81).

The framework for the first five chapters comes from Eisner's (1992) dimensions of schooling. According to Eisner there are five aspects of schooling that must be addressed if schools are to truly be reformed—the intentional, the structural, the curricular, the pedagogical, and the evaluative. I chose his work as the frame to begin the book because, in my opinion, if we want schools to improve, we must utilize student input in the process.

The focus of Chapter 1, the intentional dimension, refers to goals or aims, stated and hidden, that are formulated for the school or a classroom. Or, as Eisner (1992) asks, "What really counts?" The structural dimension, covered in Chapter 2, concerns issues such as the way the school day is divided and how subjects are assigned to time blocks. Chapter 3, the curricular dimension, involves the quality of curricula, content goals, and the activities employed to engage students in them. The pedagogical dimension, discussed in Chapter 4, is what and how teachers teach. Chapter 5 presents the evaluative dimension, which refers to the ways in which evaluation practices influence students' outlooks. These chapters, when put together, become "the average day" that students experience.

The remaining chapters developed from common threads among students' submissions. Stress at school is the spotlight of Chapter 6. I was truly unprepared for the degree to which students, even those in elementary school, are "stressed out." In Chapter 7 students talk about what they have learned from school. What are their remembrances about the schooling they have already had? What lessons will they take with them once they leave? Chapter 8 examines the future—what do students envision for themselves? What does "school improvement" mean to them? Chapter 9 presents the "good and the bad"—experiences that made a positive impression and missed opportunities that can never be offered again. Finally, Chapter 10 is a compilation of students' "stories" that needed to be told. Funny, sad, enlightening, and impressive, they needed a chapter of their own.

$\sim$

The Intentional Dimension

To tell you the truth, I do not like school. I don't like anyone in my school because everyone is fake. A____ High School is a prison. I honestly cannot even wait until I graduate.

—Anonymous

Despite the widely publicized notion of equally high standards for all students, few outside of education recognize and understand that there are two systems of standards operating—the stated and the hidden. For Eisner (1992) the intentional dimension refers to goals or aims that are formulated for the school or a classroom, both stated and hidden. The stated curriculum explains that part of the curriculum that is public like state standards, district originated course guidelines, and school-based scope and sequence documents. Teacher experience, beliefs, and practices, materials used in the classroom, and assessments that may not be formally articulated make up the hidden curriculum.

The stated curriculum is that which is formally articulated, either by state or local governments or boards of education. Usually in the form of standards and benchmarks, this curriculum is what is endorsed and taught in schools. However, no matter what instructional materials are purchased and used by schools, or what teachers are directed to teach to address these standards, other instruction always takes place. It is this "other" that constitutes the hidden curriculum.

Gerald Posner (1988), in The Curriculum: Problems, Politics, and Possibilities, *raises questions about the hidden curriculum: What are the features of schools' hidden or implicit curriculum, and to what extent do these aspects of schooling mediate teaching the official curricula? To what extent does curriculum organization presuppose* and serve to "legitimate a rigid hierarchy between teacher and taught"? How does the curriculum enable a school to achieve its primary purposes of social reproduction and hegemony?

As a result of the social organization of schools and instruction, some students learn they can achieve, and are due achievement, because of their position, while others at the lower end learn their limited achievement is their fate in life. Thus, because of the different educational experiences, students are socialized to accept societal roles (Oakes, 1985). Taylor (2003) found that urban students felt their environment as a "trap" and that it was partly to blame for their lack of success. Students also believed that school was not a place for an "education," but for meeting friends and hanging out. Failure in school, then, cannot necessarily be interpreted as resulting simply from individual deficiency. Students sometimes experience the conflict between school and street-corner cultures—school is about knowledge, and the streets are of knowledge (McLaren, 2003).

Another aspect of the hidden curriculum is the behavior and actions of administrators and teachers—the difference between what is supposed to happen and what actually happens. Students will be more encouraged to learn when they can connect success or failure to their effort, or lack of it, rather than to outside things such as people (Ornstein, 2003; Wittrock, 1986). What concerns me the most after reading students' stories is that many who felt schools did "not care" saw it as a normal part of life, and they accepted their fates as the status quo.

For the most part, the student writings in this chapter point to the hidden side of school—its atmosphere—including cliques, teachers, and staff members. It is a preface of sorts for the chapters that follow. Welcome to the world of students.

～

I Hear This High School Singing

I hear this high school singing, the varied cliques I hear,
Those of GHS, each one singing his as it should be gay and strong,
The Goths singing their Marilyn Manson as they stand against their wall,
The Preps singing as they adjust their Abercrombie polo shirts,
The Posers singing about imitating everything they see,
The Jocks singing about the games they lost this season,
The Snobs singing about their own friends,
The Dorks singing about the formula for slope-intercept,
The Skanks with their short skirts singing as they smoke,
The day that belongs to the day—at night the party of GHS students,
Singing with open mouths their strong melodious songs.
—Alison, Casey, Savannah, Natalie, Knoxville, TN

⌒

One of the major problems in school is racism, because when the white boys get in fights they do not do anything to them, but when the Mexicans get in fights they take them to juvy. The sheriff from the school just hangs around the Mexican people to see if they are doing something bad so he can take them to the office. They also judge you by what you are wearing. I am saying this because it happened to me. There was a guy and he was telling me stuff so we started fighting. When they took us to the office, the sheriff said that it was a gang fight because of what I was wearing. I had a brown shirt with blue on it, and the other guy had a red line on his backpack. When the sheriff saw that, he said that I was going to go to juvy. They took me to juvy but they did not do anything to the other guy.—Jaime Fernandez, Aptos, CA

⌒

The way a school is run, or managed, will affect attitudes towards school. When you make a school too strict the learning atmosphere disappears. An example of this is bathroom privileges. Something that petty will cause you to be put in time out or sent to the office. If you have to ask to go to the restroom then there is a problem. If the administrators are focusing on the small things like this what are the students being taught. Students get upset about actions like that, and they cause the negative attitudes. All the rules and restrictions lead to drop-outs and things of that sort.—Sloan, Vero Beach, FL

⌒

One of the great "things" about P____ is our principal's and teacher's positive attitude towards our school. They are always saying we are the best school in America.—Philip, Vestavia Hills, AL, 6th grade

⌒

School is an envierment were kids and sometimes adults go to learn how to do math, science, and learn how to read and write. Some people just go to do something all day instead of going to learn. People I know come to school for the guys or the girls; they don't come to school to learn. Some do but the rest of them come because there parents make them go. I am going to school so I can go to college and become a nurse or a doctor. I'm going to go into dissing when I go to high school. I think school is a good eniverment for kids to learn and to study. 10 out of 20 kids go to school because there parents don't want to see them during the day. The other 10 go to school to learn and become smart and go to college.—Janelle, Hudson, FL, middle school

～

The things that goes on at my school are sometimes good and sometimes bad but mostly good. I like it because it's not filled with a lot of drama between students and teachers. My school has fights almost every Friday because of rumors that people starts about the person that they want to fight but I really don't understand why they just can't talk about it between one another.

The people here are mostly cool, smart and laid back because they're not hated by anyone really but they're also very outgoing and very respectfull to other students' opinions. The sport games we have are really good at attracting people because the athletes who are playing loves what they do and are dedicated what they do. My school is cool but boring too but I like it and I wish more people will decide to come here to graduate and get a better education so they can get a better chance to be accepted to any colleges/universities of their choice.—Dontay, Melbourne, FL

～

At first I was rather excited about starting high school. This was because I knew I would be on the cross-country team. However, when the first day of school came my feelings started to change. In first period everything was still okay, due to keyboarding being a simple class. Then came second period, Algebra II, when my excitement turned to dislike. Next up to third period, English I, when my dislike turned to horror. This chain reaction continued on through the day with Physical Science and World History. My spirit diminished with each new class. Until sixth period, P.E., when I returned to my sanctuary, running. It was then that it dawned on me; school will no longer be the breeze I had come to recognize it as.

From that point on I dedicated myself to my studies, which brings us to the present. Though it still requires the same effort and hard work, it has now become routine and that dreadful first impression of high school has almost completely faded. Arriving at this point I have had to employ the use of a few skills instrumental for successful learning, my ability to meet deadlines, produce a quality product, and self-discipline.—Aaron, Moreno Valley, CA

∼

Sometimes school is fun, and sometimes it's very boring. I like going to school to see my friends but I hate doing all the work. I'm very lucky to be going to M___ High because it's such a nice school with good teachers, but sometimes I wish I went to the high school where all my best friends go. If I had a choice to pick whether to stay in school or drop out, I know I would stay because it seems like you can't do anything without your education these days.—Ashlee, Inwood, WV

∼

What really goes on during the average school day? Many things. Some good things, but mostly bad things. Let's start with the good things. Students coming to get their education and graduate. Also another good thing is many students learn new things every day. That helps us out and the long run in life.—Dominic, Tallahassee, FL

∼

A day at school. There is not much to it. Just do your work remember to take your hat off and try to keep you nose clean. I usually try to develop a really good respectful relationship with my teachers, it makes the class feel more desired than required. I usually see a couple of drug deals a day. I used to be involved in most of them, but have changed my ways. I don't really mind school as much as I used to. I learned early just to be laid back and go with the flow.—Jason, Tallahassee, FL

∼

During the average school day you see different events occur. Everybody has his or her own opinion about everyone else. They call one group of people something and then other groups something else. Fights don't happen every day. You might hear about people not getting along, but usually nothing too big.—Jennifer, Inwood, WV

∼

I am a senior student at A___ High School in San Jose, California. I am student at an American school, but I don't have enough experience about a high school because I came to United States at 2002 May. So I have just 1½ years of experience. However, I have a lot of things to tell about my high school. Now I like to talk about an average school day. In one word, it is very boring. Firstly, students do not have to do anything. When I was in India, schools were not very funny. In America students are really just go to class and chat with friends. My computer class for example, I don't know what students are doing at this class. Class teacher just sits at the back and students are getting on Internet, sending emails, and chatting with others. I don't know why my teacher is doing like this. Maybe she doesn't care about students. Freedom of students is one other saddest thing at school. It really ruins students. Students are totally free to do anything or to say something at school, basically at class. Students are saying very bad words in class. They are behaving very inappropriate, but teachers do not have the full rights to punish them. They can just say stop it or send them to administration office. These students are really bothering other students.—Jose, San Jose, CA

∼

The main thing I like about school is that we aren't babyed around by teachers, and we are trusted to do our work or we will get the grade that we deserve.—Katie, Vestavia Hills, AL, 6th grade

∼

School is a good place to be except that there is no fun. Education is the most important thing in life, because it can get you to places that you want to get to. In an average day at school, kids work, talk, eat lunch, and do things they have to do.—Justin, Inwood, WV

∼

What I really think about school . . . for one, school greatly contributes to the monotony factor of my life, yet day in and day out, still I go. Some function of what little knowledge we attain is, I'm told, truly useful and applicable to my future use in some seemingly trivial aspect of existence. So we trudge on. At times I think the most useful purpose of school is that contrast it provides with the invigorating and interesting events that occur, that I can better appreciate them. Other times I'm sure school's best function is that it keeps us young rascals and misanthropes off the streets and in another state of rather aimless distraction. Thoreau stated that "the mass of men lead lives of quiet desperation," but still I think aimless distraction more appropriate. What are our lives but seemingly endless parades of movies, video games, shows, books, work and sporting events? Does this have any purpose at all. Luckily (or hopefully) our lives and who we are remain separate from the frivolous activities in which we engage. In that respect school has some use in the occasion that one's teachers are of more than ordinary refute, for us impressionable minds have some occasion to express opinion and think more than is customary.—Sarah, Merritt Island, FL

⌇

Well, there is so much to say about school, I don't know where to begin. In school, we learn information, whether it's useful to use or not, we learn it.—Anonymous, Vestavia Hills, AL, 6th grade

⌇

There are a lot of things that goes on in the average school day. From the time you step off the bus there are people looking at you bad. Or there is your friends greeting you. Teachers going to the office to get there mail. Then is the part of the day when you have to change classes. People bumping you and not saying excuse me or blaming you. People stepping on your new sneakers.—Uriah, Melbourne, FL

⌇

Try being a senior that has just moved to Amesbury and does not know anyone and then you start a brand new school year last year. You feel out of place and you don't want to be there because everyone is so judgmental and it hurts. The teachers just make you feel worse because you don't know anybody. You feel left out and you can't talk to anybody because you don't trust anyone. What should be done about that is make it so one teacher and a group of students are welcoming so that person knows they are being welcomed to a new school. To me school is fun at times. Being able to see your friends are the best part, but what cannot be stopped is the drama and fighting. Most of the time it is girls doing all of the fights. I guess you need to get used to that when you are in high school. But it is wonderful to be able to learn things you never knew about, being able to have an open mind about things. School really isn't as bad as everyone thinks it is. All you have to do is take the time and do what you got to do. Without school how do you expect to get along in life. ___ High School is a good school to go too once you give it a chance.—Anonymous, Amesbury, MA

~

My average day at school is usually very long and boring, but at times it can [be] very interesting. 8:00 AM is usually when my day begins. I get a ride to school so I will be early and this way I'll have time to socialize with all my friends, get any homework done that was not finished, and take care of things before the bell rings. 8:30 I'm usually in 1st period, this class is boring and long, so my day starts out slow. Then, I move to 2nd period and this class really isn't bad at all. Next, I go to 3rd and I love that class which is my math class. During the 3rd hour we have lunch which is the best part out of the day!

After lunch my day is half over. I continue my day after lunch and go to my 4th period which is a decent class. Here comes my craziest class ever . . . early childhood. I can never leave that class without a headache. Then I go to 6th period which is a all freshman class. This class is my hardest. I can never get anything done due to the fact that there's freshmans running around and getting into trouble. They cause a lot of distractions.

Well here comes the end thank god. My day is over and I get to go home! On the bus is crazy because there's always a fight or something on our bus. Well the day is over and I'm going home so yes I'm done!—Yvonne, Melbourne, FL

~

Here I sit in a coma-like state,
Chin in my hands, eyes closing like gates.
High school is just a bore,
So damn monotonous, I can't take it anymore!

When I arrived I though it'd be like saved by the bell,
Turns out high school's my living hell.
They're not preparing us for the real world, they're holding us back,
Limiting our freedom, facist bull crap.

___HS football roolz!
Our principal's a major tool,
If you're not on the math team, you're outta luck
And the school lunches? One word: yuck.

The required reading is really lame,
"Old Man and the Sea" . . . boring and tame.
Every day is just the same
The principal still doesn't know our names.

They tell us to reach for the stars.
But this education won't get me far.
This poem slash rap makes me look like a fool,
But really though, I just hate school!
—Anonymous, Amesbury, MA

〜

In all honesty, I'm not the type of student who gets really involved with any-thing. My only complaints would be irrational because I'm just lazy. Al-though this may be, it doesn't mean I am ambivalent about school altogether. There have been times when certain teachers have shown attitudes toward students that would be cause for concern.

I have seen the school system treat students who have attention deficit disorder as if they were just troublemakers. It's not that they purposely don't listen, they have a hard time focusing. It is understandable that they can be very disruptive but our teachers don't have to reprimand harshly or embar-rass them in front of the entire class. Respect should be a two-way street. Also, students who come from broken homes and harsh pasts can reflect the same behavior as students with ADD. They are so preoccupied with family dysfunction that concentration can be very difficult and attention may be _____ by the emotionally unstable.—Anonymous, Amesbury, MA

〜

Blink. There went thirteen years of your precious life, a possible sixth of your entire span, and you came out with what? So many years of communication skills and basic life-comprehension courses and one's school career should cease. After that amount of schooling let us choose our own course of life, in-stead of readying us for five out of eight things we will not need. I believe it is time for some retrospective ways of growing up, involving schooling and learning and such. Sure, it would probably evolve to our ways currently and we would probably look at it as a setback, but that would be where willpower and determination comes in to assure we do not let it change to "normal" ways. I mean, look back . . . Way, way back—Keep looking. There it is, the times of Aristotle, when children of the age of six knew five different languages fluently. They held conversations then that most "intelligent" and "intellectual" adults do not engage or encounter today. All considered them adolescents at the age of nine, but never actually given the label "Teens" or "Adolescents."

People need to learn to live as if they have only a year left to understand everything. Blink. We start a career today when they were middle-aged then. We begin to make a living when they were beginning to die— they were not going to waste their life trying to make money, they wanted to gain knowledge. Although, one's wisdom could prevail and give one status during earlier times, which makes it hard for one to *want* to acquire knowledge. They did everything they could to make life better and easier, so why do we not live for others anymore? Learn simply so we can better ourselves?

What I am saying, trying to pummel through to any potential reader, attempting to make manifestly clear, is that we, the putative advanced, "learned (better)" species, are wasting time, that time which, if spent to bankruptcy, would seem to profit the contentment of our souls, on the petty attempt at omnipotence. However, I am simply venting—school seems to be an utter distraction from other, more interesting things, such as personal interests, in example, astronomy. Why wait until college? I believe everyone would pose a challenge, mentally, to all else if we knew a lot about one thing. By knowing one thing that someone does not, feelings of intimidation spur, thus encouraging alternative motives to learn. One gets three times the glory of beating someone, personally, than solving a math problem, and by having heightened emotion about something, one is more apt to remember it, although, I may be seeking variety, in opinion.

The same techniques of learning are practiced on us, the students, daily, and candidly, is extremely boring. Challenge does not overcome me, moreover, I desire it, but I really have no reason to challenge myself if there is not one to give witness to my innovative, possibly idiotic ideas. What fun is that? What gloves does that give? With a little motivation, some will, I would be a genius—anyone could. That seems to be the real problem— motivation, lack of incentive, boredom.—Casey, Clover, SC

⌒

All day long, the clock sweeps by, yet tends to stand still.
Music starts the day, but ends too abruptly as I drag to class
Essays loom over the heads of tormented minds
Students, ever complaining about the foils of mundane lives
Bells grind my ears, yet release us from doom . . . only for a minute
Unheard cries for funding reverberate through the school.
Renovations never end, perhaps because they never begin.
Yellow and green are the colors of the aged tiles on the walls and floor.

Heavy backpacks pull with their weight of knowledge
Inexperienced freshmen pass by with their words of foolishness
Gym is a waste of eighty minutes in my busy day
How can we survive on grade D beef day after day?

Some day we shall leave this place . . . but where will we go?
Crowded halls full of pushing and pulling, as sheep herded to their pens.
Holiday break is a refreshing time to regroup and prepare
Over and over again, our football team loses
Oh how close to the end, but never close enough
Life cannot be completed without the experience of school
—Anonymous, Amesbury, MA

⌒

During the average school day, you're constantly in a rush of crowded hall-ways filled with noisy laughter. The thing that bugs me the most about these halls is the students. Some of them can be so inconsiderate to the other people around them. I absolutely hate it when people stop right in front of you in the middle of the hall. You're walking, trying to get to class, and they come to a sudden stop to gather around a group of friends in the hall. If you're lucky, you're small enough to weave in and out of them. I guess that's why I'm thankful for being short.—Bev, Inwood, WV

⌒

I attend J___ high school in Jackson, Michigan. Today I will be writing about my favorite and least favorite subject and why. So, I guess it's time I began with my favorite subject. It's science but I can't believe it. In grades 4–6 I hated science, maybe because it was difficult. The reason I like it now is because of my teacher, Mrs. A___. She understands me more than my past teachers and she has a great personality. Mrs. A___ teaches to a point where she makes sure that you understand what's going on. So that you have a chance to pass the class, such as other teachers do. Those are the reasons why I like science class, because of my teacher. Now, for my least favorite subject in school. It's gym/P.E. which is an easy class to pass. All you have to do is be there. That's the problem, but I know you're thinking—she's in high school and can't get up on time to get to class, but guess what, I get up on time. I don't have another way to get to school other than walking. So my next way is bus, but I'm 2½ miles away from school but you have to be more than that to catch the bus.

My mother called the school and the lady said, "Shyeasha could ride the bus." Then, when I went to the bus stop the bus driver said, "Shyeasha, you can't get on cause you're within walking distance." So now I am absent/tardy too frequently with it causing me to fail gym. It's not about my teacher because I like her too. She's nice and does a great job teaching. This is the reason P.E./gym is my least favorite subject. Just do something for me, and put something about me in your book.—Shyeasha, Jackson, MI

~

CHAPTER TWO

The Structural Dimension

School is not very fun.—4th grade student, Florida

Another morning spent looking in the mirror thinking about misery and joy. The thought of going to school another day makes me think about those double lunches and those overcrowded hallways that I absolutely dislike. But then I think about the bright side of the day, the fact that I get to hang out with my friends and plan for my future.—Steven, Vero Beach, FL

When talking about the structure of the average school day, one has to consider the time spent at school and how a school is organized (Eisner, 1992). Both, on their own, constitute averages worth noting, but, when put together, present an interesting portrait of K–12 education. Students spend anywhere between 6 and 8 hours per day in school; that time accounts for 32% of their waking hours (Evans & Bechtel, 1997; Gilman & Knoll, 1984; Leonard, 2001). So, what really goes on at school each day? And, how do students feel about it?

The Routine of School

The most common theme to emerge from students' writings was the idea that school runs like, and by, a clock. Students often expressed just going through the motions—from class to class and event to event until the day ended—and this started early, as young as fourth grade. Then they did it again, and again, and again, until graduating from high school.

⁓

From short lunch lines to strict administration, a typical school day is not "the brightest crayon in the box of life."—Brian, Cocoa, FL, 8th grade

⁓

Everyday at school is a new adventure . . . every once in a while a roll of toilet paper is lit on fire and thrown in to a bathroom trash can. At the same time, one of those space heaters blow up in a teacher's face. These types of occurrences are almost common in my school.

School is great and all, but it is too much like a prison. Mr. ___ has said twice so far to me that "there are only two places on earth where bells determine your movement: school and prison." Sometimes I day dream about being able to have knowledge and wisdom and knowledge poured into my brain. That way a bell of any kind will never be needed.—Zach, Atlanta, GA

⁓

On a average day of school I visit six different teachers. First I would eat some breakfast and head to Mrs. ___ class where I'll learn English. Afterwards, Mr. ___ is my next teacher. He teaches Algebra 2. Mr. ___ would be next teaching Economics. At the end of class lunch begins for me and ends for others. Once I'm done eating, I'll head to Mr. ___ Spanish class to learn more verbs. Computer programming would be next. Finally my last class would be science with Mr. ___.—Chris, Melbourne, FL

⁓

I'm going to tell you about a school day in the life of me at B___ Elementary School. First of all, I get on my old rusty Bus 39. Then I walk through the doors of horrible knowledge to room 7. Next, I usually have a Daily Word Problem. After that, we usually do electricity in science. Next we learn about our countries past in social studies. Then a couple kids leave for language arts. Later we have lunch. After that we have recess for like 10 minutes! I think the lunch aids should extend our recess time so that we have more time to play outside. At 12:00 to 1:00 we have math. After that we have recess again for like 10 minutes! Next we go to special. Our specials are made up of computer, art, music, gym, and library. Then if it's Monday we have world language. That's made up of Spanish, German, and French. After that we silent read. Later we pack up. Next we do our jobs. Then, after a long day's work, for 6 hours of torture, we go home, thank god!—Christian, Turnersville, NJ

⌒

What goes on during the average school day? Well, the teachers get to school in the morning before the students to get everything ready for the day ahead. Then the students arrive and meet with friends until the bell rings for them to go to 1st period. They [do] the work that teacher gives them until PTV comes on. After PTV the bell rings again for them to go to 2nd, then 3rd. During 3rd period they have their lunch. Then the day continues and they go to 4th, 5th, and 6th periods. Finally, after 6th they get on their buses, bikes, or in their cars and go home.—Steven, Melbourne, FL

⌒

Every day I go to school and wonder what am I going to do today? When then I think, "Crazy me!" Every day it is the same thing in school. We sharpen our pencils, we sit in our seats, and we talk. After about 5 minutes of talking the teacher scolds us by hollering, "Be quiet"! When she does this everybody gets real quiet and we do our work. The quietness is like an alien has come from outer space and everybody is astonished by it coming to Earth.

First, we do our Daily Word Problem. They are sometimes easy, but not always. Next, we study science. Currently, we are doing an experiment with electricity and learning how balloons attract to each other. After science is social studies. When I open my book my teacher yells out, "Today we are learning about the Mexican-American War." I am excited because I love learning about wars. Following social studies is language arts. Next, we go to lunch and fool around until we go outside and play sports. After that, we have math class and we learn about division. Today, of all days, we have to learn long division, and it's HARD!

At recess we all gather around the computers and watch two students play games on them. When we go to special, (which is gym) we run, stretch, jump, and play games. After special we have reading. We are reading a book called "Number the Stars." The book is filled with suspense. Right before the characters do something amazing, our teacher says that it is time to pack up. My school is a good school. Sometimes we do fun things, sometime we do dumb things. That is just the way school days are. I like it that way. —Michael, Turnersville, NJ

⌣

I'm going to tell you about a normal school day. Agh!! Dun, dun, dun. At lunch kids always talk. The food tasty. Tables rest. Teachers excuse the kids. In math algebra teaches us. The children maon. Our teacher teaches us how to do the method. He also expects our pens to be working across the papers. During reading the books tell us some things. They inform us and they give us a perfect picture in our heads. Our teacher also reads to us. At recess the jungle gym stand. The kids kick balls. Kids run and play, teachers watch. That's my terrifying day at school.—Emma, Reno, NV, 4th grade

⌣

Late in the afternoon hearing the last bell is like going to Paris for the whole evening.—Liliana Zamora, Aptos, CA

⌣

My normal school day is really boring and sometimes fun but for the most part it's just plain boring. I kind of like 1st period because it's Language, to me it's like hitting a line drive in baseball it goes by that fast. I hate 2nd period because it's math, I would rather eat my dogs dog food for lunch everyday rather than sitting in math class for 75 min. I wonder if anyone has gone into a coma because school is so boring. That's the end of my normal boring school day.—Austin, Newnan, GA, 6th grade

⌣

My normal school day feels like a week has gone by and as dull as looking at white colored walls. When I get to school I go to my locker, unpack, get my things, and go to homeroom. While in homeroom we usually just sit in our desks and talk until the announcements come on. After announcements end the bell rings and we switch for first period. In first period math with Dr. ___ is almost as dull as changing a light bulb. She starts talking to us about percentage that sometimes doesn't even make sense to any of us. While she writes stuff on the board most of us just sit and start to drool. Everyone is relieved when the bell rings. In second period Language Arts we come in write in our agendas and do our homework. Language isn't as boring as Math because we go to lunch. After lunch I go to third period Social Studies. When we get in we write in our agendas. As soon as we finish the teacher takes attendance and then she start talking to us about Canada or something that is boring. It goes by so slow that feels like 2 hours have past by. Sitting and listening to the teacher talk about thing that we are not interested in. At the end of the period we are happy. Fourth period Science goes by pretty quick but everyone is tired of paying attention. It goes by quick because all the teacher does is talk. After we go to our lockers and get our things and go to 5th period. Health is not bad but it hard to pay attention to the teacher instead of the clock. At the end of the period everyone is all tired out. Art for sixth period boring and the teacher is always in a bad mood because all of the other classes get on here nerves. At the end of the day everyone is excited that the school day is over.—George, Newnan, GA, 6th grade

Lack of Engagement

A large number of students seemed disengaged with school, describing it as boring and tedious. Several students gave the analogy of "being in prison." For some on the "outside" it may seem as if students just complain. However, in my opinion, we do not give them enough credit. Students are very astute about the goings-on at school. Their reasons for lack of engagement—seatwork and worksheets, early start times, and block scheduling—are valid concerns. Having taught in systems where school started early (7:10) and classes were long (90 minutes), I can understand why some teachers resorted to seatwork and worksheets, and why students were bored. Throw in weeks' worth of standardized test preparation, and it is a wonder students even attend.

⌣

In a sense, our school is like a prison. The shades are always closed, the food is icky, the top of the doors are covered by white paper, and most of the time we can't even go outside. The only "free-time" I have is lunch, and that is only 15 minutes. Aah!

Waking up way too early, tests, homework, homework deadlines, and going eight hours with no real break can be tiring and extremely boring. I worry too much about how I am going to organize my time between homework, extracurricular activities, and me time. It seems like I am losing hair and gaining wrinkles from all of this stress caused by school. Stress from school that I wish could be avoided, but I need an education; so what is a student to do?—Relane, Max, ND, 10th grade

⌣

It's five o'clock AM, you wake up so tired, you take a quick shower because the bus comes at 6:30. After getting ready, you go to your kitchen and eat whatever you can find. When you get to school it's cold as ice while you wait for your friends to come. Some freshman bump into you and hit you with their backpacks. The bell rings at 7:35 and they give you seven minutes to get to your class. After an hour in your first period class the bell rings and you have to get to your second period with in seven minutes. After second period, you have ten minutes for break. As soon as the bell rings to go to third period you grown in disappointment and walk to class. By the time break ends you're wide awake but you still don't want to go to class. You sit through third period and then fourth period and you ache with anticipation to get to lunch.—Kristina Jaras, Aptos, CA

⌒

I don't think it is necessary to be at school so early in the morning. School is not an optional thing, it is really mandatory and I believe it is ridiculous that students have to be in school before eight in the morning. School is supposed to be an enjoyable environment but it is not enjoyable at all if you're half-asleep and cranky. Students who are half-asleep when they get to school learn nothing in their first period class because they have to sleep through the lesson because their sleep was disturbed so early. If school started later in the morning or if students got to choose what time their classes were, I believe they would learn more and not be so tired. If students weren't sleeping in class maybe our high school's reputation and grade would go up.—Adam, Vero Beach, FL

⌒

I get up on an average school day at 7:30. Before I take my shower, I have to mentally prepare myself by putting on a CD. My parents already left for work so I can play it as loud as I want. After I get dressed, I go to my car and head to school. During first and second period, I'm feeling pretty good, participating in class discussions and being friendly. By the time third and fourth period roles by, I am feeling drained and need some lunch. I ride with a couple of friends to McDonalds or something. Most of the time I don't feel like going to 5th period so I come back late for lunch. By 6th and 7th period, I have my head down and not participating as much. By the time the bell rings, I'm running out to my car and speeding home.—Yolanda, Tallahassee, FL

⌒

For students, every day is the same old thing. Wake up, to go school, do homework, go to bed. Rinse and repeat. This is the unstoppable cycle of life.

It's always the same things, good and bad, over and over throughout the day. The periods are all the same, really. The teacher goes on with a lecture about something, and then assigns multiple tasks to do at home. They act like their assignments will only take us as long to do as it will grade. One teacher never thinks about how little free time one will have if all five or six of our teach-ers gave the amount of homework they do.

Luckily, the tyrants who run this "prison" called school, at least give us breaks. The best part of the day, these 19 and 39 minute saviors are all that the students really have going for them. Though short, these breaks are a great way to relax and hang out with friends.

Only too soon, these "escapes" must come to an end. Back to class we go, driven by a primitive, yet some how effective, all-ruling bell. As the school day comes to an end, the stress on your mind really starts to pick up. Though school may end as early as 3:14 for the teachers, it lasts much longer for the students. At an average of 30 minutes of homework per class, if we arrive home at 4:00, we end up not being able to really be free from school's strong grip until 6:00 or 7:00. By then, we barely have any time for ourselves. This is a big part of why students are never fully awake for school. Kids do need free time, and most take it, even if it means cutting back on sleep to only a few hours. Then it is time for the horrifying cycle to continue its hold on us.

Finally, after five grueling days, we are able to have a short 48-hour break. While this may seem good, we really do not have a chance to escape the re-alities of school. Teachers love to pile on the homework during the week-ends, and give a total of 5–6 hours of homework and projects. If the average student sleeps 12 hours a day on weekends (to make up for the lack of sleep on weekdays), that cuts down a total of 30 hours combined with homework. From there, we have to use a good portion of that for family time, leaving us with less than 25% of our weekend to really relax.

In conclusion, though many adults will agree with students that school is tough for the 40-hour week that we must attend, many do not realize that it is only a small portion of the work we really must do. Though we do get a small amount of free time, it is not enough when compared to the number of hours we must put into our schoolwork.—Alex, Woodland Hills, CA

⌒

I think that school is extremely boring. We only have 4 classes a day and they are the same everyday, same order everyday. Personally sitting in a chair for 80 minutes gets pretty boring and I tend to not pay attention after half the class goes by. I need variation. When we get projects, we get projects that last the whole term. The last thing that I really don't like is the teachers. Some of them can be really rude and won't let you go to the bathroom when you really have to do. Then I can't even pay attention because I'm too busy trying to keep my mind off the bathroom.—Anonymous, Amesbury, MA

～

During an average school day, it's not much that goes on. I mean, we go to our classes, do our work then the day is over. Every once in a while it might be a fight, then people would think it was a good day.—Kristie, Tallahassee, FL

～

BBBEEEPPP it's 7:40 a.m. students are rushing to their first period class so they're not late. Sitting in the classroom for 90 minutes and then only 4 minutes to get to their second period class. YES sitting in one classroom for 90 minutes! A teacher does not teach for 90 minutes. Reality check.—Kelly, Vero Beach, FL

～

An average day of school for me is nothing but normal no more. On the way to school "thirty minute drive" I try to gather myself before "it" approaches. I arrive at school, two minutes later after landing the bell sounds for class. My first two classes fly right on pass me easily, not even knowing. Now it's time for fourth period. Fourth period is one of the longest periods of the day if you're hungry because, this period is right before first lunch. Finally, fourth period is over time for lunch, which will blow by like time in the dark; forty-five minutes isn't a long time. The bell rings for fifth period I can't move, the hallways are too crowded and I might be late because the lockers are so far from the lunch room. I am at my locker now still no progression because I have a special security system I call thump and bump which takes almost a full minute. I am glad I don't have to use the restroom. Period six is gone and half of seven now. I try to prepare for the three seated, loud, thirty-minute journey home.—Harold, Tallahassee, FL

School Is Enjoyable

Despite the fact that many students who wrote to me dislike going to school, quite a few wrote about the daily aspects that make school enjoyable for them. Ironically, the most pleasant characteristics of "school" were nonacademic—friends and lunch. What else makes school fun? Easy classes and friendly teachers.

⌣

Well, a normal school day is really fun and enjoyable. Going to the bus-stop my friends friend picks me and him up. We listen to the radio laughing and having conversations about the conversations on the radio. Then we get to school. Walk to the commons area: talk, hang out before going to first period. Then to first period I go, economics: worksheets and discussions about money and such. After first, I to go second period, learning vocab words and writing about a typical school day for me. After second, I would go to third (obviously 1, 2, 3, etc.) talking to D___. Spanish! Oh boy, I'll just go to by fourth period now. That's when the fun begins, the class is sooo easy for me; so I just actually talk in that class. Walking to fifth I will meet up with D___ again and talk, go to art class and draw! Off to sixth period. . . . Yes! Again I know science, so I just talk in sixth. After sixth school is over then I get on my bus, socializing with other students and friends. Get home, eat, play computer and or do my homework (if I have homework) until eleven o'clock. Bed time! Then I do it all over again.—Chris, Melbourne, FL

⌣

As a sophomore, a typical day for me is not bad at all. I usually wake around six o'clock and leave my house around seven fifteen. First period is gym and second period is my favorite subject: English. Third period I sit through social studies and usually my fourth period, creative writing, goes by fast. I have first lunch, so I go to lunch after fourth period. I sit with my best friend, B___, and a bunch of my other friends. After my enjoyable lunch, I have science and then Algebra 2. Lastly, I work my fingers in keyboarding.

I am a varsity cheerleader for our school. For basketball, we have 1 practice a week and on average cheer about three games a week. When I arrive home from school, I have to start my homework immediately to keep my life on track. Our practices usually run from five to seven o'clock and I get home around seven ten or so. When I get home I try to get to bed early to I can function for school the next day.—Amy, Inwood, WV

⌣

At L___ High I kind of like it. Well I guess I have to say that I do like it. After being in three Elementary schools, three Middle schools, and so far one

High school, I must say that L___ has some unique feature that interests me. Yes, I especially love the schedule. Periods Alpha, Two, Four and Six on a Gold day and Alpha, One, Three, and Five on Blue day. Yes, this gives us much more time to learn things and to explain things unknown rather than learning over five things a day. Wow the way my school days starts doesn't really bother me anymore after having to get use to it for half a year. I get up at four o clock in the morning. I use my cell phone as an alarm clock; cell phones can be used for practically anything. I take a shower in the morning to wake myself up sometimes. Get dressed. Do my hair for about fifteen minutes. Get my book bag prepared for the day. I have to be careful because I have two different book bags. One for a blue day and one for a gold day, to save me trouble. After I have fixed my room and cleaned up by five o clock am I watch TV, brush my teeth, put in my contacts, rarely eat breakfast, watch the news and wait till 5:50 am which is my bus stop time.—Briaunna, Longwood, FL

⌣

As I walk through the main doors that lead to the hallways of C___ High School, I hear the first bell of the day ring. Time to get to class. I quickly make it through the crowded hallways to get upstairs to my first period class, French III.

Each class period runs for ninety minutes, so I sit in French III and listen to my great-aunt, Mrs. ___ try to make me understand the odd words flowing from her mouth, but she's never helped. As I sit in her class waiting for the bell to dismiss us, I watch the minutes go by, one at a time.

Finally the bell rings. As I jump straight out of my seat, I rush to get out of the door and on with the rest of my day, away from my French class. I quickly shuffle through the hallways to get to my locker where my math book always is. After I get my math book, I'm on my way back upstairs to the other side of the school to get to my Algebra II class.

Mrs. ___ is my Algebra II teacher, she doesn't have exactly the best method of teaching, but then again it is Algebra II. Algebra II is a great class, simply because I have a lot of friends in there. The class goes by fast, the work is challenging though. Mrs. ___ loves to joke with our class all the time. She makes the ninety minutes seem to fly by.

After second period is over the day goes by pretty fast and easy. Third period is creative writing. That class is great. It's not too hard, and it's always fun, regardless of our assignments. We have lunch during this period, so after a half-hour of class goes by, we are released to lunch. I am usually one of the first kids to get into the lunchroom, so I always go and get fresh fries for my lunch. Then I go to my table, where I meet up with my other friends. We all always have so much to talk about; it's a wonder we have enough time to finish our meals. When lunch is over it's back to Mrs. ___'s class for another hour.

From there I go downstairs, on the other side of the school to my fourth period class with Mrs. ___, she teaches US History. The majority of my friends say they hate that class, but I find it very interesting. I am always answering questions, that class is a piece of cake! Depending on how much Mrs. ___ talks, the class goes by pretty quick. The clock in the classroom is broken, so everybody constantly asks me for the time. I keep them all posted every fifteen minutes. Once the last bell of the day rings I rush to my locker to put my books away, then I quickly get out to the front of the school where my dad picks my up everyday after school. From there it's just an average afternoon.—Trisha, Clover, SC

Things That Go on at School on a Daily Basis

High school students, more than their elementary and middle school counterparts, documented the types of events that occur at school. Other than attending classes, school serves as a meeting place, a place to "hook up," and even a place to fight.

⌒

On an average school day much takes place. Mostly it depends on what kind of student you are. There are those who study hard and do their work and there are those that do not. But no matter what kind of student you are a lot of the same things take place. You begrudgingly wake up and get ready to go. Sometimes you are on time other times you are tardy, it is not that important. If you get there on time most people talk with their friends. Then you to go to class. Once you get there interesting things unfold. Sex. Contrary to popular belief it does happen and happens a lot in high school. When you put guys and girls together for six hours in a day what do you think is going to go down. In an average school day there is a large amount of flirting, touching, grabbing, rubbing, et cetera and in some cases actual sex. Yes on-campus fornication does take place and there is nothing that school officials can do about it. Besides sex there is actual work that takes place during school. But mostly it happens within the class period. No one actually does work at home but frantically in class trying to complete it before the teacher picks it up. And in most cases there is way more talking and socializing with friends than work. Lunch is a welcome time each day when students get race either off-campus for lunch or to the cafeteria, both trying to beat long lines and impatient workers. When the actual school day ends many students engage in extra-curricular activities, whether they be sports or clubs, some lasting until late in the afternoon.—Ayana, Tallahassee, FL

～

During the average school day many students are worried about how they look. Most people are running around trying to be cute. Many students are trying to go around thinking of how to make the teachers happier. It sometimes comes to our minds to be the best and achieve all we can. Success is always on our minds as we glance into the future.—Derrick, Tallahassee, FL

～

Learning goes on at school. Friendships go on during school. Stress and relief goes on during the day. Sleeping, laughing, and drama are the three most common events that occur on a regular school day.—Sara, Tallahassee, FL

～

One of the craziest things I went through at A___ High was when one day, a friend and me decided to drink before coming to school. So we got some shots from my house of some wine that my dad had in a cabinet. We rode the bus to school, and we sat all the way in the back. Then we got to school, we were giggling with friends. But when first period had started I had to go to the restroom so I asked for permission to go. I was trying to act normal and walk straight and when I got to the restroom I found my friend there that I had gotten drunk with. We were giggling in the restroom when a girl that did not like me came into the restroom with her two friends. As I was leaving the restroom I had the idea of asking that chick why didn't she like me and why she had a problem with me. I asked her and she started screaming and acting all stupid. That question ended up as a big argument. When we were arguing a nark passed and heard us, so we had to go to the office. There they were talking to me and ask me if I had been drinking, I was denying everything and that got me into trouble. Then I got mad because I had found out that she had written a statement about me. I started screaming at everyone that I was going to f___ her up, and I got out of control. My asthma also got out of control because I was mad. The sheriff took me to the hospital and there they were examining me. In conclusion they suspended me for five days, they put me on probation, and they told me that if I touched her that they were going to take me to juvy. And the hospital charges were expensive, so yeah that was my experience.—Maria Fernandez, Aptos, CA

⌣

My average day is alright. My alarm clock yells beeping noises at 6:00 a.m. I take a 15 minute hot shower, dry up, get dressed, and my sisters alarm clock goes off. While they get dressed, I'm downstairs micro waving waffles I eat about 4 of them I go back upstairs. . . . So we leave at about 7:15 maybe later. Once we get out of the house we have to go to the bus stop. Walking to the bus stop is like walking 3 miles. I walk on the bus and I sit on the 3rd seat to the left with two 2nd graders. I like little kids. The buses first stop is cannongate and drops off the elm. kids before M___ kids, so I let them out of the seat and fall asleep until I get to M___. Everybody gets off the bus to homeroom. My homeroom teacher is Mrs. ___. I sit in the back of the room. The annoucments come on with Mr. ___. The announcements are as boring as going to a 20 year old rolling disco with your mom, with old people. After the announcements I go to 1st period but I don't have to go any where because Mrs. ___ is also my teacher in 1st period. Mrs. ___ is nice, funny, and blonde. 1st period alright its fun on days where we get to watch a movie or listen to the radio. Last week we listened to Bill Cosby's stand up comedy o the radio. After 1st period class I go to Mrs. ___'s 2nd period class, social studies, Mrs. ___ is some strict person, I mean it, but she can be nice sometimes. "Ring, Ring," Time for lunch. For lunch we usually have soy moo meat its nasty lunch except J___ he will eat anything in the lunch room. Here comes 3rd period which is Science, Mr. ___ to make it clear. He is cool and lets us do a lot of projects like a boat project. Dr. ___ is my favorite but can be very strict. WE do a lot of stuff like coloring graphs and eating cake. It's a lot better than Mrs. ___, I sleep in her class. After math we have connections, mine are Art& Health. Art is my 2nd favorite even though Mrs. ___ is very mean and nice at certain times. Health is not all that we all do Work Sheets and its over. Well, that is my average day.—Blaine, Newnan, GA, 6th grade

⌣

I wake up at 5:30 AM when my first alarm clock goes off. I fumble around in the dark to realize that it under something. Then I feel around on my bed.

Then my second alarm clock goes off in a blast. I bonk my head on the corner of my bed. Now time for family scripture study and family prayer.

After I was ready and done I would go outside and make sure that every one got out to and on the bus. I read until I get to school. After we drop off the elementary school kids, we go to switch high school kids for the middle school kids. When they get on I close my book and wait for the torment that was just about to begin. He was a seventh grader only because he failed. He was short, hairy, fat, and a bully to me. There were many more bullies starting with ___, a tall, fat dude with square classes. He picked on me since I knew him. I will stop naming the bullies now that I am at school. Now here I go to the gym where I read my book again. Now that the bell rang I go to the band room and put up my instrument and go to homeroom. My homeroom teacher is Mr. ___. I read there unless we are doing the announcements. My first period is boring. It is math class, though it used to be my favorite class. Did I mention that I like school! My teacher is Mrs. ___, tall, brown hair, brown eyes, white skin, with a little tan, and looks a little old, with glasses. Science is my second period and comes third on my list. It is a really fun class. Mr. ___ is my science teacher and he is shortening, not to be rude, old, and wears big, thick glasses. Social Studies is my third period and fourth on my list. Mrs. ___ is my teacher and is a grouch, or a nice old lady, depends on how you see things. She makes social studies a bore or fun. My next period is language arts and number one on my list. Mrs. ___ makes English fun and is a chubby, short, funny, and old teacher.

Band is my first connection and 5th period and 5th favorite. I play the clarinet and I sit in the back scared. Mr. ___ is a cool, tall, old man that keeps everything rad. Spanish is my 6th and last class and Spanish is number 2 on my list. Senora ___ is a big, nice, fun, and forgetful teacher. I have forgotten to include my lunch hour, lunch is after my second period and has a time for social life outside. Lunch is a loud, big, and good place for echoes. I have very few friends, A___, J___, B___, and E___ are my school friends. I usually say hi to all of them except B___, because he is in 3 of my classes.

Well after school is manic. It all starts on the bus home. I sit in the very back of the bus thanks to my driver. We start out to the buses and then our buses to Timberlake where we wait for the high school bus to come, switch students, and take us home. I read on the way home. We stop many times before then, but when I get home and have to deal with homework and my brother. My jobs would never get finished I brush my teeth and go to bed, in the morning the same thing would happen, better, or worse then yesterday.—Branson, Newnan, GA, 6th grade

〜

A typical high school day for me include being stared at by girls, giving hand shakes to my friends, and wrestling in the hall ways of my youth . . . when I come into school I have to go through the metal detectors and allow the teachers to look through my bags. . . . High school to me is like a big play pin in which I get to do what ever I want and it really won't make a difference. I like high school as far as social life goes, but class work is a whole different story.

Every since I cross the threshold out of child hood into young adult hood, I have become less interested in learning. All I really want to do is hang out with my friends but the gum of a successful life keeps my shoe stuck to the ground. Credits that I earn is like a pay check that I get in the mail. I know what is there, but I just want to see it on paper.—Ervin, Atlanta, GA

〜

Ugh . . . all right all ready, I'm getting' up. As I turn off my alarm it says its 5:55 in the morning. So I go back to sleep for about 50 mins. Then I hear . . . hugh hugh . . . MITCHELL!! So finally get up and get dressed. Then I brush my teeth with the toothpaste that feels like a cloud but stings like bee. Then I put my deodorant on, put some cologne on, and fix my hair. After I accomplish all of my hygiene needs I go down stairs. I let my dogs out and put some food and water in their bowls. Then I let my dogs back in. They scarf that food down like there was no tomorrow. Then while they're eating I go to the pantry to get the best cereal I have. After I finish my breakfast, I put Marley (AKA *demon dog*) in her cage. Then I say bye and get my book bag and head out the door. The bus gets there about 2 mins after I get to the top of my driveway. I step on the bus and try to scope out a seat but they're all full, so I stand up on the way to the Elementary School. I don't want to try to get through the little kids because it would be like trying to get through the Mall of Georgia at 5:00 on a Saturday. Instead, I get off with them and come back on the bus before the bus driver can shut the door on me. I finally get to sit down, rest, and talk with my friends. We pick up some more kids on the way to the High School and drop off some kids at the High School. After they get off, the Middle School kids rule the bus (except that the bus driver is still there). We rule that bus for about 15 mins, then we're dropped off at school. Once at school, I go to my locker and then to homeroom.

Homeroom is the time for boring announcements and finishing your homework. My homework is done, of course! After homeroom, it's time for my least favorite class—Social Studies. This class seems to last so long, it feels like we are making history instead of studying it. Second period is the most fun class, so time flies by and then it is time for lunch.

Lunch at middle school is like lunch in prison. Except not as harsh. There are not as many restrictions, but the food sure is bad. I have a tuna fish sandwich and it tastes like wax. I sit with the same people that I sit with every day and try to stay out of trouble. Today I make it without a scratch. I reward myself with a Savagely Sour Ice Pop and head outside. I visit with my friends and then it's off to third period

I get to third period and do my warm up (something to keep us busy), as my teacher collects homework. If everyone turns their homework in the whole class gets a reward. Boy, it's been a while since I've seen any candy in this class. At least today, it's not my fault we don't earn a reward! My third period teacher is funny, so you don't really notice the time. The rest of my day goes just the same. Doing assignments, having fun, and learning. During class change, all of the kids rush into the hallway like a herd of bulls. I can't believe the teachers don't get trampled. I guess they've had practice. I manage to make it to the bathroom between classes, so I won't get a demerit for asking to go later. I finish my day at school feeling like I've just survived a hurricane. I head for my bus, thinking that tomorrow's another day.—Mitchell, Newnan, GA, 6th grade

⁓

Besides dealing with tests and homework there are other daily stress factors; such as the condition of the bathrooms at G___, most lack mirrors, tissue paper and are decorated with many styles of graffiti. The bathrooms also go through periods of filthiness and disrepair, and the lockers rarely ever work properly the first week of school.—Mary, Atlanta, GA

⁓

What goes on during an average school day? This topic is very simple. The main thing that goes on is negative behavior and other students cause this. The second thing that goes on is note writing to other students during class and this is stopping those students who pass notes from learning because they get distracted. The last thing is bad language; this is mainly towards teachers, deans, and students. In my opinion this happens everyday even by me.
—Bianca, Cocoa, FL, 8th grade

⌒

The average day at school is fun. When you go in the door Mr. ___ and Mr. ___ welcome you and you feel at home.—Madalyn, Vestavia Hills, AL, 6th grade

⌒

It's Monday morning and I flop out of bed when my alarm clock goes off. I slither into my robe still half asleep. My dog is sleeping on the couch again and I drag him off. I hit the power button to the remote and the television flashes on. Good Morning America starts now and there's something about Iraq on it. I sit there thinking about the day ahead, and I remember that I have an Algebra test today but I'm not sure how to evaluate some of the equations. The linear inequalities that have to be solved by graphing are floating through my head. I hear my sister talking to my mom about this girl she hates and how they are now best friends. My stomach growls and it's time for breakfast.

When I get done eating I hit the shower. The warm water feels good on my sleeping body. I turn off the water and hear the door close which means my mom must have just got back from taking my sister to school. I dry off, throw on some clothes, brush my teeth and hair, and wait until it's time to go.

The bus zooms around the corner and stops for two girls and I to get on. I sit in the second seat as usual and listen to the noise grow as more kids get on. In the back a girl is yelling at a boy for no apparent reason and a couple of kids behind me are talking about a fight that happened this weekend.

When I enter the school courtyard I hear a couple of faint voices. I stand over in one of the four corners of the courtyard and wait for some of my friends. . . . The bell rings for second block, which is when the middle school kids start class, and the group of kids and teachers scatter. Language arts is the same as always, read, copy homework down and wait for whatever "fun" and "exciting" assignments Mrs. ___ has planned for us today. After making a chart about advertisements the bell rings and time for the easiest class ever: U.S. History.

In U.S. History you read the newspaper, except I only like to read articles about space and the comics. Kids are talking most of the class period because the teacher doesn't really pay attention to what's going on. Paper airplanes and erasers sometimes fly by my head and some dumb kids are duct taping their legs together. Even though many different things are happening it's still a good class to be in considering my grade is over one-hundred. Halfway between this class we have lunch. The lunch room is really loud and I got there just in time to beat the huge lines. I get my chicken strips, pay the cashier, and say thank you. I sit with the same crowd. . . . We talk about how stupid some other kids are but they are funny as heck. We pick up our trays and throw them in the trash can then head out to the courtyard. The group of kids that's usually out there is at it again. They are playing extreme hacky-sack which is a more dangerous version of the original. In this version they kick they hacky way up in the air and shove each other out of the way to get it. The only reason I watch it is because it's hilarious and then the principal yells at them. So, then they go find some other destructive thing to do. The announcement comes on and tells us to go back to class. The rest of U.S. History is pretty easy so the day starts to fly by.

The Algebra test is kind of difficult but I get through it. Most of the equations were not hard so I finish first. Since I'm done early I take out the homework I couldn't finish and try to complete it. A few minutes later, after everyone turned in their tests, Mr. ___ starts to explain the next lesson. It is about nonlinear relationships which looks simple so I just sit there for a while, like most people do, staring straight ahead but I'm still listening just in case Mr. ___ calls on me. There isn't too much homework assigned so I'm happy.

"Finally" I mutter as I get out of the Algebra classroom, "the last class of the day." In the hall kids are catching up on the latest gossip while some couples kiss and go their separate ways. . . . We are going to art. . . . During art we learn one point words which is a lot harder than one point boxes. But I finish the assignment for the day and work on extra credit. A kid has to go to the bathroom and Ms. ___ doesn't let him. He leaves anyway and yells back "I don't care!" I guess that means he doesn't care if he gets a referral. He is one of those kids who gets a referral two or three times a week, but he doesn't really care so he laughs about it on the bus. The end of the day announcements come on and we get dismissed to go to our buses.

The bus is loud with voices all over the place. In the back two boys are getting enraged in an argument so they will probably beat the crap out of one another when they get off the bus. It's not my stop so I sit and look out the back window, a crowd of kids are gathering in a circle to get a better view and the bus turns a corner. Two stops later and I get off the bus. Soon J___ and B___, another kid on my street, get off too. We start talking about who is going to get their butt kicked. We all agree that one of the kids is going to rearrange the others face. I go down to my [house] thinking about what to-morrow will be like and grin.—Nick, Cocoa, FL, 8th grade

~

We know what is expected of us before-hand. This makes it easier for us. The teachers try to catch us doing something good, and reward us with an A-Slip or recognition card. This helps our self-esteem. Having these rules make us become accountable. Learning accountability now will make it easier to be-come successful later.—Smylie, Vestavia Hills, AL, 6th grade

~

Everyday, when kids come home from school, parents immediately say, "Hi Honey! How was school?" and we reply, "Fine." It is the same way everyday. Then we get on with our lives . . . and homework. School is more than just a simple "fine". It is stress, fun, hard work; the list could go on forever! "Fine" doesn't explain how a day at school is in the least! School is more than homework and tests; it's a way to make friends, join a club or a team, and ed-ucate you for a good future.—Lucy, Vestavia Hills, AL, 6th grade

Photo by Luigi Arcala

~

CHAPTER THREE

The Curricular Dimension

Kids want to learn. They don't have to be bribed, threatened, or shamed into learning. They need to be given a reason to learn. (Ohanian, 1999, p. 28)

In high school, I think they should teach you the best way to buy a car, or a house, or how to make a loan, even pay taxes or how to even fill out a resume and prepare you for the interview. Those are all things that you will do in life, and it's a shame high school doesn't "teach" you how to accomplish those things.

—Shawn A., Melbourne, FL

According to Eisner (1992), curricular dimensions involve the quality of curricula, content goals, and the activities employed to engage students in them. He raises two important questions concerning this factor: To what degree are students really engaged in what they do in school? Do they find intellectual satisfaction?

Glasser (2003) suggests that there may be close to 5 million students between the ages of 6 and 16 who come to school but do nothing. Because the primary responsibility for academic success does not reside with teachers, principals, superintendents, parents, or any other adult involved in the education system, but with the learners, students will do well academically only if they want to and feel capable of doing so. If they lack either desire or confidence, they will not be successful. The challenge is finding productive ways to motivate them (Stiggins,

2003). However, in an era with budget cuts and a return to the basics, just how "successful" are schools in challenging students and fostering an atmosphere of high enthusiasm?

When it comes to discussing school curricula, debates wage over what "students should know and be able to do." Nonetheless, since this book is primarily concerned with what students think, and not what the rest of us believe, I will present information based upon the most common curricular observations students presented.

Boring or Exciting?

Eighty percent of students say doing well in school makes them feel good about themselves, and the same percentage are upbeat about their education (NCES, 2002). Yet, according to recent numbers, 71% of students said that they did the minimum to get by in school; 56% admit they could try harder (Public Agenda, 2002; Scherer, 2002a). One reason why students may not try is because they have no reason to. Numerous students complained that school, and schoolwork, was "boring." In fact, "over the past two decades, 12th graders have reported a declining interest in school. In 2000, only 28% percent said their schoolwork was 'often or always meaningful,' down from the 40 percent who thought their classes were meaningful in 1983. Similarly, in 1983, 35 percent of 12th graders said their courses were 'quite or very interesting.' More recently, that figure dropped to 21 percent" (NCES, 2002; Scherer, 2002a, p. 5). Three high school students make similar points.

⌒

To be completely honest, I hate science. The funny thing is that I do excellent in that subject. It's just boring to me. Don't get me wrong, my teacher is great, but it seems as if that class just drags on and on. The class I love is art. I'm not good at drawing, but I love painting. I just get this great feeling when I paint. I feel free.—Bev, Inwood, WV

⌒

In some classes, it just seems so long and boring that the teacher could talk a glass eye to sleep.—Andrew, Vero Beach, FL

⌒

Liking school is almost unheard of, but liking at least two of your classes is an important part of deciding weather you will actually attend or not. My two favorite classes are HOSA and anatomy and physiology, because I wish to pursue a career in the medical field and I have found something that makes me tick, I have become involved in different programs surrounding these classes. V___ HS is blessed with these career-training programs such as agriculture, auto mechanics, and carpentry. With these programs teachers have interrelated academics and things students like into one, which makes us interested and hooked on what we're doing.—Dana R., Vero Beach, FL

What Makes a Class Good?

Even though many students complained that school was boring, countless others commented on why particular classes were their favorites. In almost every instance, the fact that the work was interesting and meaningful prompted students to favor a class. Many schools make education an "outside enterprise forcing students [to] memorize and repeat facts without ever appealing to their truth—and we get predictable results: many students never want to read a challenging book or think a creative thought once they get out of school" (Palmer, 2003, p. 73). Tomlinson (2002) writes about five items that "invite" students to learn: affirmation, contribution, purpose, power, and challenge. Many students in this study admired the fact that they knew why they were doing an assignment, or how the work would help them down the road.

What about favorite and least favorite subjects? According to one recent study, typically students rate history as the worst school subject for engagement, while anything related to computers is ranked very high. Vocational subjects seem to be better for stirring interest than academic subjects (Scherer, 2002b). Students who wrote to me had definite ideas and examples about what makes a class good or a favorite.

∼

There are endless opportunities at H___ High School to pursue your dreams. Many of these classes could be considered technical college and university classes. [Our school] is a high school of the future and is a model for all other high schools to go by. [We] have an extensive Technical Education Program. This program includes the Vision House, auto shop, machine shop, metal fabrication, millwork, drafting, architecture, welding, graphics, and yearbook.

There are many opportunities in our business education area. Our school store is a major accomplishment . . . students work there during senior study hall, in the morning and after school. We also have a business management class were you create a business plan.

The agriculture education department has many opportunities . . . including landscape design, greenhouse management, animal science, horse science and companion animals, small engines, ag mechanics, dairy science, wildlife and forestry, plant and soils sciences, water, soil and air quality, and animals, plants and you.—Joseph, Hartford, WI

～

One experience I remember and thoroughly enjoy is science labs and experiments. In sixth grade we did many labs. One specific lab I remember is when in class we dissected an alligator. The teacher cut it up and showed many interesting things. A following lab was a dissection of a pig head. Now in the following years at the high school we progressed to fire (one of my favorite hobbies). In chemistry we got to spray chemicals on fire to see the color reaction the fire had. Science through the years has been great fun. With all the exciting labs I was always entertained.—Louis, Merritt Island, FL

～

My favorite subject is history. The reason that I like history is that if it is taught well it is like one fastinating story. I love learning about what has happened in the past, what we should do differently in the future, and how our lives are impacted by the world around us. Before I studied World War II in history all I knew about was the Holocaust and Hitler. Now I know about "Little Boy" and "Fat Man" the atomic bombs, I know about Pearl Harbor, and I also [know] that if Great Britain, France, and the United States had not tried to be isolationists the whole war could have been stopped before it began. Another thing I like about history is learning about people, their opinions, and their way of handling certain situations. I enjoy comparing Hoover's view on the Great Depression to F.D.R.'s way of handling things. It is interesting to me to think "What If?" What if the United States had gone ahead and entered World War II? Would the war have been less devastating? Would the United States have ever entered the war? If the U.S. had never entered the war would Adolf Hitler be king of the world or would there be anyone left for him to rule after he had tried to create the perfect race? What if the stock exchange had just been closed on the first few days of the Great Depression? Would there have been less suffering and starvation? In history I realize that each moment counts and each person makes a difference. Whether that person is the president of the U.S.A. or the one innocent person in Germany fifty years ago.—Rachel, Vestavia Hills, AL, 6th grade

⌒

I came into high school loving to do things with my hands. I am a hard worker when it comes to building things with my hands and the use of tools. At H___ High School we have a wide variety of classes that are set to mine and other students standards. Like myself there are many people that like to build and experiment with woods and metals. That is why I like H___. It makes a huge difference when our tech. ed. Department is one of the best in the state. We are lucky . . . the school's tech. ed. departments are the greatest thing that ever happened to myself and probably many other students. —Brad, Hartford, WI

⌒

Wow! It's hard to believe it has been thirteen years already. It has had its ups and downs. Through it all I think that the best choice I made was joining ROTC. It has taught me respect, leadership, and has prepared me for the future. I was never a really bad kid through the years. I would get in trouble every now and then. The reason always seemed to be disrespect. I would talk back to my teachers and they would call home. When I got in high school I joined ROTC.—Cordell, Merritt Island, FL

⌒

Reading is so awesome. We summarize chapters in the book and write them down the next day. The class silent read chapter books. Often we partner read short stories.—Courtney, Reno, NV, 4th grade

⌒

The first positive thing about school is the Air Force Junior Reserve Officer Training Corps, or AFJROTC. If it was not for the JROTC program, I would probably be going to another school, or not even be in school.—Andrew, Vero Beach, FL

⌒

Web design class is a pleasure. I feel like I can be at peace with myself, and have a lot more freedom than in any other class. I like the fact that we contribute and help work on a school-wide intranet, and also help work on other miscellaneous projects like backgrounds for the student desktops. I contributed to the AP Presentation that will be presented to middle school students who will be entering their freshman year of high school next year. —Shane, Vero Beach, FL

〜

My least favorite subject is chemistry. Firstly, it is very hard to understand. We have to memorize all the name of the element and also much other stuff. Secondly, I do not like my chemistry teacher. He does not explain anything. He just stands in front of the class and say something. Most students complained it, but he does not care about that.—Jose, San Jose, CA

〜

My favorite subject is math. The one reason for is it because it's fun and exciting. It's fun and exciting because of the teachers and the math problems. The problems are so well . . . fun. I can't really explain it it's just like that. The teachers help with the problems and that's why they are fun. Another reason is they way they teach. The teachers I've had make it exciting because of how they teach. There teaching patterns is what gives it away.—Richard, Melbourne, FL

〜

English is often branded as a boring class. But in my English class, there is never a dull day. We recently wrote a love story for Valentine's Day about two inanimate objects. Some examples of the creative stories are: shampoo and conditioner bottles, a filing cabinet and a file, Barbie and G.I. Joe. The turn out was quite interesting. We also read a play entitled "The Diary of Anne Frank". After we got done with the play we had a list of project to choose from about Anne Frank. Most of the projects were either Jewish food or Poster boards. The food, for the most part, was great. We all know more about "The Diary of Anne Frank". Miss ___ has assigned many projects for us to help us learn about English. We also do Mad Libs to help us improve and remember our grammar. We read a story out of our Literature book about a mentally handicapped man named Charlie. Afterwards we watched a movie about it. Miss ___ got the movie School House Rock about grammar. That day was interesting. We were all a little scared knowing we were getting a new English teacher, but things turned out to be quite fascinating. Whatever it will be, I'm sure our next project will be very . . . interesting.—Kate, Max, ND

⌁

Math is my favorite subject. I never really liked math much up until this year . . . math was my worst subject. . . . I stunk. . . . I got a brand new teacher right out of college. She was a gymnast at the University of Arkansas. She is so much fun and she is really funny. She makes us want to learn because we get to play math games on the floor, dance, sing, listen to music, and just have a ball learning math. Her lessons are short and easy to understand. If somebody doesn't understand something, she takes the time to explain it until they do understand.—Casey, Vestavia Hills, AL, 6th grade

Too Much, Too Fast . . . or of the Wrong Thing

Some students in my study, especially those in high school, were frustrated at the pace of instruction. They felt as if the pace went too fast to even ask questions of the teacher. According to them, testing is to blame. There is too much to teach and too many options (Schmidt, McKnight, & Raizen, 1996). "Given the sweeping nature of the high school curricula . . . few schools are able to allow the time necessary for students to grapple. As long as the end result of high school is measured in 'coverage' and as long as 'coverage' is assessed by measuring the student's memory, there will be no time for students' own questions" (Sizer & Sizer, 2003, p. 146).

A prime example of this is textbooks that schools use. U.S. math textbooks, for instance, cover between 175% and 300% more topics than those in Germany and Japan, yet our students do not perform as well. In science textbooks, we cover between 433% and 930% more than Germany and Japan (Schmidt, McKnight, & Raizen, 1996, as cited in Schmoker & Marzano, 2003).

⌁

I do not agree with FCAT activities. Students are forced to do FCAT prep activities before school starts. Most students in 11th and 12th grade have already passed the FCAT and if they have not, then they are probably in an FCAT class. It is unfair to take learning time away from other students who have passed. Being that I am in an honors class, most of my peers have passed the FCAT with the highest scores. . . . Yet, we have to take half an hour out of Pre-Calc to do FCAT related assignments. These activities are wasting the time of the already capable student.—Aaron, Vero Beach, FL

⌢

My worst subject is Language Arts because I do not get what Mrs. ___ is saying. The teacher goes to fast and it is hard to keep up with what she is saying. The teacher and my mom and dad keep telling me you can do better. The more they keep telling me I can do better I just do worst. They keep saying and saying you can do [it] I know you can. I get pressure to try to do better and I can not. I got so mad once I wanted to yell "SHUTUP."—Joshua, Newnan, GA, 6th grade

⌢

What causes stress at school? When the exams come near. Sometimes we may be at the point where we may not have covered everything that may be on the exams and teachers try to cram it into your head at the last minute. —Briaunna, Longwood, FL

⌢

The curriculum moves to fast that I can barely understand anything my teachers say. It's like all they care about is if they finish their lesson plan for the day, or "if problem two will be on a test this Friday." It is a sad thing when teachers do not seem to care about you.—Lauren Kaplan, Orlando, FL (Originally published in *Florida Educational Leadership*, 4(1), Fall 2003, pp. 40–41.)

⌢

When I am at school all I try to do is cram all this stuff in my head by the time I get home I have almost forgotten all of it!—Casey, Newnan, GA, 6th grade

⌢

Whatever happened to creative writing? What happened to connecting the dots, rather than memorizing the facts and writing them down, word-for-word on tests? What happened to reading because you wanted to? What happened to really thinking? Every day at school we memorize facts. Then, we write them on homework sheets. We look through the book for the sentence that matches number one and fill in the word that is missing. A week later, we transfer the facts from our brain to the paper, never to think about them again.—Elizabeth, Vestavia Hills, AL, 6th grade

∿

A resinable amount of homework is fine by me; in fact, sometimes, for certain classes, it is extremely helpful! But busy work that does not help is a nuisance. Cross-words and word searches generally waste my time. That, I find, is very hard to manage.—Lydia, Vestavia Hills, AL, 6th grade

The So-Called Dumbing Down of American Students

"American schoolchildren, from kindergarten through grade 12, are no more learned today than before, perhaps even less so" (Gross, 1999, p. 5). If Gross's claim is accurate, then we are indeed in trouble. However, in his book he fails to consider possible reasons behind course-taking patterns or the outside forces that impact students' options. Singh, Granville, and Dika (2002) note that by ninth or tenth grade students have already made unspoken decisions about pursuing or not pursing advanced courses, and these choices are determined by earlier success. Moreover, their attitudes about subject areas are also formed by viewpoints of parents, peers, and teachers. What about lessons beyond the textbook? Is teaching about life just as valuable as teaching about algebra or prepositional phrases? Students who wrote to me have concrete opinions on how well schools are doing in preparing them for the future—futures to include higher education and life in general. Note: several students submitted full-length essays; because the writing was so powerful, I decided to print one of them in full.

∿

I am in a special program called the Engineering Institute. A majority of my classes are honors and I get a sample of some of the major choice classes such as aerospace, interior design, and TV production. My class rotates, what, every 2 weeks or something? Just to get samples of the classes.—Briaunna, Longwood, FL

〜

Not "Dumbed Down"

At a recent church youth retreat that I attended, the speaker was a funny, bald man who gave powerful sermons; one day, he was apparently focusing on how unaware our generation is of the world around us. He said this was partially the fault of modern schooling, repeating the sentence, "You've been dumbed down, folks," over and over again. When I heard him say this, I felt uneasy and shifted nervously in my chair. Had my generation been "dumbed down" by modern schooling? Is my college degree going to be worth less than a high school diploma from 1970? I certainly hoped not. I have always enjoyed school, both its academic and social aspects. And to hear someone, especially an adult, degrade my education, which I dearly value, I felt a mixture of astonishment and resentment. School has taught me so much and I believe that it has worth. Since then, I have been assessing the true value of my education and have found that school has many intrinsic qualities that most people overlook.

To the common, untrained eye, school seems like just a building where children are forced to learn English, math, science, and history. But this is not the case. School teaches more than just the basic subjects of knowledge; it teaches the wisdom of life and the keys to success. This overlooked fact may make our education today of equal or even greater value than the education provided decades ago. In studying basic knowledge and subjects such as science and math, students learn how the world functions and exists around them. These subjects are needed as a foundation to learning; they are the basics students need to understand what happens in life. This knowledge also tends to improve with time; new scientific discoveries are being made each day. Thus the more recent the education, the more thorough and accurate it is. The atmosphere of school teaches unique qualities all together. In being around the same people hour after hour, day after day, year after year, a sort of bond tends to form, a feeling of togetherness. Bonds of this sort are formed daily but are also challenged continually by the age-old fallacies of distrust and hate and the current abominations of sex and drugs. The strength of the bonds and friendships we make together in school today are stronger than those made in school decades ago because of the new relationship gremlins that we have had to conquer, together. After school hours offer valuable enrichment as well. Participation in clubs and organizations like band and orchestra impart important values such as responsibility and leadership. These values build the character traits needed to succeed in the real world. This educational value of school did not exist in the beginning. But these useful and essential skills have found their way into modern schooling and have taught their ways to many. These values of life were not taught in schools decades ago, and therefore a modern education offers more to the student.

Much has been overlooked in modern education. The knowledge taught today, like science and math, is advanced and accurate. The wisdom of life, like making and keeping friends, are daily and fervently imparted upon the student. The keys to success, like leadership and responsibility, are commonplace today and can be found in schools everywhere. These make up the essence of modern education, the worthy backbone of my schooling. We have been "smarted up," not "dumbed down."—Yujing, Marietta, GA

⁓

High school. Does it educate young people more academically or socially? I think that some people may be surprised at the answer. As an average, middle class high school junior I have found that I have grown more as a person and learned more about people, and life in general than I have academics.

Social life—its what drives students. For me and my friend, it's the reason we show up every day. If I were to go so far as to make a generalization I would say that socialization is the main reason students stay motivated in school. High school indirectly teaches teenagers how to behave civilly, to act as part of a group, how to interact with others, how to effectively manage their time/finances, and how to come to a decision democratically. These are all skills that turn teenage dirt-bags into happy, healthy adults. Personally I feel that this is more valuable than some of the knowledge gained through academic courses. This leads me to say that an active social life is imperative to the maturation into an adult. . . . While the student may get the grade in school, they do not learn to communicate with others, or how to practically apply the knowledge they have. Anyone can see that this is not the picture of a competent adult. School is preparation for life, and life is interaction between people, not who can write a better essay or solve an equation faster. Knowledge is better gained through experience, not bookwork.—Justin, Clover, SC

Why Extracurricular Activities Matter

Extracurricular activities are as much a part of school life as academics, but involvement is sometimes a double-edged sword. Some debate the use of curricular money for extracurricular activities, and with stricter accountability measures in

place, schools are faced with dilemmas in terms of how resources are utilized. Moreover, in the push to return to basics, critics claim that sports, clubs, and the arts are not necessary. At the elementary level, time for recess and art and music classes is being replaced by time for "preparing for the test" or remediation. At the secondary level, the cuts are not as dire . . . yet. With increased pressure to "make acceptable progress," schools have to make tough decisions about what type of curricula to offer their students. However, studies have shown that facets of extracurricular activities—the collective quest, ritual and passion, and performance opportunities—positively affect students' experiences and that growth can also be transferred to the classroom (Kunzman, 2002).

In a recent article in the Christian Science Monitor, *Elizabeth Nesoff (2003) reports that music programs are being cut from schools all over the country. The primary causes? Tight budgets and strict testing mandates, like No Child Left Behind, bring about budget decisions. Often what is not tested (music, art, physical education, etc.) goes. What will happen without music programs? According to Nesoff we will have a society that is deprived, without cultural roots, or the educational and discipline benefits that come from music education. Music does help academic achievement. Consider these statistics: Preschoolers' spatial reasoning IQ rose 46% after 8 months of keyboard lessons (UC-Irvine study); music instruction is linked to higher scores in math, reading, history, geography, and the SAT; and students who participate in band or orchestra report the lowest use of alcohol, tobacco, and illicit drugs (Texas Commission on Drug and Alcohol Abuse, n.d.).*

Extracurricular activities, likewise, provide opportunities for students to appreciate teamwork, individual and group responsibility, physical strength and stamina, a sense of community, and enjoyment of leisure time. They offer a means to reinforce classroom lessons, using academic skills in real-world situations, thus making nonacademic experiences an integral part of students' education experiences (O'Brien & Rollefson, 1995). Research (DeMoulin, 2002; Redd, Brooks, & McGarvey, 2002; Ryska, 2002) has revealed a positive link between extracurricular activities and students' personal development and academic achievement. DeMoulin (2002), in particular, found positive correlations between academic and personal achievement and specific activities. Those involved in leadership and music/chorus experiences had higher grade point averages than nonparticipants.

～

I would have to say that I have had many school related positive experiences with the art department: band, drama, and stagecraft (technical theater). I can be involved with the things that I love, and am good at while learning vital life lessons and improving my skills as a musician, actress, and stage manager. I'm very thankful that my school offered these programs and that I was able to take full advantage of them during my time here at M___ High.—Rachel, Merritt Island, FL

~

Who would of thought that making a video would be this much fun? The video yearbook club is a club that works together all year trying to make an end of the year video for B___ Elementary School. There are 13 kids participating in this club, and I am one of them. Our computer teacher Mrs. ___ runs this club with help from Mrs. ___. Mrs. ___ gives a slip to two people in the club then they have to go to get the camera and video tape at least 5 minutes of each important event. Every Friday the video year book club gets together and figures out ideas for the movie (example—for the first 5 minutes of the movie are acted out by the video year book club) and we write down ideas for the beginning of the movie and other parts. Then we share our ideas and then we pick one and then we act out the idea we picked out. Once we know the idea we are not allowed to tell anyone. It's a secerect shshshshsh! Finally, at the end of the year everyone sees the movie in the all purposed room from first to fifth grade and all the teachers see the movie to. Then we send home a permission and people can purchase the movie if they liked it when they saw it in the all purpose room. I think a video year book is better than a regular year book because a video year book can last a lifetime and have so many memories to.—Michelle, Turnersville, NJ, 5th grade

~

Participating in various club activities is a great way to get involved in school. There are daily club meetings in school ranging from Korean Club to Freshman Steering. I am part of the Freshman Steering Club and Colors of Hope. In Freshman Steering, we plan different events such as bake sales and car washes that may help our class raise money. In Colors of Hope, we make greeting cards for children in hospitals. It is just a reminder to show them that we care. Being in a club also allows you to make new friends and to socialize with people your own age.—Sabrina, Woodland Hills, CA, 9th grade

~

Students who perform community service or are very involved with their schools devote more time to homework than those not involved; moreover, the more

involved students are, the more homework they do. In addition, students who are involved earn better grades and have higher opinions regarding the overall job their schools do in providing them with a quality education (Horatio Alger Association, 2002). Research also suggests that participation in extracurricular activities can increase students' sense of engagement or connection to their schools, and thereby decrease the likelihood of school failure (Finn, 1993, as cited in O'Brien & Rollefson, 1995; Lamborn, Brown, Mounts, & Steinberg, 1992). Indicators of successful participation in school include consistent attendance, academic achievement, and aspirations for continuing education beyond high school; research shows a positive correlation associated with each of the above factors among high school seniors, including better attendance, less truancy, higher GPAs, higher standardized test scores, and increased numbers going on to higher education (O'Brien & Rollefson, 1995).

⌒

I really do like the fact that high school offers a lot of extracurricular activities to fit everyone's needs and personalities, activities such as the Fishing Club for the anglers, the Key Club for the volunteers, and FBLA for business type people. These activities allow people to be a part of groups with those of similar interests. These activities also give students the opportunity to do something productive with themselves after school besides getting into trouble. After school meetings and events play a major role in keeping kids off the streets and in beneficial organizations.—Keiera, Vero Beach, FL

⌒

At H___ H.S. there are numbers of after school activities that take place like sports, DECA, Model UN, drama club, FBLA, chess club. These organizations have many benefit[s] to improving students grades and their overall personality. These activities have proven to keep students more productive in school, while being healthier and less likely to get in trouble.

There are many benefits to these activities. These activities keep students away from drugs and alcohol. This is a time where student get a chance to socialize and hang out with their friends. These activities provide students with better leadership and communication skills. Athletics provide all of the above benefits including building muscular endurance and muscle, and giving students a higher self esteem and healthier bodies.—Dustin, Hartford, WI

～

My favorite school activity is cheerleading. I know you're probably thinking, "Oh great, a ditsy cheerleader." Cheerleading isn't only about stunting, tumbling, and screaming. I think it teaches girls and boys, at a young age, how to have teamwork. It also gives you a boost of spirit so that you can have a new, happier perspective on life. Even if you aren't the coolest person in the grade, you can still make the cheerleading squad and feel important and appreciated. Cheerleading is a lot of hard work, so you have to learn how to be committed and dedicated to what you do. You can't decide one night to skip practice and go to the movies with your friends. If you do skip a practice you will learn your lesson by getting demerits. If you get too many demerits you can get in a lot of trouble and kicked off the squad! Cheerleading can help you learn to keep your priorities straight. You have to have a "C" average to be on the squad. That means you can't be getting lazy on your homework and keep saying that you had cheerleading as your excuse.—Meredith, Vestavia Hills, AL, 6th grade

～

Given these data, we should pay more attention to the number of students who participate in extracurricular activities. If there is a positive link, then O'Brien and Rollefson's (1995) finding that 4:5 seniors in 1992 participated in extracurricular activities (42% in sports, 16–18 % each in honor societies, publications, student government, and clubs) offers a critical argument for noncore subjects and extracurricular activities.

Sports-related activities, in particular, have a tremendously positive effect on students, especially females. The President's Council on Physical Fitness and Sports (1997) and the National Council for Research on Women (1991, 1998) list some benefits that occur when girls and boys participate in sports: improved self-esteem, positive feelings about body image, increased self-confidence, increased opportunities for experiences of competency and success, and increased willingness to take risks and try new experiences. Participation in extracurricular activities translates to the classroom (Webster, 2000). As students from California write:

～

I believe that the most important aspect of being on a sports team is the achievement of personal goals. I feel extremely confident that I am on the road to achievement. The goals that I set for myself this year were to join the girls' volleyball team and condition my body. To complete this goal I needed one thing, the most important thing that my Coach ___ taught me, D.E.M.A.N.D.! The word demand has brought me where I am today. D.E.M.A.N.D. stands for discipline, enthusiasm, motivation, aggression, never to give up, and desire. When I went to summer practices for volleyball, I gave it all I had. I was learning new skills that would better prepare me.—Cassondra, Moreno Valley, CA

～

In practice the coaches make us run. It is cold and my body is tired from school. I end up sore and bloody from cuts and scrapes. I never really want to go, but I know I have to because I like to win. That is how I think of school. I hate getting out of a warm bed in the morning and doing homework instead of watching TV. I'm always tired, but I also know that it will pay off in the end just like practice. I will win by getting a good job and earning good money. That is why I know that the skills I have learned in my classes this semester are important.—Nicholas, Moreno Valley, CA

～

Despite the good news about extracurricular activities, there are drawbacks when schools and the public place too much emphasis on them, particularly the weighted importance of sports. Even though some students addressed the aspects of stress and time management when involved in extracurricular activities, they could not downplay the role of extracurricular activities in schools. Were these activities missing, many students would not attend school, as these students attest.

～

The only reason school is fun is because of sports. Going to school involves getting up early, going through boring classes, and taking tests. The only school days that are fun are game days. These days are the only days I'm mainly awake. How would you like to sit through seven different classes that are about an hour long each, and listen to someone talk? It seems like everyday we go over the same things in class. So what's the point of going to school?

Basketball is the only reason I go to school, besides my parents. Basketball games and practices are what I look forward to during the school day. I'm sure I'm not the only one who feels this way. School would be a lot more fun if we didn't have to take tests or start so early. It's all work and no sleep. If you ask any teacher in the school I'm sure they could tell you they've had more than one student fall asleep during class time. This is my perspective on school and sports.—Janae, Max, ND

⌒

Sports and school spirit are the two best things a school has to offer. After all, a school without school spirit is not really even a school. School spirit is one of the many things I like about school. At the football games there are thousands of people cheering on their Indians in hope of a victory. Students paint their faces red and white before the games to show off their school spirit. When entering a basketball game the sound of fans cheering fills the air. People screaming and yelling "D-Fence, D-Fence," or the dance team doing their latest cheer at center-court.—Aaron, Vero Beach, FL

⌒

My favorite thing about school is the sports I get to participate in. they are fun and keep me in shape. The sports I participate in are in order form best liked to worst liked: Wrestling, football, baseball and track.

The best thing about sports is meeting new people; having fun and learning new stuff to make you better. When participating in sports you get out of some school and should do the best you can when you are participating in. Also do not lose your temper it only makes things worse.

The sport I like the most is wrestling. Wrestling keeps me in the best shape and I meet a lot of new kids and see a lot of good looking girls. When I am wrestling I can only blame myself for losing, even though I can only blame myself I still let the team down. Wrestling also makes me push myself to limits I did not think I could go.

When I am in school I think about sports and not about school. I also think about my grades and keeping them up so I can still participate in sports. I think if there were not sports during school it would not be worth going to. People in school should participate in sports for there own benefit. I think it would do them a lot of good and help them be more social. A person joining sports also gives coaches more numbers to work with and more options.—Heath, Max, ND

⌒

It's Friday. The fight song is playing over the intercom as our school's football team prepares for the big game. All students are sporting school colors as an air of excitement sweeps the hallways. The night finally comes. The stadium is packed. Loud cheers help bring our Indians to yet another victory. It is in this win that most students forget about the bad points of high school. Teachers, pressures and grade point averages are now gone. Students are able to enjoy just being kids again.—Maura, Vero Beach, FL

～

Friday Night Fever
On Friday nights across America, from the warm Pacific shores of the Hawaiian Islands to the bright lights of East Coast cities, thousands of people from all races and backgrounds come together for one common purpose—football. No, this is not the big time professional leagues or the high stakes college grudge matches. It is something unique to America, a slice of pure Americana that provides some of the greatest school memories one could have—high school football.

In the opening scene of the movie *Remember the Titans*, the narrator set the tone by saying, "In Virginia, high school football is a way of life." Even though this movie was set in the 1970's, little about high school football has changed, and not just in Virginia, but in the entire South as well. It seems that the entire southeastern portion of the United States has taken up a love affair with the rough-and-tumble sport. Southern high school powerhouses like Georgia's Valdosta, North Carolina's Independence, and Louisiana's Evangel Christian have all left their marks not only on their respective states, but the nation as well, winning national championship after championship, not to mention bragging rights over their rivals. After one of these magical seasons ends, many folks wait months on end for the next one to begin. Coaches, who to the normal eye are regular teachers, are revered as Friday's heroes or scorned as goats. Either way, win or lose, the high school game is one of the most beloved Southern traditions.

While some say that high school football consists of three months of play and a nine month week off, to get into the true spirit of a high school varsity football game is to visit any American high school on a crisp autumn Friday. All day, thoughts focus on that night's big game. Teachers' lectures fall on deaf ears, and colorful game posters and local newspaper headlines only add to the effect. The real magic, however, starts when the sun begins to sink. Thousands file into a small, charming little stadium to clamber up to their cold, hard, unassigned seats to watch their sons, peers, neighbors, or siblings compete against eleven other like-minded people from another high school in some other town. Golden shadows are silhouetted against the grass, gradually fading into darkness and letting the stadium lights light the stadium into a shimmering beacon that lights the inky sky for miles around. Plays on the field, spectacular in their own right, are only enhanced by the noise or cheers, boos, and the bombastic blasts from the supportive band. A constant buzz hovers over the stadium during the season, and even after the crowd is gone and the lights have dimmed, the electricity and exuberance in the air from past seasons can still be felt.

In the end, no matter how much America changes as it begins to age, it will still have high school football. No matter when cars fly or people live on the Moon, the crowds and fanfare will always be there to serve as a touchdown, rather, a touchstone, into a great future.—Michael B.

Photo by Daniel Escorcia

~

CHAPTER FOUR

The Pedagogical Dimension

A poor surgeon hurts one person at a time. A poor teacher hurts 130.

—Ernest Boyer

My favorite teacher is all my teachers because they all help me in some way.

—Justin, Inwood, WV

The pedagogical dimension refers to what and how teachers teach (Eisner, 1992). Research has documented that a good or bad teacher makes all the difference in student achievement (see Brophy & Good, 1986; Cochran-Smith, 2003; Darling-Hammond & Youngs, 2002; Sanders & Horn, 1998). This book is not the place to discuss how this happens or to argue for or against colleges of education or certification routes. Rather, the focus is simply on teaching—what materials teachers use and what students think about their teachers.

For some people, being a good teacher is about being able to connect with students and subject matter. According to Palmer (2003), good teachers share one trait: a strong sense of personal identity, while bad teachers distance themselves from what and who they teach. Wong and Wong (1998) say it another way: Some people go into teaching because it is a job. Some people go into teaching to make a difference. Although I suspect that none enter the profession to be ineffective, what exactly makes a good teacher? Depending on whom one asks, answers may vary tremendously. Here are a few that I have heard from those both in and out of schools: they have a good grasp of subject matter; they care; they maintain strict rules; they are likeable; they challenge; they have good scores on teacher tests; they maintain high standards; they have many years in the profession. Get a sense of the complexity concerning "good teaching"?

Those studying teaching and learning have identified several common qualities of good teaching. Good teachers make sure students do their work, control the classroom, are willing to help students when and how they need it, explain assignments clearly, vary the instructional routine, and take time to get to know students and their backgrounds (Corbett & Wilson, 2002). Linda Darling-Hammond (1996) further clarifies—successful teachers develop engaging tasks that give students meaningful work to do, design tasks that allow for student choice, constantly assess students to identify strengths and needs, and pay attention to developing students' confidence, motivation, and effort. For younger children, in one study, a good teacher was one who let them have some autonomy over doing specific subjects, more choice in work done in class, and was caring and kind. A bad teacher was one that was too strict or punished too harshly, unfair in assigning work, and did not care about the students (Wragg, Haynes, Wragg, & Chamberlin, 2000). For older students in the study, the top three important teacher attributes were: explains things clearly, provides good exam preparation, and treats all students fairly. A good teacher helps students when they are stuck, explains clearly, and can control the class. A bad teacher is one who is too strict, shouts too much, does not clearly explain assignments, and does not respect students (Wragg et al., 2000). One student writing to me summed up the important role of teachers:

～

The most important aspect of school that I believe students take for granted the most are the teachers. It's not always easy to find qualified individuals to come in and be as dedicated as it takes to be a good teacher. Most spend many hours after school each week to help students and still most people don't show the teachers the appreciation that they deserve. When you get to college, you will see that the teachers care less about you as an individual and cannot tend to your every need. I'm thankful for the teachers that I have. Even if I may not care for them, I try my best to get along with them and always show them respect.
—Jeff, Vero Beach, FL

Good Teachers: What Students Say

Good teachers, according to one student in a recent study, "care about me, listen to what I have to say, don't try to make me do things I don't want to, and ask me what I'd like to do" (Glasser, 2003, p. 232). While teachers are not generally able to grant wishes like this student's, many students who wrote to me stated that the teachers they liked were the ones who cared about them, not just as students but as people. Palmer (2003) writes, "Good teaching cannot be reduced to technique; good teaching comes from the identity and integrity of the teacher" (p. 67). This emotional support is more than "touchy-feely" stuff, it is integral to student achievement. Research shows that students who feel emotionally supported by their teachers are more likely to experience academic success, enjoy their time in school, and exhibit good behavior (Bru, Stephens, & Torsheim, 2002; Fraser & Fisher, 1982; Merrett & Wheldall, 1989; Rutter, Giller, & Hagell, 1998).

⌒

Twenty years from now, I know I can look back to my high school years and remember one specific class; my Algebra II honors class taught by Mrs. ___. Now I have always had an interest in the math department, but she not only made it fun, but she made sense of everything. Mrs. ___ was an amazingly smart lady that was absolutely social with her students. She would be willing to help anyone at any time just to make sure they would understand a problem. Being the most dedicated teacher in the math department she was also a friend to me when I needed someone to talk to. Mrs. ___ and her Algebra II honors class started a new view on school for me, and kept my grades alive. Besides teaching the necessities, she taught me how to make fun of a problem and how if you just keep trying, the reward is worth every hour of your struggle! She is now retired, but I know she still shared her knowledge even though she is not working as a teacher anymore.—A. L., Merritt Island, FL

⌒

I would personally my ROTC Col. ___ has to be my favorite teacher. He doesn't only teach military traditions. Col. ___ let every one of his cadets know that you need to achieve lifelong goals. A few of the goals are maintaining a 2.0 gpa or higher. Also do things right the first time around. The most of all thing he said is to have higher education after finishing high school.

When Col. ___ talks about doing things right the first time, it usually means buckle down and pass your core subject and not worry about little things that aren't important. Then there's taking the FCAT and to pass it the first time instead of thinking about it your senior year. Col. ___ always saids you have a chance to make something out of yourself.—Alisha, Melbourne, FL

～

Mr. ___ Rocks

My favorite teacher is Mr. ___ because he lets us do a lot of neat things. One thing is he tells us to pass the ball in different ways. The other day, we played a game were we had to hit a checker piece with a basketball and get it on the opposite side of you (partners side). Whoever had the checker piece on their side lost. I can't wait. Last year in my old school, I thought I would never have a gym teacher like that again. Mr. ___ changed that in a heartbeat. Mr. ___ is as funny as when my rabbit spaz out. He is the nicest teacher I know. It's neat having that one special teacher you like, especially if he likes you as a student.—Brooke, Turnersville, NJ, 5th grade

～

My favorite teachers have always been my history teachers like Mr. ___, Coach ___, and Mr. ___. I enjoy having or have had those teachers as well as enjoying their classes. Some other favorites are the ones who help place the FCAT standardized test like Ms. ___, Ms. ___, Mr. ___, and Mrs. ___. All of my history teachers made sure we were taught about important parts of history.

Another thing that makes these teachers my favorites is because they care about the students and what we are taught. We were also pushed to make the grade and wasn't just given grades. Another one of my favorite teachers is Mr. ___ because we are motivated to stay on top of our work. So, what I'm basically trying to say is my favorite teachers this year are Mr. ___, Mr. ___ and Mrs. ___ because they are paving ways for my future if I choose to walk the path, and I will.—Chari, Tallahassee, FL

～

Even though I've questioned some of the teachers I've had along the way, they have all taught me everything I know today and have also helped to make me the person I am today. I know that every day of school I get under my belt is one step closer to a fantastic future that I will have. The more I am writing, the more appreciation, I realize, I have for teachers and all that they do. Therefore, teachers are definitely a positive aspect for going to school for twelve long years. Not only are they educating you to a fantastic future, they can also be mentors, counselors, friends, or just great people.—Chrisy, Merritt Island, FL

⁓

My positive school experiences have always been with great teachers who have impacted my life. One time my 6th/7th grade English teacher was in the kitchen of the cafeteria at our camp. At this school we took a week to go to camp for "outdoor school" and learn from nature. I was on duty of helping in the cafeteria to set silverware and other miscellaneous items out. Anyways, she was in the kitchen cooking scrambled eggs with a few other teachers and I just remember her singing "I feel like a natural woman" at the top of her happy lungs. It made an impression on that moment and also to this very one because I want to be like that.—Lauren, Merritt Island, FL

⁓

Favorite teachers, I never had. This year I do, my history teacher Mr. ___. Out of all the history teachers I've ever had he's the best. You can also call him Coach ___. The reason why he is my favorite teacher is he brings history to life. Coach ___ catches me up with work that I miss and makes learning fun. He doesn't have you sitting down reading a book all period and answering questions. Instead, we get into groups and do worksheets together. He talks about the important things that happen in history and he never side tracks from what he's talking about.

Coach ___ makes us think about things we never thought about like all the people who were involved in the civil rights movement and what they went through. He looks at the situation from every aspect that you never thought about. This is probably the only favorite history teacher I ever had who make history interesting.—Melissa, Melbourne, FL

⁓

The best thing that I've experienced in my last 13 years of school is having Ms. ___ for a teacher. For the past three years of being in her class she has taught me many things about writing, English, and how to get into college, but what is the most meaningful is what she taught me about myself. She taught me to believe in myself, and to only strive for the best. Without her guidance and support, I would be completely lost. Thanks for everything. Mrs. ___, you mean more to me than you'll ever know.—Alison, Merritt Island, FL

～

My teachers I have right now are pretty cool and reasonable, especially my English teacher Mr. ___ (even though that's my favorite subject). He's just plain out a nice person. He's courteous, funny, and makes you want to learn about the things he's teaching. Another teacher I admire is my earth science teacher, Mrs. ___. She's really nice and helpful to her students, so every time I have a problem that's about the only teacher I would ask for help in the school and expect positive results.

I know you're probably getting tired of hearing me talk about my teachers but there are four more special ones like the best history teacher ever! Mr. ___. It's probably because he's the youngest male teacher I have I can relate to him more as a students also a friend. Another teacher I have is Mrs. ___. She's really nice and understanding, although I don't get the good grades in her class. I don't talk bad about anyone, especially if they're kind to me. The old but exciting Mr. ___ also known as my computer teacher is probably the funnest class I have where you're expected to do work. Because while I'm doing assignments I'm listening to music, and if you know me, that's one great hobby of mine. Last, but not least, is my physical education teacher, Mrs. ___. She probably thinks I put her last as an insult, but it's nothing like that. I never notice it but the things that she gets on me about are valuable lessons in life like to do everything to the fullest, respect and if you have gift to be avail of it.—DeShawn, Jackson, MI

～

Well, Dr. Lisa Scherff, I remember you as my intensive reading teacher. Your classroom was next door to Ms. ___. I remember coming to your class 9th grade stressed out and you used to calm me down. You would talk to me on a one to one basis to relieve my stress.—Isabelle, Tallahassee, FL

～

My classes aren't too hard, thanks to the teachers. All of my teachers try their best to make sure we understand the things we're learning in class. If I have a question about something, I don't feel uncomfortable asking my teachers for help. The teachers encourage us to do well, but don't expect us to know more than our grade level should. I know that if I need help with anything I can go to my teachers and they will make things more clear. My favorite class of the day is science. I'm not that interested in science, but I love the way my teachers explains things. I've always had trouble with that class, but this year it's different. He teaches to every single kid individually instead of looking at us as a "whole" class.—Jennifer, Inwood, WV

⌒

I've had many teachers who I will remember for the rest of my life. Such as my 8th grade history teacher Mrs. ___. She was so creative and I actually remember stuff from her class today. I also like my 11th grade history teacher Mr. ___. I like him because I actually learned something from his class. Although many complained about his complexity it was well worth it.—Jessica, Tallahassee, FL

⌒

My favorite teacher in the first grade was Mrs. ___. She was my favorite because she gave us game time every day for one hour. Every day she would read us a chapter in her favorite children's book. She had a good sense of humor and was very kind. . . . She always gave us a second chance if we did something bad. She never yelled at us and was always smiling. The best thing I like about her was she always helped us we needed it on our work. My favorite part of her class was our little reading groups. That is why she was my favorite teacher.—Lindsey, Newnan, GA, 6th grade

⌒

I remember a time when my English teacher assigned a huge project on poetry. Now, no student likes to do long projects over weekends, but it had to get done. While reading famous poems from Poe, Whitman, Longfellow, etc., I was intrigued by the styles and flow of language. In having to create my own poems, I discovered a new, different way to express myself. Ever since that one project, it has opened my eyes to new writing styles. I am an admirer of poetry and have expanded my writing in creating different poems. It is a new way of thinking, a different way of expressing, and a beautiful way of writing. And, I look back and wonder how I have progressed in writing poetry. I have to thank that one English teacher who, not knowing it, influenced me in the aspect of poetry and creative writing.—Laura, Merritt Island, FL

⌒

If you have a favorite teacher then sometimes that teacher is able to catch the student before it leads to "drop out." What I mean by catch them is sometimes the teacher is able to get into the students' head. Then that teacher becomes, not only a teacher but a friend as well. Once that teacher has the student's trust then the teacher is able to show the student that there is more to it than just being popular.—Rochelle, Tallahassee, FL

⁓

My favorite teacher was my 3rd grade teacher Mrs. ___. She would let us play games, have recess, and have parties. She also helped all the kids in our class reach 75 AR points. Her husband was like a skyscraper he had to duck to get in the door. One time she read to us a book about a vampire bunny, so we got to wear broccoli necklaces all day long. We also got to raise caterpillars into butterflies, then we let them go. During the ITBS Test when we had brakes she would let us do Jumping Jacks. She had a good relationship with all the kids, and she still loved us even if we were a little bad sometimes.—Nathan, Newnan, GA, 6th grade

⁓

The title, my favorite teacher, did not cross my mind until the sixth grade. It was my last year at the middle school and I was hoping for a good one. The teacher that was soon to have the title of my favorite teacher was Ms. ___. She was my math and science teacher for the year. Ms. ___ became my favorite teacher for many reasons. Ms. ___ made math out to be the best subject in the world, which is contrary to what most students believe. Every day she found a way to keep the class interested in the material. She would use different incentives such as candy. Ms. ___ would invent class games to better our understanding of the material. In class she discussed subject matter that would be interesting to sixth graders.

Ms. ___ truly cared about the students in her class. She did not care if we were all "A" students, as long as everyone did their best. If you did not understand part of the material, she would work with you as long as you were also willing to do your part. A student was never left behind. When any of her students experienced trouble with a peer, she tried to resolve the matter herself before it went to higher authorities.

The true reason she is my favorite teacher is she is not afraid of tears. This fact may sound petty to some people, but not to me. Math is not my best subject and I am known to have "mad tears". These are tears that appear when I become frustrated at myself, for the smallest things. Most teachers dislike having a student that cries, but not Ms. ___. Instead of sending me out of the room, she would work with me through the tears. She never became angry with me but always seemed to understand.

Ms. ___, my sixth grade teacher deserves the title of my favorite teacher. She was always willing to help her students and she made sure the help was received. Ms. ___ always found a way to make class interesting. Through out the year she never appeared to be judgmental—always understanding.—Elizabeth, Clover, SC

⌒

My 4th grade teacher Mrs. ___ was a great teacher! She new just what to say and when to say it. She loved us like her own and she treated us like it to. Mrs. ___ great to be around, she made me look forward to school every day. She treated us all like her children equally. She said "she didn't have a favorite student cause it was to hard to pick". We had lots of fun in her class no one wanted to go to the 5th grade. So we always would try to make her go to the 5th grade and get us all back in her class. We had a great time in 4th grade and I will never forget it!!—Christina, Newnan, GA, 6th grade

⌒

My favorite teacher would be my fifth grade teacher, Mrs. ___. Having her as my Literature/Language, Science, Social Studies, and homeroom teacher was like a chocolate sundae everyday! She is very funny and made everyone laugh with her jokes. I wish all teachers did that! Mrs. ___ dropped our lowest grades, before report cards were ready to go home. When we had free time in class, she would sometimes let us go outside on the playground. If it was too cold, we could talk to our friends or play inside.

Mrs. ___ usually had a smile on her face, if you make her really mad, watch out! She was also laughing and kidding around, too! When we worked on projects, she would let us talk, and put on music, so we could concentrate better. She made tricks and jokes on April fool's day. Unlike other teachers, she made learning a piece of cake. I thought holidays were the best!! She made goodie bags filled with candy and pencils. We even had brain food when we took our Major tests. In L.A. class, she gave us 10–20 minutes of reading time before class began. When we got really bad grades, she gave us opportunities to bring up our grades. Now she teaches at a different middle school, and I wish she would teach here. It was really fun to be in her class. We sometimes e-mail each other. I really miss her! Like I said, I wish all other teachers were like her!—Soyolmaa, Newnan, GA, 6th grade

～

My teachers name was S ___. She is my mom, I was home schooled for 4 years 2nd, 3rd, 4th, and 5th grade. Our classroom was in our basement. My mom always helped me with my work. (Especially math.) We also went to a lot of places like an Emu Farm. We also got to hold an egg that had already hatched. We also went to a Fish Hatchery and saw an albino catfish. We also got to feed the big catfish that were outside but the food smelt worse than melted dog food. My mom really cared about the way our handwriting looked, if it looked messy and sloppy she would help us do it over. There were only 3 people in my classroom, me, my twin, and my little sister. Another thing I loved was every day we would go upstairs and we would eat a peanut butter and pudding sandwich.—Mindy, Newnan, GA, 6th grade

～

My favorite teacher was Ms. ___, my wacky, crazy, fifth grade Science teacher, and friend. One of the coolest things she did was experiments. We did almost three each week! She also had many parties! She was very close with her students and their parents. If you had a problem, she would help you. I think she gave the best advice. She thought that we could be the best. And you know what? We all were the best that we could ever be! She knew how to make us do the best we could! I don't know how, but somehow, she always did. I don't know of any of her students that didn't like her! Her classroom always smelled like freshly bloomed flowers. She was crazy and laughed and joked a lot. I think she was the best teacher in the world. Even though she isn't my teacher anymore, she is still my favorite friend!—Jessie, Newnan, GA, 6th grade

～

My favorite teacher Mrs. ___ my third grade teacher to me was like a hot fudge sundae on a really hot day!!! When a kid in her class would get sick she would bring it to your house if your parents didn't come and get the homework! That was cool how she would do that for us!!! I still wish that she was here but she moved to Pennsylvania but me and her have such a good bond that we keep in touch with each other while she is there. She said she was supposed to come to Georgia this summer so she can visit us so ill be waiting on her ok bye!!!—Christopher, Newnan, GA, 6th grade

∼

Many would have to agree that a good teacher could influence a person's heart. Jesus is often referred to as the "great teacher" because of his humble approach and use of illustrations to paint an eloquent picture, carried to the hearts of his listeners, his message of God. John Nash, an intelligent man who, despite his being mentally ill, was admired by many students and inspired them to break the boundaries of mathematics. Dr. Martin Luther King, put his "preaching and teaching" abilities to work when he spoke out against the injustices of black people, in turn birthing the civil rights movement. Parents are teachers too, for it's through their example and guidance that their children follow. Within the walls of H___ High School, there's a man who has had a great impact on the vast majority of his students. Anyone who has had the privilege of being one of Mr. ___'s students has experienced a unique and entertaining form of learning.

Despite British literature being the syllabus for his teaching, Mr. ___ has taught me an underlying lesson that as a black person I don't think fellow associates would understand. Ralph Waldo Emerson once said, "To laugh often and love much, to win the respect of intelligent persons and the affection of children; to earn the approbation of honest critics; to appreciate beauty; to give of one's self; to know even one life has breathed easier because you have lived that is to have succeeded." Mr. ___ has definitely taught me what it means to "laugh often" and because of this I've "breathed easier." To live in a town everyday where you know people are judging you and could care less whether you were dead or alive, to feel their stares, and hear their whispers. Somehow to stumble upon something that takes your attention away from the disturbing realities of life and brings you to ease is a pretty powerful thing. He has honestly made the difference in Hartford being less of a place of residence and more of a "home" for me.

The numerous visits and positive comments he receives are proof of the effect he has on his students. Whether these people leave his class forgetting everything they've learned doesn't matter because sometimes the greatest lessons in life are learned through the life and example of a person.

Success can be defined in a variety of different ways. When someone can have a memorable effect on a vast majority of people that's someone who has succeeded in life. whether Mr. ___ realizes it or not, I'm sure all can agree he's a very "rich" and successful person.—Monica, Hartford, WI

∼

My favorite teacher would have to be my 1st grade teacher Ms. ___. Ms. ___ she did a lot of stuff for me that year. She would always help us separate from the class. For example she and I would always have Friday conferences where she and I would talk about my grades, my behavior, and my other problems in school. From what I can remember she never once raised her voice. She made learning fun. We also did stuff just for the fun of it. One thing we did was we acted out the play the Wizard of Oz. The first thing we did in the morning was talk time. Talk time is where you would go to the front of the class and tale stories about what happened to you. You also got to sit at her desk on your birthday. Also on backwards day we did and said everything backwards. So for these reasons and many more is why Ms. ___ is my favorite teacher.—Darby, Newnan, GA, 6th grade

∼

I look forward to her [Mrs. ___] classes everyday. Why? Because she makes them fun! She doesn't stand in front of the class and go on and on in a monotone voice. She puts some expression into the lesson. She actually gets up there and teaches us, using things we like as example. For place values some teachers might put a number up on the board and say, this is the one's place, this is the ten's place, and so on. That is so boring! Since almost everyone down here likes college football, she brought in pictures of three stadiums: Arkansas, Alabama, and Auburn. Then she wrote the number of people each could hold on the board, and explained place value to us.—Kelsey, Vestavia Hills, AL, 6th grade

∼

Mr. ___ is my forth grade teacher, which is where I am at right now. This is the first year that I have had a male teacher. He is really into Social Studies, and politics. Every day we talk about current events in the news. I really like that he treats us like adults and talks to us about what it going on in the world.—Cameron, Ft. Oglethorpe, GA, 4th grade

∼

My favorite teacher was my 2nd grade teacher Mrs. ___. I went to school at W___ Primary School in Waynesboro, Georgia. She was my favorite because she used to make us laugh all the time. She also knew she was supposed to make today fun and tomorrow promising. I really miss my 2nd grade teacher Mrs. ___. Amanda, Newnan, GA, 6th grade

And What About the Bad Ones . . .

I doubt any teacher enters the profession to be substandard. Nonetheless, I was taught by some who were incompetent, and, although rare, I see more of the same when I visit schools. Some teach while never coming out from behind their desks; others yell at students; a number of them simply don't teach. What turns a good teacher into a bad one? Perhaps it is simply forgetting "that teaching is an art and . . . teaching without authority ceases to be teaching at all" (Banner & Cannon, 1997, pp. 1, 21). Maybe "teachers forget that teaching has three important sources: subjects taught, students taught, and the teacher. Reduce teaching to intellect and it becomes a cold abstraction; reduce it to emotions and it becomes narcissistic; reduce it to the spiritual and it loses its anchor to the world" (Palmer, 2003, p. 67). Other teachers merely fail to remember that they are not the center of the classroom and fall back on traditional teaching methods—like lecturing. Still, other teachers fall short because they don't connect with their students. This disconnect can be caused by racial, ethnic, gender, academic ability, and/or socioeconomic differences. Some research has shown that "teachers . . . communicate more easily with students who participate in elite class structures, give them more attention and special assistance, and perceive them as more intelligent or gifted than students who lack cultural capital" (DiMaggio, 1982, p. 190, as cited in Kingston, 2001). Finally, teachers are often constrained by mandates from the state, district, or their own administration, and required to use ineffective materials or methods. Students, such as the ones below who volunteered comments, see these and other reasons why teachers are "bad."

∼

One of the factors that determine whether a person likes or dislikes high school is the quality of their teachers. Today, at times, it seems as though people couldn't decide what to do with themselves, so they simply got teaching degrees. Few really love what they do. The second you walk into a room with a negative teacher the feeling becomes contagious. Why is it that adolescents with the many pressures of today are expected to respect somebody who doesn't even want to be there? It used to be said that teaching was a vocation, not a job.—Maura, Vero Beach, FL

∼

Students dislike school because of the teachers. The majority of people have had at least one teacher who he or she did not like. Especially in Florida, there is a large shortage of teachers. When there is a need for teachers in a community, the schools will less than likely fire a teachers, unless behavior was incredibly negative. The schools will not really look for character in a new teacher, but instead the fact that he or she is able to teach. This ensures the fact that somewhere, some student will have a teacher that is rude, or calls a particular student out in the middle of class. For instance, I have had a substitute that made fun of me, as well as verbally assaulting a fellow classmate and friend. This will lead to a student disliking the class, and in most cases, ultimately disliking school.—Michael, Vero Beach, FL

⌣

My least favorite teacher is Mr. ___. I have never had anyone be so mean and rude to me, especially a teacher who is supposed to be there to help you out. He announced to our class after a girl asked a question that answering her question would be pointless because women are not worth educating. He refused to answer questions when he didn't explain something very well and reminded our class once a day that we are stupid. My favorite teacher besides Mrs. ___, of course, is the chorus teacher. She is always there if we have a problem and is very trustworthy and energetic. We work very hard in her class but she knows how to have a good time. She also puts in so many after school hours to help us in competitions. She is always willing to be there when we need her. We need more teachers like Ms. ___ and *less* like Mr. ___.—Clare, Merritt Island, FL

⌣

If I was talking to my counselor, I would probably discuss to her about the least favorite subject . . . my Draft/Design class. What I dislike about the class is the teacher. She never tries to help the ones that are in need of it. She pushes a lot of assignments on us at one time and expects us to do it. She's the type of teacher that shouldn't be a teacher. She has no patience. —LaShaune, Melbourne, FL

⌣

Teachers and administrators have developed a so-called attitude. Not to say all teachers are mean, but most are out for themselves and only partially care about the students' lives they have chosen to enrich. To enter into a classroom and be presented with bookwork is not the ideal situation students are looking for. It may seem to teachers that students do not care, but most do and properly motivated by a facilitator, that certain spark can become a fire in less than a 90-minute class period.—Dana, Vero Beach, FL

⌒

Now you probably think that just because I am a student that I am going to complain about teachers. Not entirely true. I will talk about some teachers' attitudes and they won't be too terribly flattering. I will however also talk about the good things teachers do. For one thing, students dislike teachers who are smart alecs. A smart alec is a person who gets really annoying and sarcastic towards other people. When teachers become upset and begin lecturing students on behavior, or whatever it is the lecture is on, students tend to stop listening. Some teachers have an attitude that may be negative toward all students. For example, my best friend forgot to get some paper signed for her class. Her teacher came down on her pretty hard. My best friend said, "I am sorry. My mom was in a hurry to get to work so I couldn't get her to sign it." Then her teacher replied, "Don't you have a father?" My best friend replies, "No Ma'am. My father doesn't live with me." The teacher didn't even apologize! How rude! I am also wondering why do math teachers even bother handing out math homework? Do they really believe that students are going to go home and do the math in their heads? They go home and turn on their calculators! What's the point? Some teachers are nice. Some teachers can actually get students to pay attention. They are truly gifted teachers. Kind and sympathetic teachers are the only teachers who actually teach. Other teachers simply stand around and teach themselves while students sit around and ignore them.—Keylie, Cocoa, FL, 8th grade

⌒

Being a student of public school my whole life has led me to form my opinion on it solely based on the teachers. Yes, the teachers and their motivation make or break the learning atmosphere at school. I had a physics teacher last year who was, in my opinion, the smartest, most efficient man I have ever met. He made learning fun for me and I wanted to excel in his class more than anything.

Many things can contribute to a student's lack of drive or ambition. One is the blatant ignorance of a teacher for his/her students' feelings and the subject he/she teaches. It's obvious when a teacher has no passion for what he/she does, and for students, it stimulates laziness and the question "why" towards the work assigned. Nobody wants to do work for a teacher who doesn't want it.

The concept of "busy work" is another huge turnoff for students. The idea that teachers cannot talk for an hour about the subject they should have a degree in and that they have to give out thousands of worksheets to teach their subject for them is frustrating because we are expected to learn as best we can this way. This makes me irate. The last thing any student wants is a worksheet packet. If your going to test us on knowledge, then TEACH US, otherwise do not become somebody who brings up the future generation. Many sports coaches teach subjects like mathematics, things they do not know about.

The right things such as attitude, thought, and actual genuine consideration for the students can have a huge effect on whether or not somebody becomes a bum or lawyer. The main key is motivation. Many kids do not realize the importance of learning and proper education. I think that it says a lot when I, who is considered immature and rambunctious by many adults, have already figured this out by now.—Will, Atlanta, GA

⌇

I think some teachers make school worth it and some don't because you can tell when a teacher's really interested in teaching and helping kids or when there there just to get paid and they could care less. I think really it's teachers that make school all of what it is and isn't.—Jessica, Merritt Island, FL

⌇

Teachers are one thing that makes a student not want to go to school. You can ask anyone that the one thing they hate about school is having to sit in a class with a teacher that does a lecture for the whole period on a topic that is will probably be useless when they become adults. Adults will probably react the same way if they have to sit in a room for a long period of time listening to a speaker who seems to droll on forever on a topic they don't really care about. The one thing that will want a student to go to school is the teacher that actually makes the classroom experience fun. Very few teachers today know how to do that and that is one thing that I would definitely want to see improved. Sure, I know that going to school is a kid's top priority, but it will make things a lot easier if I enjoy being in a classroom.—Ivan, Woodland Hills, CA

～

Many well known and loved teachers do not belong in a classroom. I'm not saying there not good with kids I am just saying that they could do a better job somewhere where you don't need so much responsibility. I have at least two teachers that every time I walk into class they don't remember what were on in class or don't care what we do in class. You might be thinking that sounds fun and easy, but it isn't.—Devin, Vero Beach, FL

～

Everyone has one—no one is exempt. No matter what classes one takes or what teachers one has, there is always one. Whether it be first period or fourth period, there is always a dreaded class. For me, it is first period, Algebra II. Just the thought of it makes me queasy. When I wake up each morning it burns into my mind—I start the day with ninety minutes of pure torture.

Walking into the room, the hum of the projector fills my ears. The warm-up on the screen crushes my hopes that she will be "nice" today. Finding my seat, I do whatever I can to stall—talking to neighbors, staring out the window—which all seem to fill the minutes until the bell rings. As the ring echoes through my ears, the last of my stomach drops. Moving as slowly as possible, I get my calculator and books. As the woman at the front of the room opens her mouth and begins to speak gibberish, I begin to count the minutes. Unable to follow her, question after question runs from my mouth. Each time she makes me feel more stupid than the last. Finally, I shut up, tune her out and focus on the clock. Counting down each minute like I am to get my first kiss, the bell rings. As I jump out of my seat and race to the door, I give a sigh of relief. I made it through the worst class of the day.—Madeline, Clover, SC

～

Quarrel

When having a quarrel, one that's unnecessary
I don't wanna admit that I'm wrong
But on the contrary, I think it's mandatory
To evacuate the school building and leave everything
Because the enemy is what lies inside that environment

The teacher is whom the rivalry I speak
I think, no, I know, he/she should go into retirement
Everything that he/she assigns, I despise
In my eyes, it took me some time to realize
That I, should calm down, I went out of bound
For freaking out about . . .
The grade
The grade that I foreseen
I have too much pride to say
That I didn't work hard for it
So, I'm sorry
—Kim, South San Francisco, CA, 10th grade

CHAPTER FIVE

~

The Evaluative Dimension

I found it almost unnatural that a third-grader would worry about a test as though her life depended on it. And this was a child who was doing just fine in school . . . that child had spent a whole year with nothing much for homework except sample test worksheets, and primarily taking drills at schools and then worrying about passing or failing. That's not what I call education. (Inman-Crews, 2000)

Today's students are saturated with assessment and evaluation. There are quizzes and tests in their academic classes. Then, there are tests for promotion, tests for competency, and tests for graduation, which have dire consequences for many students. No one can argue against the need for assessments—instruments that gauge or measure. What is attached to assessments—evaluative decisions—is debatable. In this fifth and final dimension, Eisner (1992) is concerned with how the evaluation aspect of schooling affects students' outlooks. How do students evaluate their educational experiences? How do they evaluate the evaluations? How do their evaluations manifest themselves? One way to analyze the "problems with schools" is to look at how students react at school and to school. I begin with the opposite—assessing students.

Tests Versus Assessments Versus Evaluation

For those outside of education, the term "test" might bring back memories of weekly spelling tests, the midterm examinations taken, or even the SAT. Many adults, including the stakeholders that put tests into place, could never, in my opinion, survive school (testing) today. Part of the misconception regarding testing is lack of knowl-edge, or confusion over, what testing means. In fact, several terms—testing, assess-ment, and evaluation—are confused and deemed the same, when they are not equal.

A test is "an instrument" or measuring device (Wiggins, 1993). A test is a one-time shot, and performance on a test cannot tell whether a student truly has un-derstanding or not. In other words, the standardized tests that students take once a year provide only a snapshot of what they might really know. Assessment, on the other hand, "is a comprehensive, multifaceted analysis of performance; it must be judgment-based and personal" (p. 13). A true assessment of a student's academic progress would be gleaned from grades on assignments, teacher observations, and performance on tests. Even with clarification between testing and assessment, an-other term must be explained: evaluation. Evaluation refers to the comparison of information learned (from a test, for example) to a standard (the minimum or pass-ing "number" or "score" that someone sets) for the purpose of judging worth or quality (Huitt, 1997). This aspect of "testing" is what most citizens are probably most aware of.

From student writings, three testing-related themes emerged: tests taken at school, standardized testing, and how students "evaluate" school.

School Tests

It is no surprise that students do not like to take tests. I did not receive one sub-mission that characterized tests as fun. Writings included in this section are some unique perspectives on school tests.

⁓

Tests . . . they are the hardest things to do in school. You have to study and study more. If you don't you will probably fail the test unless you're a good listener. I listen when the teacher is going over the subject of the test, but I forget everything when we do the test. That is bad because I fail.—Chelsea, Inwood, WV

⁓

Tests, I absolutely hate them! Sitting there with a big fat red F that is like saying, "Remember me from last week?" When my mom sees it, it's like when she gets a high wireless bill, she screams really, really loud. I was thinking that my report card really, really, really hates me. Some of my teachers let you raise it to a D, but that is still bad and still gets me grounded. I remember being able to retake tests in 2nd grade, when did that stop? I have about 3–4 tests a week, most on the same days! Benchmarks are hard and Chapter Tests are also hard. I took a Chapter Test in Science and the definitions weren't right! I mean it was like this, real definition.

Force-A pushes or pull, and here's his definition, Force—Something that pushes or pulls gravity down, or something dumb like that. I wish tests were easier!—Steven, Newnan, GA, 6th grade

⌒

The only part of school that I don't really like, besides the early mornings, are tests. When it's time for a big test, no matter how much I study, sometimes I freeze. I try my hardest when I take a test or quiz, because I know how important they are to my grade.—Jennifer, Inwood, WV

⌒

I like to talk about tests. In America, tests are really very easy and simple. In India, tests are really hard. We have 12 subjects in a school year, so we have 12 tests at one grading period. A school year has 3 grading period. In a year we just have tests in these 3 grading period. We do not have tests in each week or month like in America. I said we have 12 subjects. Each subject has just one test in a grading period, but the problem is we have to memorize everything. We cannot use any class notes, textbooks, or ever calculators. We have to memorize a lot to take these tests. We have to study for each subject. It is very hard to memorize everything. In America, tests are very easy. Most time we can use our calls notes or our textbook. We have just small tests in a grading period, and also, we have just 6 or 7 subject in a year. We have tests in almost every week or in each month. Then we do not have to study those stuffs. Therefore, tests in America are very easy and simple.—Jose, San Jose, CA

⌒

What I think about tests, put it like this, I hate them. Actually, it depends on what class it is, if its geometry, I hate it. Teachers can make tests fun if they made them all multiple choice. For some reason multiple choice is the least out of anything. So for all teachers who want students to take tests serious, please make them multiple choice.—Kerron, Tallahassee, FL

⁓

What causes stress at school are tests. When we have a test I began to sweat and I write so fast that I mess up, so I have to erase sometimes. You have to study and sometimes it messes up your schedule, might have to stay up late studying, and maybe family time . . . when I get a bad grade and show it to my parents they get angry and I can't play outside, all I can do is study and that makes me think unpositive.—Sonal, Key West, FL, Elementary

⁓

To me test are like being forced to eat cockroaches for two week strait with nothing to drink but onion juice. Now you sorta no how I feel about test. See sometimes when I take a big test that counts a whole lot for what I make on my report card, I get really nervous and that causes me to go absolutely blank. I can't think, so I go on to the next question. Of course then I have to come to the question later. That's only when we take really big test, and most of the test are really easy. I think the kings of all test are the I.T.B.S test and the C.R.C.T. They take so long and they're boring. If teachers didn't give out test, it almost not even going to school. If you don't get test then you wouldn't, because you wouldn't be tested. The reason I said that is because I get Tested almost everyday.—Cody, Newnan, GA, 6th grade

Standardized Tests

The next chapter focuses on the stress that today's K–12 students face. Much of that stress is closely linked to testing. In fact, I received so many stories linking stress to testing, that to better demonstrate the impact, that particular section was moved here.

The debates about standardized testing are being waged in cities, towns, school districts, and in the legislatures. Although the notion of accountability is sensible and needed, the harmful effects are well documented. As cited by numerous researchers (Darling-Hammond, 1995, 1996, 1997; Heubert & Hauser, 1999; Kohn, 1999; McNeil, 2000; Thompson, 2001), basing high-stakes decisions like retention and graduation on a single test score can have devastating effects— curriculum is narrowed to just test preparation, dropout percentages rise, students suffer from stress, teachers burnout and quit the profession early, and authentic learning is lost. "Research on causes of school dropouts indicates that among the factors increasing the likelihood of dropping out are being retained in grade, experiencing failure in school, and low self-esteem. If tests are widely used as indicators of school ability, it certainly seems likely that testing programs may well contribute to these factors that have been shown to increase likelihood of dropping out of school" (Haney, 1993, p. 52).

In the 2002–3003 school year, more than 43,000 third-grade students in Florida failed the reading portion of the FCAT. According to state law, they all could have been retained. In March 2004, it was revealed that 28,028 were actually held back (Weber, 2004). Studies show that being held back once doubles the chances of being held back again (Mann, 1987). Where will these children be five years from now? How many will drop out before they are 18?

A story that received a lot of attention when No Child Left Behind (NCLB) was passed concerned the "miracle" in Houston, Texas, where it seemed that high-stakes testing had lowered the dropout rate from nearly 50% in 1997 to less than 10% just a year or two ago. However, recent stories by the Houston Chronicle and 60 Minutes revealed that fraudulent practices by schools and administrators kept the real dropout numbers hidden (closer to 50%). Even worse were data showing that minorities' dropout rates were much higher than white students'. This might eventually also be the case in Florida where third-grade failure rates on the FCAT were 36% for black students, 31% for Hispanic students, and 32% for those qualifying for free or reduced-price lunches; only 14% of white third-graders failed the test (Weber, 2004).

Sadly, due to testing pressures, students most at risk of failing (and thus hurting schools' reputations), such as minorities and the poor, are sometimes held back to "skip the test" or are "pushed" out of school. As Stiggins (2003) says, "the cost of achieving high quality at so many different levels of large-scale assessment has been astronomical, not just in dollars spent but also in opportunities lost" (p. 199). "The time has come to fundamentally rethink the relationship between assessment and effective schooling . . . we assume we can stimulate maximum teacher effort and student learning by threatening public embarrassment for both students and teachers if students don't succeed academically. We assume that the reason students do not learn is that teachers and students are not putting forth the effort required to succeed" (p. 197).

Although NCLB determines whether a school is in need of improvement based upon performance on a single statewide test (standardized test), a majority of those polled (66%) recently by Phi Delta Kappa and Gallup believed that was not a fair way to judge a school. Another 77% thought that it was not possible to judge a student's proficiency in English and math based upon a single test (Rose & Gallup, 2003). Compared to similar topics on last year's survey, it seems that support for standardized testing is dropping. Likewise, the number of students who support the use of standardized tests to measure their progress dropped from 65% in 2002 to 60% in 2003 (Horatio Alger Association, 2002). With an overemphasis on testing, the message that we send to students is that what really matters in their education is their test scores. As a result, students and teachers in high-stakes testing programs find ways to cut corners (Eisner, 2003).

Not surprisingly, high school students object to graduation tests. All but one student who wrote to me regarding standardized testing were against it. According to the majority, onetime tests not directly based on their school subjects were an unfair assessment of their abilities. However, what surprised me most was the empathy students felt for their classmates. Although expressing their contempt for the tests, they expressed sorrow at seeing others fail or get "stressed out" over them.

⌒

I know we have to take tests, but some I feel are not necessary. For example, the FCAT. I know passing is not supposed to be all that easy, but if you do good in school, turn in all your work and pass your tests and quizzes. Then you get in class and take the FCAT. This one test determines if you pass or fail. I feel that just is not right. I say that because some people are not good test takers, especially if you must pass it, to be promoted. Even some students panic, some drop out if they don't pass. Most of those are honors students. So, if you see what's happening to them, imagine what regular students would do. —Andreia, Tallahassee, FL

⌒

Standardized tests! How do you feel about them? Well most students dread them. Adults think they are good. They show how much your child knows. I think that we shouldn't have them and if we do have them show how much you know but not judge you or determine your classes or if you graduate from high school. One test shouldn't have that much control over your education. What if you aren't a very good test taker or just wasn't feeling well and you bomb the test. It should be your grades that matter. Also these test have all ranges of questions. Isn't that unfair to the students who are in lower classes? Compared to students in honor courses the test should be more level with each student and not determine your classes or if you graduate.—Chelsea, Melbourne, FL

⌒

The tests that the government require students to take are ridiculous. It seems as though they make the tests too hard for some kids. Everybody isn't on the same level when it comes to math and English, so I think they should make different versions of the tests. School for some is very difficult and I think they should make it easier for some kids to graduate, if they do this they'll have less dropouts.—Kristie, Tallahassee, FL

～

An Every Day School DRAG

Every day I wake up, get dressed, eat breakfast, watch t.v., brush my teeth, then talk to my friends on the computer, and finally go to the bus stop. In school we unpack, do our daily word problem, then start our subjects, but todays different. Todays the day of the N.J. ASK TEST! Every teacher tells all the kids its easy and that it will take about three days. But it ends up being a cusial week long test. Finally you come to a stop sign. You've made it through the first quarter of the test. Your grip on the pencil loosens when you relize its lunch time and your way behind. As you rush to fill in the answers the teachers voice gets firmer "PENCILS DOWN!" When finally she calls our your name, you have just one question to catch you up left. But now you have to drop your pencil and go to lunch.

You sit at a cold bench, a steamy hot dog in front of you. The lunch aid says "Eat that hot dog its brain food." Any kid will tell you that food is anything but brain food. So you take a bite the lunch aid still watching to make sure you swallow. You make a twisted sour face saying "its okay" then mumbling "Yeah right I want McDonalds." Soon you throw the half soggy bread and hot dog away with out a piece of food in your stomach. You go to your classroom for recess, its to cold to go outside. Your heart beating for you know what you will be finishing . . .

After a long hard day you go home then you think about your homework then stop . . . your teacher told you at the end of the day there will be no going back to other sections. And YOU FORGOT THE LAST QUESTION!

F

—Jackie, Turnersville, NJ, 5th grade

～

Since when were the FCAT tests that we took at school really hard? That's right, never! Governor Bush I would like to commend you on the fine job that you have done with holding students accountable through FCAT testing. The state of Florida had gone to long (like many others) not realizing that our children are not learning properly. This test helps educators to see what areas kids need to work on. Some teachers feel that the FCAT makes kids nervous, I disagree. The material is plain and simple for each grade level. If they don't know the material they deserve to be held back.

The FCAT allows teachers to see what areas or/of what subjects need to improve for each student. The mind is like a plum ripe for picking. If we do not discover what area children need improvement in, then they will never get the help needed. Its plain and simple, also if the student fails all three parts to the FCAT then he/she deserves to be held back.

Many teachers and children may argue that the FCAT is: "just going to make kids nervous which will cause them to do poorly in school up until the test and do poorly on the test." If the teachers show the students example problems and how easy they are they will not only be less nervous, they will also be refreshing their memory on the material. So governor, I ask you to keep doing the fine job on the schools systems that you are.—James, Melbourne, FL

⌒

First issue is the saturation of stupid people in public schools. Although many people view themselves as average, that is purely because the metaphorical bar has been lowered. If we were to stop lowering the bar, then eventually Darwin's laws of natural selection would come into play and there would be less stupid people. But since we keep lowering the bar we are slowly letting the populace decrease in intelligence to the point at which we will self destruct. This can be traced back to FCAT and similar tests. If we weren't being trained to only pass these tests instead of focusing on real life situations, then we would be more suited to go into the real world. Passing the FCAT is, indeed important, but the only reason the school emphasizes this is to that they can get more money and are thus selling our future so that their school looks better.—Allen, Vero Beach, FL

⌒

Let's talk about the OLSAT. The questions are like "what would this pentagon look like if you reversed it, turned it twice to the right, but it into fourths, and folded it in half!" I mean I'm only in the sixth grade!—Deborah, Vestavia Hills, AL, 6th grade

⌒

Governor Bush I think we shouldn't have to do testing in school like the FCAT because some students do very well in school but when it comes to test they do bad. I don't think the FCAT should determine if we get our diploma. When I take a test I usually do well. It's when I take a long test that's when I fail. Testing as so the FCAT should not be in school. Students do not enjoy taking tests, especially the Florida Comprehensive Assessment Test because it puts a lot of stress on them. A lot of my friends do good in school but when they take a test they fail. Also I don't think it fair because some students are in a lower math class and half the stuff on the FCAT they haven't even been taught yet. Students that do very well in school and fail the FCAT don't get their diploma. That's 13 years of your life wasted. Without a diploma you can't get a good job. I feel like we shouldn't have to do major test in public schools. Little tests that decide what you know are good but not ones that take your diploma from you if you don't pass. Most students become very anxious when they take big tests. Some students to do well in school but do bad on tests. I don't think we should have to take big tests in public schools.—Jeff, Melbourne, FL

~

One other thing is MCAS testing. A standardized test that you must pass in 10th grade to graduate. I think it is completely unfair for someone's future to be decided by 1 test. I am a junior so I've already taken it. I passed with advanced but it was very hard and I needed a lot of extra time. I know many people who failed it and now have to take extra classes and retake it. —Anonymous, Amesbury, MA

~

As far as standardized tests, I'm totally against the idea of them. I know for a fact that not all students test the same way, some good and some bad. I think that your acceptance into college shouldn't be based on a test score. While some students aren't good test-takers, at the same time, some students do well in school but do very well on standardized tests. I've been told some of the smartest and most successful people in the world didn't do well in school. —LaKendra, Tallahassee, FL

~

We have to take the most important test in March—the FCAT. That is also what makes school boring and hard at the same time. Teachers talking about the FCAT everyday. They make it sound like if we don't talk about it everyday that we are not going to pass.—Erica, Key West, FL, Elementary

~

What I think about Tests? First, I'm not a good test taker, but I think they are hard sometimes. But the tests are to see what you have learned or what you know. Some tests are to test your ability. About the FCAT, I don't see why we have to take this test to get our diploma when we haven't learned every-thing on the test in class.—LaTasha, Tallahassee, FL

⌣

I Didn't ASK for Stress

On most school days, I sleep as late as I can. My mom wakes me up and I get dressed. While I eat breakfast, I watch Sponge Bob Square Pants on TV. My mom takes me to school early for safety patrol. Most days are nice but then there is the ASK test.

Our school is having the New Jersey test today and that's different. When we get to school the teacher puts the test down on your desk and you begin. Most of the kids are frowning because of the test. Some of the kids fall asleep. I hate these tests because I worry if I'll do well.

We only have two hours to finish. You have to rush and I keep breaking pencils. The teacher doesn't like us sharpening them. Seems like I always have one question left when time is up. I try to quickly answer it but can't. You can't go back to it and this is why the ASK test gives me stress. —Joe, Turnersville, NJ, 5th grade

⌣

To begin with passing or failing one test shouldn't predict your graduation. After 13 years of taking tests it boils down to one test that tells whether or not we pass or go on to college. Although many pass it we still have to go through stress of whether or not we're prepared to take a test that was prepared by people who ask questions that no one knows about.—Jessica, Tallahassee, FL

⌣

Who likes taking tests? I sure don't! Governor Bush uses FCAT as a state standardized test. If you do not pass the FCAT you will not receive a high school diploma. The FCAT makes students nervous, not get a diploma, and don't have to waste a week of school taking FCAT.

FCAT makes you nervous because if you don't get a 3 or higher on math or reading you do not get a diploma. You only get a certificate of completion. Also, some students could get straight A's but not be a good test taker. So that means if a straight A students could not get his/her diploma because they freeze or just get real nervous when taking tests.

FCAT is just a waste of a good week to learn. The FCAT tests take a week to do. We could be learning more stuff, if we didn't waste our time taking a test with no real result. I'd rather learn more real ability. As you can see FCAT is a ridiculous and waste of time test.—Ryan, Melbourne, FL

〜

My thoughts on Gov. Bush's testing in public schools is a big joke like his so-called policy on affirmative action. Why do we prove ourselves to some middle aged man? All this test proves is that if you are dumb and can't pass it, and to me it's not right and it should be given to those who need it more. This money we are spending on tests could be used in a valuable cause like, for example, more classrooms, more books and supplies, and more teachers due to over crowded classrooms.—LeDarius, Melbourne, FL

〜

What I think about Tests? I think the idea is very stupid. Why is because it is a big set back. Even though you may or may not pass the written test, it doesn't mean you actually can't do the job. For example, the FCAT. I think that it is the most dreadful test ever. It doesn't make any sense to go through high school for eleven years and its time for graduation and you can't feel good about your graduation because you know you didn't pass the FCAT and you only going to get a high school completion not a diploma. That is very unfair for all students even is you pass it or not. Why make us take a test may affect our future and dreams.—Lawrence, Tallahassee, FL

〜

Okay, test wise, Bush is taking it way too far. It's kind of outrageous for an "A" student to not pass the twelfth grade or not graduate because of a test. That doesn't really make sense. I'm talking about the FCAT. I mean that test really has nothing to do with everyday life. The tests at school, I can understand, because those things deal with the choices that we have to make in the future. So, I think that the FCAT is a waste of time, and should be voided.—Rochelle, Tallahassee, FL

〜

I wanted to write about what should be improved in school about the state test. One important factor is the state test times. They make you take the test for about two weeks. Now that's very stressing. A different factor is the state test questions. The way that the state test people make the questions and put them is very complicated and also tricky. I think they should just put them directly to the point instead of going backward and forward and to the sides and messing you up.—Anthony, Cocoa, FL, 8th grade

∼

Another thing that stresses me out is the FCAT. You study all year long, but when you get the FCAT, you forget half the things that are on it.—Marcy, Key West, FL, 5th grade

∼

Here in Massachusetts a lot of focus and emphasis is put on testing, especially statewide standardized testing. The MCAs, Massachusetts Comprehension Assessment, is a standardized test taken in all grades now up until 10th grade where the student *must* pass in order to graduate. In my opinion the tests are good to assess how well teachers are teaching and how students are learning, but for it to be a graduation requirement is absurd. I, myself am not a good test taker, but I am on honor student. If my chances of graduating were jeopardized by this test I would have been most unhappy. However, I did pass and if I hadn't I would get second, third, and possibly more chances like everyone else, and that is beneficial. I just believe that putting someone else's possibility of graduation on the line because of one test shouldn't happen. In theory these tests are a good idea, but in practice, I believe, they are a failure, like communism.—Anonymous, Amesbury, MA

∼

I don't like testing
Because I haft to work off my little tush
I just hate that testing act
That was signed by president Bush.
So when I go to take a test
About Reading English or Math
I just wish that I had
A magic powerful staff.
Where I'd grant all my wishes
So I wouldn't have to take a test
I think that's just for me
I know that would be the best.
So I went to the White House

And declared all my rights
But Bush didn't give up
And put up a good fight.
He said I'd have to take the test
And he told that for a fact
Then he ripped out a small scroll
And read the "No Child Left Behind Act."
So just let me assure you
From kindergarten to college ranks
You'll have to take a test
If you want to be like Tom Hanks!
—Justus, Ft. Oglethorpe, GA, 4th grade

⌒

I still have one major problem. As you know, there is one test in Florida that you have to take to "get out of high school." It is called the FCAT! To be sure, it is my worst nightmare! The state law says that you must pass this test to graduate high school with a regular diploma—otherwise you receive a certificate of completion.

And so now, I have a major problem. I still must pass FCAT math. I have taken it twice, and still not passed. Now, I am not a strong math student, and I know it. But, if Jeb Bush, our Florida governor is reading this (which I highly doubt), then, here is some advice: "why must students work hard for four years in high school, and still, it all comes down to one test that determines our future? Now, how fair is that?" The FCAT test does not measure how smart we are; it just measures if we get out of high school, or not. Believe me, talking about the FCAT can really raise by blood pressure!—Lauren Kaplan (Originally published in *Florida Educational Leadership*, 4(1), Fall 2003, pp. 40–41)

School Evaluations: How Students Act Out

Because I will discuss student stress at school in Chapter 6, I want to focus on ways students "evaluate" school: skipping school, using/abusing alcohol or drugs, tuning out, and/or dropping out. As a former teacher, I used to hear friends and acquaintances not familiar with school life complain that "all students" were apathetic, juvenile delinquents, or lazy; however, none wondered what might happen at school to cause students to skip, drink and/or use drugs, wander aimlessly, drop out, or fail.

Skipping school is an occurrence that, unfortunately, starts early in students' schooling and builds from grade to grade. The NCES reports that the tendency to miss school (either by skipping or for other reasons) increased with grade level. Eleven percent of eighth graders skipped at least one day of school in a 4-week period in 2000; this figure increased to 17% for 10th graders and to 33% for 12th graders (Scherer, 2002a).

Although alcohol and drug use among teenagers has not increased dramatically overall, a large number of students report using both. Data from the 2003 "Indicators of School Crime and Safety" (NCES) shows that 47% of students in grades 9–12 reported using alcohol within 30 days of the survey; 5% reported drinking alcohol on school property. For marijuana, the percentages were 24 and 5, respectively. The reasons behind students' use of alcohol and drugs are more than peer pressure and "feeling good." A study by the National Institutes of Health found that 44% drank to relieve tension, 25% because of boredom, 17% because of frustration, and 3% to get through the day (O'Malley, Johnston, & Bachman, 1998). A new analysis published by the Child Trends databank (2004) reveals that in 2003 over 25% of all students in high school felt sad or hopeless almost every day for 2 or more weeks in a row that they stopped doing usual activities. Figure 5.1 illustrates this information by race and Hispanic origin.

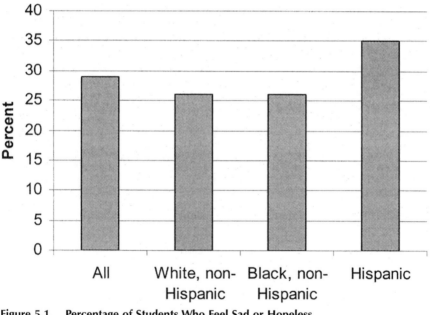

Figure 5.1. Percentage of Students Who Feel Sad or Hopeless
Source: Child Trends, 2004.

An even bigger problem, and one that is sometimes hidden by school districts due to policies such as No Child Left Behind, is dropping out, and the costs are astronomical. The United States loses nearly $77 billion annually because of school *dropouts (Weis, Farrar, & Petrie, 1989). It is estimated that close to 25% of fifth-grade students will not graduate from high school (Fine & Zane, 1989; Mann, 1987). In urban areas, nearly 50% of adolescents will quit high school; less than half of these will return for a regular diploma or GED (Fine & Zane, 1989; Kolstad & Owings, 1986).*

Many drop out because they simply do not like school. However, in-grade retention and relationships with teachers are also factors (Fine & Zane, 1989). Thirty-one percent of those surveyed said they did not like school; 30% reported low grades as another reason (Fine & Zane, 1989; Ekstrom, Goertz, Pollack, & Rock, 1986). Some additional causes for dropping out include tracking, overcrowded classrooms, mislabeling minority students and placing them in special education classes/programs, and high expulsion rates (Weis et al., 1989). "For students, increasing pressure to score high on tests, combined with a lack of focused opportunities to learn, can lead to a sense of futility, a feeling of hopelessness that can cause them to stop caring and stop trying. For many of them, consistent evidence of poor performance repeatedly reported to their families or to the public can result in a profound and long-lasting loss of confidence. Those who stop believing that they are capable of learning will stop trying" (Stiggins, 2003, p. 199).

⌇

Speaking of tests, I hate them. Let's face the truth, no one likes to take them. Tests are long and time consuming. Yes, I don't like them, but that doesn't mean I don't try to at least pass them. Most people know someone who could care less about tests. I know that I do. He never does any class work, for any of the classes I have with him. He does do the tests, but they are hardly passing. His attitude through school is that he doesn't want to be here. It makes me wonder whether or not he'll graduate with the rest of us, or will we lose another student when he drops out.—Bev, Inwood, WV

⌇

"Drugs in School" by Erica, Aptos, CA
Rosa: Anna, do you remember when you got drunk in school?
Anna: Oh yes, I think I remember that day was so fun, but I almost died.
Rosa: It was scary because you went to the hospital.
Anna: I know, but at that time it was fun.
Rosa: But did you learn you lesson?
Anna: Yes, kind off. I need to go to counseling.

Rosa: What kind of consequences did you get?
Anna: I got in trouble with the school and the law.
Rosa: Well, try not to drink because something worse can happen.
Anna: Sure, I will try.
Rosa: Do you still bring tequila to school?
Anna: Sometimes.
Rosa: You're not scared that they will catch you?
Anna: Yeah, I will try not to bring it to school.
Rosa: You better not.
Anna: Don't worry I'll try not to do that any more.

⌣

School is important and not because we would all be retards without it but because we would be socially inferior. When I stay home from school and go surfing nobody goes and it's not a lotta fun, but when my friends and I are at school and we all get talking about how boring school is and how much fun it would be to go surfing, we get really hyped up about it. We would sneak out of school something would happen where we almost got caught and we'd laugh about it all day. And when we got to the beach and were surfing, no matter how good or bad the surf was we would always say, "hey this is so much funner than school." I think because school is so dull and boring it makes other things more enjoyable. Plus this is where we all meet to make plans and that's what's teaching us.—Jimmy, Merritt Island, FL

⌣

Juan Medina, Aptos, CA
Yvonne: Tom, do you remember when Yolanda got drunk?
Tom: Of course, it was crazy; everyone in school was talking about that. It was so funny, but at the same time, it was dangerous because she was risking her life.
Yvonne: What was she thinking?
Tom: I think she wanted to feel hyper or in heaven.
Yvonne: No, I heard something about why she got drunk, but I'm not sure if it's true.
Tom: What?
Yvonne: I heard that she was having many problems at her house. That's what I heard.
Tom: Whatever, I know her well and I do not think she got drunk because of that, what do you think?

Yvonne: Well, I think she got drunk for people to say that she is cool or something.

Tom: I guess you're right. I asked her why did she do that, and she's all, "to have fun" and I was like, right.

Yvonne: Well I have to go, see you in sixth period. Bye.

Tom: Bye.

⁓

Many of my friends parents know that they do drugs. Most parents just worry about their children getting caught, compared to what actual drug does to them. If the school thinks telling kids what drugs do to them in seminar will keep them away, they really need to look harder.—Bill, Hartford, WI

~

CHAPTER SIX

Stress at School

School will always be stressful to students. I doubt there will ever be a stress free day for most of them. You're always worried about something. Whether it be an upcoming test or trying to get to class on time, your body is full of stress.

—Bev, Inwood, WV

Stress being performed at school is caused by "haters" don't stand to see anybody succeed.

—Shenedria, Tallahassee, FL

I can remember elementary school as if it were today. Each day I couldn't wait to get off the bus and get into the school. I loved what we did: art, music, writing, reading, and math. It was fun and stress-free. No one cared what I wore or how much money my parents did or didn't make. When I started middle school, things began to change. Clothes started to matter, as did who were my friends. Still, I felt little stress. I did well in school and liked my classes and teachers. Even the first 2 years of high school were not that stressful. I was in honors classes; I liked my peers and my teachers. Tests weren't a problem. I don't remember feeling pressured to drink, smoke, or do drugs. I think the real stress began once I could drive and was better able to get out of the house. I became conscious of a need to dress and act a certain way, to maintain high grades, and do well in my sport, and the choices I began to make to deal with the stress negatively impacted my life inside and outside of school.

Research has shown that stress in school-age students is a growing problem (Credit & Garcia, 1999; Muto & Wilk, 1993), and judging from the amount of writings I received about it, I doubt many adults really understand what it is like to be a student today. Frankly, when I think of today's students, I wonder how they manage the stress in their lives. Consider these statistics: as of 1997, 1 million children have been involved in new divorces each year (divorce.com); nearly 1 million teenage girls become pregnant each year (AGI, 1999); recent government statistics show that 1 in 10 high school students have been the victim of dating violence (Guzman et al., 2003); and the use of illicit drugs among 12th-grade students has increased steadily since 1992 from 6% to 11% (Child Trends, 2002). Compound that with cliques at school, the desire to fit in, the pressure to do well academically, standardized testing (which can determine whether a student graduates at all), trying to get into college, or even just figuring out what to do with one's life after high school, and you can easily see why today's students are stressed out.

What Is Stress?

According to researchers, there are two types of stress—constructive and destructive. Constructive stress occurs when a situation is perceived as challenging, offering potential for some personally meaningful benefit. Destructive stress, on the other hand, occurs when a situation is perceived as challenging, but focuses on the potential for loss (Bluestein, 2001; Gazzaniga, 1992). For students, an example of constructive stress would be participating in sports or band. Although preparing for a competition itself might be "stressful," the end result is most often positive and meaningful. A high-stakes test presents students with destructive stress; if the test is not passed, promotion or graduation might be withheld.

Several factors influence stress: anticipation, worry, helplessness, and responsibility (Wilson, 2002). At school, stress is exhibited in several forms, including increased absences; health problems, such as stomach aches; aggressive behavior; test-anxiety; lower grades; and anxiety regarding extracurricular events (Elkind, 1981; Martirano, 1997; Nenortas, 1986). Predictors of stress include any type of change (school, grade level, puberty, etc.); peer pressure; growing independence; family matters; parental pressure to achieve; and overcommitment to school and extracurricular activities (Credit & Garcia, 1999). One study estimated that between 10% and 30% of students experience school-related worry enough to impede performance (Credit & Garcia, 1999). I was surprised, and saddened, that one student, as young as he was, could articulate "stress" so well.

~

Kids get stressed when bad or saddening things happen during their life. For example, in my case, I would get stressed if my girlfriend broke up with me or if I had to move far away and leave all my friends. Sudden changes in a person's life could stress them out, such as a parental divorce, move far away or other stressing events. Just about everyone has his/her own stressors. There are also long term stressors such as a family member dies or is diagnosed with a incurable dieses.—Dustin, Newnan, GA, 6th grade

∼

According to national statistics, the biggest cause of stress for high school students is their grades, with overall numbers jumping dramatically. Forty-two percent of students report that the pressure to get good grades is a major problem for them. For all students there was a 16-point increase from 2001. Other causes of stress include financial pressures (42% indicated it as a major or minor problem), pressure to look a certain way (53% indicated it as a major or minor problem), sex (7% say it is a major problem), and drugs and alcohol (8% say they are major problems) (Horatio Alger Association, 2002). From the responses I received, five major contributors to stress emerged: doing well in school, fitting in, teachers, the workload, and a final category I call "it all adds up."

Doing Well in School

"Doing well" in school means different things to different people. I am sure when I was in school my idea of doing well was dissimilar from what my parents experienced when they were adolescents. It became clear, after reading students' submissions, that doing well for them is more complicated. Students wrote of having to "do it all" to succeed; children as young as the fifth grade already feel pressure to "go to a good college." Worse than that is the overextending that many high school students feel they have to do.

A recent report by the Rocky Mountain News *shows that some colleges are changing their admission requirements to discourage students from burning out. Examples they point out: Duke University shortened the amount of application space devoted to extracurricular activities and Colorado College asks students to estimate the weight of their backpacks; Harvard officials suggested students take time away from their busy schedules (Sanchez, 2004). What I found was that many students were pushing themselves physically, mentally, and emotionally, not for the inherent feeling of doing well, but to get into a good college so they can have a "future."*

∼

My goals are complicated at this point, but I think I would really like to go to a first rate college. I want to be able to have a choice on which college that I attend. I think it would be cool to medical school because I would really like to be able to help people, as cliché as that sounds. I also think it would be kind of nice to work those strange hours. I want to have one of those jobs where you can give one of those I'm-important-so-move looks.

I know that school would seriously affect my chance of getting into a good school, and even more so if I continue to go the path of medical school. I am trying to develop good study habit, but sometimes I just have one of those days where it's like if I don't have some kind of fun soon I think I'm going to die of boredom.

I still want to accomplish this goal but I know it's not the end of the world if I don't. I have many other goals but this particular goal is at the top of my imaginary list, so I am going to try to accomplish it, especially since those around me are so supportive of everything I decide to do with my life.

I know that many others around me see me as this "perfect" student, but I'm really not. I just try my best and hope everything works out for the better. I am going to continue to work hard so that maybe one day in the future I will be able to get into the school I think is best for me.

I hope my goals work out for the best if not only for me but for those who put in so much time and effort into supporting me. I thank those who take the time to read this so that maybe they will understand better about what students may feel.—Candace, Newnan, GA, 6th grade

～

Most students are stressed because of college stuff. Some dude suicides because he didn't get into MIT. Students are stressed because of peer pressure. So I think teachers should pay more attention and intercese on certain individual students who have bad environmental problems.—Han, Tallahassee, FL

～

Let's face it; school is tough! The studying, drawn out days, and stress from our parents and family to do well is plenty enough to give you a serious headache. However, once you reach high school, the things that seem so hard to deal with turn into monstrous efforts that we are forced to face on a daily basis for four years. Then studying turns into what seems a curse, dragging out for hours a day! The days seem to last even longer, and the pressure from our parents to get good grades and get into a good college feels sometimes like torture. High school is tough work, but once you get through it, the feelings of disgust we all carry for high school might turn into feelings of abandonment, and the good things about high school will be greatly missed.

Probably the greatest stress of them all is beating into our ears day in and day out. You've heard it. It's the one coming from our guardians that threaten our social life if we do not receive good grades. Keeping our grade point average up, being successful on the SATs, and getting accepted into a good college are things that will not only help our parents feel secure knowing, but also give us confidence and stability.—Stacie, Vero Beach, FL

～

Stress at school is caused by a combination of things. The responsibility required to do well in school alone can cause much stress. Many things are at stake if you do not do well in school. Not doing well in school also affects your success in the future. The aspect of school that causes most of the stress is the time consuming factor of it. Not only do you have to do work in school, but you are assigned homework to do. To excel you have to meet these demands and make a good grade on them. School is almost like a work environment. You have to set up a schedule and plan things in your agenda book. If you do not meet these demands, it could cost you your education. That is a lot to lose considering that you have worked many years just to get to that point. That alone causes stress. There is the pressure to do well in school as well. You have a reputation to maintain and grades to keep up. Trying to impress parents, friends, and family goes along with the pressure. You would not want to let down the ones you love, and this puts a lot of weight on your shoulders. Knowing the pain or disappointment you can cause to others if you fail can be, above all, the most stressful.—Devin, Melbourne, FL

～

Tests can be very stressful to people of every age. To me, however, it's not the actual test I worry about, it's the studying. Studying means overloading my mind with facts, emotionally damaging my confidence, and taking time away from what I really love to do. (And it certainly doesn't help that I tend to be overdramatic). Basically, I am not fond of studying, and I wish there was an alternate way of learning.

Instead of trying to learn and understand what was covered in class, I try as fast as I can to cram every little fact into my memory. I keep those facts stored in my mind until the test, when I release them onto the paper. So far, this technique has not failed to get me a good grade, but sometimes it feels as if it has failed at teaching me what I was supposed to learn. After I take a test, those facts are now behind me, and I feel no need to remember them anymore; they already served their purpose in my mind. To make matters worse, because I let these facts leave after a test, the final at the end of a semester then becomes ten times harder. I have to memorize and store those facts all over again! And because I am a major procrastinator, I leave studying for every final in every class to the last minute! My stress level becomes so high; I can't concentrate, making studying nearly impossible.

Studying can be so stressful for me, that if I am having trouble with even the slightest thing, my confidence breaks down and I start going crazy. I start rambling on about how my intelligence isn't really as high as people think it is, that I am a fake and a fraud, and that I'm not going anywhere in life. "All I know is how to memorize! How is that smart?" "Now I won't receive a good grade on the test; which means I won't receive an A in the class; which means I won't have straight A's; which means I can't be valedictorian; which means I won't be accepted to UCLA; which means my whole life is ruined!" I then start going into how I don't know what to do with my life, and that I am a hopeless cause. I am only fourteen! I shouldn't have to deal with the stresses of the real world yet!—Jackie, Woodland Hills, CA

∼

Grades are important to everyone don't ever let anyone lie. They are probably the most stressful of the lot. School can be very stressful. I think everyone has different things that stress them out. These are only some of the things that stresses students out in school.—Abigail, Melbourne, FL

Fitting in at School

Students' perceptions of belonging, fitting in, or connectedness with their schools are related to positive academic, psychological, and behavioral outcomes during adolescence (Anderman, 2002, for example). When individuals are deprived of the above, negative outcomes can occur—emotional distress, health problems, and increased stress (Baumeister & Leary, 1995). Seeman (1975) identified several causes of stress that impact students: powerlessness, the sense of incomprehensibility of personal and social affairs; *normlessness,* the sense that social ideals to which most people profess are continually violated in practice; *cultural estrangement,* the individual's rejection of values commonly held in society; *self-estrangement,* the individual's engagement in activities that are not intrinsically rewarding; *and* social isolation, the sense of exclusion from or rejection by social groups. *Each of these factors can induce stress; however, together they can make going to school a nightmare for students. From the writings I received, it is clear that going to school is not like it was for most adults who are reading this book. I was completely unprepared for what students had to say.*

〜

My parents even get mad at me for saying it, but the truth is adults have no idea what the average high school student has to deal with. Most people think we got it easy, yah we don't have the same problems but the ones we do have are just as stressful as the ones that everyone else has. It would be nice if everyone could spend a day at my school and see how it really is to be a high school student, cause it's not easy. You have teachers that don't care, some do. You have peer pressure, drugs, sex, etc. It never ends until your out of school. This year my school went to a lot of trouble to make it a better place to learn and to make it safer, but I don't feel any safer and it's still hard to learn. Between the stresses at home combined with the stresses at school it's hard to concentrate. That's why a lot of people resort to drugs to get away for that short time of not having to care. Sometimes I think I should just to escape for a few minutes. I won't though. I know that the stresses will still be there when I come back. I can only explain some of what an average high school students goes through. There's so much in order to understand you would have to be a high school student yourself cause it's nothing like what's on TV.—Amber, Jackson, MI

〜

School is one of those things you wonder why you wake up early in the morning and go to. School can be the best thing in the world if you're a football player, cheerleader or if you're on any other popular club in school. School can be a living nightmare if you are not popular. It seems like everybody is trying to make your life miserable for no reason. Sometimes I want to be more popular, but then I think if I were more popular would people see me as I saw them.—Will, Vestavia Hills, AL, 6th grade

〜

Since I now know that I have grasped your attention, I'll let you in on a little bit of both sides to school. . . . I'll start with the bad and finish on a good note. Yeah, don't forget . . . I am the optimist. Let's see, what could possibly be unnerving about school? Hum . . . that's a toughie. . . . Okay, I'll put a lid on the sarcasm, for now at least. The biggest thing that has always bothered me about school is stress. My stress arises from the fact that people are the reason for most of my stress at school.

I can never understand why teenagers, most of them at least, are very closed-minded and just plain mean. It shouldn't matter what you wear to school or whom you associate with, but that you are all supposed to be there for the same reason . . . to learn. Well, then you get into the stresses of trying to uphold some unwritten title of earning better grades than the person sitting next to you. Ahhh . . . school gives you many things to worry about . . . grades and whatnot, and it opens your eyes and gives you a sample on a little taster spoon of what life will really be like, in the future . . . and that is scary in itself.—Alison, Merritt Island, FL

～

Sometimes stress at school can bring horrific days. Tests bring me the most stress. I try not to let social stress interfere with my attitude, but people can be crude sometimes. Often, I walk down the halls and see kids being teased and tortured. I often imagine putting myself in their shoes and try to feel the pain, but it just doesn't work.—Amy, Inwood, WV

～

Stress at school is caused by students getting picked on.—Justin, Inwood, WV

～

Stress can be caused at school by a lot of different things. Being that R___ [High School] is a popularity issue people try to fit in. So on one side you have the popular kids with all the name brand clothes, and the cars, and a lot of friends. So the unpopular is already stressed out because they don't have. Then they become more stressed out because they're trying to get. Then they're not able to get. So one thing leads to another and they drop out.—Rochelle, Tallahassee, FL

～

People say the school's a safe place
But once your inside
There's no turning back
There's words going everywhere
Right behind your back

Whispers in silence
And rumors going around
People making fun of others
And maybe hurting them too
Just because they're different
And because they don't act like you
Sometimes you don't have other
To help you when you fall down
It frightens you
And you don't know where to turn
You're just stuck where you are
Until the whispers and rumors pass
And the tears from your eyes fade away
And then you can go about your day
—Sarah, South San Francisco, CA, 10th grade

～

Students have to buy the right things, have the right looks, go out with the right people, and act the right ways just to get in with the "in" crowd. The "in" crowd is a group of students who either break every rule weekly, or have all the right things to be cool. Everyone wants to be attractive to the opposite sex. Even if students are attractive to everyone else, they also have to have the right attitude. The "right" attitude at our school would be really nice to your friends and a peacock to everyone else. I say a peacock to everyone else because it means cocky. Everyone is a drama queen. Our school is just like a soap opera I tell you . . . students have it rough, but one day we will not have to come to this student prison called school.—Keylie, Cocoa, FL, 8th grade

～

Everyone has stress, right? Well, school stress is worse than all of the others combined. In school you can't be too smart or they call you "Teacher's Pet" (which I've been called many times). If you are below average you get shunned. If you are a girl with to baggy clothes you get call a tom-boy in a bad way. If you are a boy and wear too tight clothes you are a Tom-girl. Even if you're a girl and wear clothes to tight you get called a "Girly-Girl." I am so glad I never been called that. If you haven't know the popular kids from kindergarten or if you come on the first day and they get a wrong impression then you can bet your not going to get popular. Even if you do get popular you can't trust popular kids at all.

If you end up not getting popular you get rumar going around about you that aren't true, people talk behind your back and you get made fun of. If you happen to be one of these people you can only count on your true friends if you're lucky to have some. School stress happens in every school and no matter how good your school's there's bound to be some kind of school stress lurking around. Ahhh ☹—Julie, Turnersville, NJ, 5th grade

～

Every morning students get up early and come to school. Some days are fun some days are so stressful that you start to bite off anybody's head who messes with you. So what you should be saying is what causes these stresses? There is the subject of whether you fit in. Do you play sports, are you popular, or do you have a tight group of friends. If you don't then you will most likely feel left out or get mashed. What is you don't feel like matching up to the critia our these thing. Aggravation from your friends erupts.—Abigail, Melbourne, FL

～

I hear teachers and parents always saying that, "school can't be *that* bad!" well, from a student's point of view, yes, school can be *that* bad! When I hear those words coming from these ignorant adults I must say it is quite annoying. It is only annoying because they say that they know what we're going through, when in actuality . . . they don't. When they were in high school, they had different pressures put on them. There are so many different stages of pressure that a student goes through in one day!

The first stage is, what I call the "getting ready" stage. This involves getting dressed and so forth. Now, getting up in the morning is when the stress of a "normal" school day starts. I get up and I have to take a shower, because if I miss one day of cleanliness I think, "What will people think of me at school if I don't shower today?" once I am out of the shower I have to go into the dreaded closet where what I decided to put on for that specific day could very well determine the way I am going to feel for the rest of the day. If I wear a skirt on a really cold day (which I have done many times) people look at me as if I'm crazy for wearing a skirt when it's negative ten outside. So after I pick out my outfit, I must go into the bathroom and spend 20 minutes or so putting on this stuff called makeup (by the way: whoever invented that is STUPID!). I have to decide what shades and colors to wear for the day because if the color of my eye shadow doesn't "go" with my clothes, that's a huge fashion don't! after I finish my makeup, I proceed to the mirror in my bedroom where I will spend who knows how long on my hair. Once again, there is the pressure of the "look" of the hair. If the hair isn't done right I am already a mess up!

Once the "getting ready" stage is done you must go on to the "arrival" stage. This is linked with what kind of car you drive into the student parking lot and who it is that you meet once you are there. Some students have to ride the bus. I rode the bus until I was old enough to drive, and for some reason the girls whose parents dropped them off from day one, have problems with me riding the bus! What is it their business anyways; we're all going to the same place. The other students, who drive, drive really nice cars, such as brand new Explorers and Lexus'. Me, I drive a teal Mazda 626. Now, there is nothing wrong with my car . . . but the people that can afford better, look at me strange when I come into the parking lot, as if I have no right to be there because of my car. Once I am in the parking lot, I go to my friends' vehicles, where we all usually pile in someone's car. The "popular" people hang out around their cars, which are grouped so nicely together. They stare at you if you even attempt to pull into one of their "designated" parking spaces.

After the "arrival" stage, you proceed on to the "hallway" stage. This is where you encounter the biggest problem with the social levels. The girls and guys at the top of the social chain walk down the halls as if there is no tomorrow. They take up the entire hall and you had better not attempt to pass them. They stand in the middle of the halls and socialize with their friends and boyfriends when I am just trying to get to class. In the halls is also where the critiquing comes into play. This is where the girls will look you up and down and give you the look of approval on your outfit of choice, or of complete disarray. This is your daily profiling, and you had better get used to it.

Starting at the end of the "hallway" stage is the "lunchtime" stage. This is where the pressure of who you will sit with and what everyone else will think about it comes into play. Also during this stage, what you eat is being noticed. Are you eating a salad like the "skinny" girls, or are you eating two breads and two things of chicken nuggets because you know that's what is going to fill you up?

After the "lunchtime" stage you have your "leaving" stage. This, similar to the "arrival" stage is when your afternoon schedule becomes noticed. Are you going straight home from school, showing that you are a "loser", or are you staying after school for some extracurricular activity? This is also very important to how you are viewed.

I have attempted to show you how the normal daily school routine can be very stressful. Almost every single waking minute has it's own stresses. So, next time a teacher or parent says that they understand what we're going through, they don't . . . and the reasons listed above are why. So yes, school can be *that* bad!—Courtney, Clover, SC

Teachers

Another factor that students identified as stress-causing was teachers. From their viewpoints, teachers' behaviors, attitudes, and teaching practices created or added to the stress they already felt.

⌒

School as a whole is stressful. It all depends on who your teachers are and the classes you take. Some teachers are ridiculous in the amount or assignments they give you. Others will not accept your work if you are absent for a certain day even if it's excused.—Bintu, Tallahassee, FL

⌒

School is in one word: horrible. I hate it! It's the main cause of my stress. I'm so stressed by school, that by 12 o'clock noon on Monday, I'm just begging to go home on Friday afternoon. One of the many things that causes stress is the teachers. They are a huge pain (no offense). They pressure you to learn everything. I know that this will pay off one day, but I'm just too stressed right now to be as smart as Albert Einstein. And what's with teachers not realizing that kids have feelings too? They yell and criticize you, and probably don't even realize that a kid might be on the verge of an emotional breakdown. I have this teacher. I'll call her "Mrs. ___" (name changed to protect the innocent). She says I'm being sarcastic when I say I don't understand science. I've had lots of teachers like her, but she just makes me feel like she's a dictator or something, like a megalomaniac (I do know what that means, too). Teachers drive me crazy being bossy all the time. I mean, we're not a dictated country or anything. A child's mind is fragile, you know!

So, in conclusion, school is a NIGHTMARE. Honestly, if I had to go to an all girl-school or something, (which would mean more cheerleaders and popular criticizers, and less boys), I'd drop out. Other kids would probably share my opinion, because school can sometimes be very depressing, unless hating school is just a new trend.—Jessica, Cocoa, FL, 8th grade

⌒

The main reason that a lot of students be stressed out at school is when teachers seem to assign projects around the same day. Then some students have to decide which one to do first. They make it so hard to you to make good grades.—Kristie, Tallahassee, FL

⌒

I am in the ninth grade at ___ High School and a big portion of my life revolves around school. I live a very busy life and school just adds to that pressure. I am an A students and I play soccer on the varsity soccer team, and the track team. For me, a normal day begins at six o'clock in the morning . . . I arrive at school at about seven-thirty each day. I feel that these classes are what cause me the most stress. Teachers require such perfection and precision in the work that we do. They often assign huge amounts of work to test our skills. Sometimes I wonder if teachers realize that we have other classes because one teacher provides enough homework for a week. As my day goes on, the homework just keeps piling up. Two hours of English, one hour of Spanish, two more of biology. At this rate, no wonder why so many teens drop out, they're burnt out in their first semester!—Erin, Woodland Hills, CA

⌒

Lots of things cause stress at school. I think that teachers should have high expectations but just because you're in an honors class you shouldn't have to know everything. Other things that cause stress at school to me is teachers that don't know how to teach. That is the main thing that stresses me at school. A teacher can give you an assignment to do and not explain any of it to you. You can outline a chapter and instead of reviewing the chapter before the test, you just have the test and just do another assignment. I don't like every subject, but I like to learn and teachers that don't teach me, stress me out.—Ciara, Tallahassee, FL

⁓

There are many different things about school that cause stress. One of the biggest problems is the few teachers with attitudes. Some of the teachers feel as if they have the power to be disrespectful to the students and not get disrespected back, but this saying also applies to adults. "If you want respect, you have to give respect." Many teachers fail to realize how reality works when they have a little power in their hands.—Roshaunda, Tallahassee, FL

⁓

Thursday
Dear Diary,
Like every week days, I went to school today. The teachers gave me so much homework, and I have tests to study. I have history, math and science tests and an English homework that takes about four hours! Ok, on Monday my biology teacher assigned us Chapter 5, and she told us that we are going to have a chapter test on Friday. Then I went to history class on Tuesday, and my teacher assigned us a chapter and told us that we are going to have a test on Friday. On Mondays I have flute lessons, Tuesdays I have volleyball class, and Thursdays I have community service. I wish the teachers understood how busy I am. So today, I realized I haven't read any of the sections in the chapter for history or science. I know that if I go to school tomorrow, I would fail both tests. Tests make me nervous, and I feel like I can't breathe until I finished taking the tests. Well, I guess school is all about homework and tests.
Monday
Dear Diary,
School started again. I think what is the most stressful thing about school is trying to keep As in all my classes so I can go to good University. That means I have to do well on the tests and do well on all of the assignments. I realized I have all the hard teachers. I am not just saying this, but all my friends agree that I do have all the hard teachers. When my friends have straight As in all their classes, I end up having many Bs and few As. I think my teachers are good, but if the classes are too hard for all the students to receive As that is not good.—Amber, Woodland Hills, CA

⌒

As I recall my high school years the things that comes to mind first is rules. If I'm not mistaking, rules got me first referral, for not standing up for the pledge in time. My teacher thought I was being disrespectful. But disrespectful to whom? Before my teacher started teaching school, he used to be in the army. So he saw things from a different perspective regarding his country. I guess that's why he made my 8th grade year a living hell. Every time I turned around I had a detention, he even took sports away from me, which at that time I treasured the most. Track was something that inspired me, something that made me whole, something that would change my life forever . . . but he took that away from me. So you ask me what causes stress at school? Teachers cause stress at school.—Oteya, Tallahassee, FL

Managing the Workload
"Managing the workload" pertains to both the amount of work students felt they had to do, but also their extra responsibilities. When I was in high school in the 1980s, a small portion of students had jobs. Now it seems like most students, even those who are not old enough to drive, have after-school jobs. Beyond school work and jobs, students overload their schedules with extracurricular activities in order to better their chances of getting into a "good college," which adds to their already full agendas.

⌒

One of the major concerns of stress in school has to do with the workload. A lot of teachers don't realize that we have lives outside of school and other responsibilities to attend to. A lot of students have jobs or sports activities outside of school. My pet peeve is when teachers assign projects and papers at the same time. It causes a lot of stress when you have four or five projects to work on. The intensity of the course should remain the same while the workload should be lessened.—Aaron, Tallahassee, FL

⌒

School itself is not a stressor; it is what goes on within the school that causes the stress. School is nothing but a place, a concrete floor fenced in and run by some of the most intelligent college graduates. If "school" was just walking into a room and listening to a lecture everyday it would so much simpler. It's the time that students have in between classes, the nutritions and lunches, the different methods of teachers, and all the adjusting a person has to go through that creates the little soap operas of day-to-day life.

One of the biggest stresses of school life is balance. Every day of school we are expected to have even more work to complete at home. We are also trying to come home and relax and have some times to ourselves; whether it be a hot bath, some time on the phone, or just watching TV, everyone needs to unwind. And besides that, we do enough work at school without us having another hour of work when we get home. Many students ride the bus for an hour, or go to after-school activities, and may get home anytime between 5 and 7. Trying to make enough time for yourself is hard since there's always homework to be done.—Chase, Woodland Hills, CA

⁓

The reason why most kids stress out at school is because usually you have six classes and most of the time you have to study for one class, have a research paper, or even have a presentation alone for another. All that work can put you behind and all that work is some how due in the same day or week of all your other classes.—Kizzy, Tallahassee, FL

⁓

As a freshman in high school, I thought I had it tough being an adolescent in school. But when I entered my six new high school courses, being a freshman didn't look so bad. During the first week, I was already up to my head with assignments. I was given tests, homework, and a book review. My teachers taught me new methods of learning, evaluating, analyzing, and even how to draw. The school year had only just begun and I was already stressing. . . . Completing assignments in English is like caring for a hardwood floor—it's difficult. It's hard to keep up, and if I fall behind, it's almost impossible to catch up . . . There are many different and high expectations in high school. A great deal of improvisation and determination goes into a person's work.—Margaret, Moreno Valley, CA

⁓

My major problem with school is the expectancy that the student's life should revolve around school, school related activities, and most especially, homework. To demand, under punishment of law, six and a half hours a day for five out of seven days a week pushes a person's (*especially* a teenager's) tolerance to the limits.

Homework is the bane of my existence. After sitting down almost continuously for about six hours, listening to a teacher, taking notes, and doing work, the student is expected to go home and do homework. I am aware that teachers have to go home and grade endless amounts of papers, and I am sympathetic to that, but that does not mean that the student deserves the same fate. It also seems to me that the teachers see our two "free days" on the weekend as an opportunity for the student to do more work, instead of a break from work. This is entirely unfair to the students because these are the "prime" years of our life, the time when we are supposed to be having the most fun we will ever have, and if this is the most fun I'm ever supposed to have, I'm pretty skeptical about what comes next.

Another thing that angers me is how much pressure and importance is put on the student's output in school. First of all, the student is required by law to attend school regularly, with no consideration towards how the student feels about school. Second, if you do not center your life on schoolwork, requirements, and activities, you are screwed when applying for colleges. Lastly, if you do not get into a decent college, it is very unlikely that your job will be especially profiting, or that your lifestyle will be what you want it to be. As a last word, I would like to add that my pet peeve is when a teacher tells me to "be a teen while I can." It makes me want to smack them in the head with a heavy, blunt object, such as their own textbook.—Travis, Atlanta, GA

⁓

One of the major issues that causes stress is too much homework. Teachers think giving homework to students is easy. Usually when a teenager gets home all they want to do is sleep. Then the next day they have to rush and get it done while another teacher assigns class work.

Another issue that causes stress is taking tests. If a student has about three or four tests a week it gets very difficult to study different subjects at a time. Usually whenever a student has a test they get lazy to study and keep pushing it off to the last second. Then you feel very stressed out and think that your going to fail the test. So, if the number of tests per week go down then it would be much easier to study without being stressed.

The last thing that causes stress is being absent and missing work. You have to finish the assignments you missed plus the assigned. Usually you get a day or two to finish the work or it will be marked as a zero. We usually don't finish the work on time and have to rush at the end. Then we still don't finish and get marked as a zero so then it could possibly give you a failing grade.—Ranya, Melbourne, FL

～

I often wonder why I do not have grey hair from my surplus of work in my high school years. After all of the stress that I have encountered, it is a miracle that I do not look like my grandfather. Throughout a student's high school years, he or she will more than likely be faced with hundreds of different writing assignments, research papers, novel readings, and projects. Most of the time, these things are usually assigned to you around the same time. Thus giving you a truckload of different assignments due to multiple teachers for different types of classes. Things get even worse if you are involved in an extracurricular sport or organization. Me being part of an extracurricular sport, I can attest to this statement. You see, where most students can go home after school every day and have seven or eight hours to do their homework, those extracurricular students will only have three to four. This in turn leads to lots of stress on the students. So I would say that the main cause of stress in school is the surplus of work.—Brandon, Tallahassee, FL

～

We're at school for about eight hours a day and do work for the whole time. When teachers pile on the homework it's like they're taking away half our lives. Some people play sports or have jobs so they don't have a lot of time. It's okay if we didn't finish the class work and they assign that as homework, but giving us more is just crazy. I play basketball for the school's team so I know how it is. After school we go to practice for two hours, then home, then you take a shower, eat, do homework, and then it's time to go to bed. On game days it's even harder because sometimes we get home really late. —Ashlee, Inwood, WV

～

What causes stress for me at school is the fact that we are no longer on block schedule. This means that we go to all of our classes every day. This is not good because I also have after school activities that sometimes do not allow me to leave school until about 7:30 or 8:00 p.m. Because 9 times out of 10 I have homework in all six classes and at least two tests the next day. And who's to say I will go right home after this? This means that I will be up until about 12:30 or 1:00 a.m. trying to get my homework done. And I would have to do it all over again the next day. On a good day I will have no homework in any classes, but on a bad day I will have six tests on the same day. Now that is stress.—Taneshia, Tallahassee, FL

∼

Stress, stress, stress is a big issue at R___ [High School]. R___ treats students like college students. We have so many tests, research papers, and quizzes. In English I, 9th grade, Ms. ___ used to give quizzes two times a week. Tests in her class were every week. I used to keep migraine headaches all the time in 9th grade. I've compared schools to R___ with the homework deal and L___, L___, and even C___, do not have as much homework as R___ does. This is why R___ is very stressful.—Isabelle, Tallahassee, FL

It All Adds Up
Tests, homework, teachers, peer pressure, parents, relationships with friends, breakups, sports, extracurricular activities, drugs, sex, alcohol, jobs, graduating, and getting into college to make money—"it all adds up."

∼

At P___ High School there is a lot of drama. Everybody is in everybody's business. No one can have a real relationship without another person trying to interfere. The females are crazy when it comes to drama. They always start fighting over who they like. Sports are also a big stress causer. Try having homework plus going to practice for about 3 hours. It takes most of the day time away. Plus, if you lose a game, you have to come to school hearing of lots of nonsense. For example, the football team.—Androse, Melbourne, FL

∼

Stress is caused by many things, mostly school work, teachers, and friends. Countless students find the work to be troublesome. Why would any student want to do work when they could be talking to friends or shopping or sleeping, a very important part of high school life. For those students who have a lot of work or find the work to be difficult then the stress is increased. Then when you get to school you have to deal with teachers. Many teachers are very strict. And it is hard not to have stress when your teacher is strict. They mostly nag you about being on time, prepared, doing your work in a specific way, not turning anything in late, and participating in class. Another thing that stresses out students in attendance. There is an extensive policy which has many rules and regulations. Yet being absent is extremely problematic because even when you do bring in a note of excuse many times it is not recorded and then you fail because of absences. Even when you get your attendance straightened out you have to worry about your friends. There is always drama. High school is full of drama. Backstabbing friends, cheating boy/girlfriends, jealousy, someone not talking to someone else, it is just one big soap opera. People are always on the phone trying to deal with everything that is going on. Trying to manage your time between all that happens in school is very hard sometimes and it leads to having a stressful life. And in some cases even when you escape from school and go home you get it from your parents. So life is stressful, especially in high school.—Ayana, Tallahassee, FL

⁓

I believe the stress at school has gotten worse over the years recently. There are many factors that lead up to stress. For example, homework is a major stressor; tests are a major stressor; and above all, your peers are a major stressor. Many people don't realize how tough school is, not because the work is hard, but because of all the stress on top of the work we get. Students have to balance school life with family, extra activities, and much more. Homework, for example, is a main factor of stress. You go to school for six or seven hours and after that you go home and do an hour or more of homework. At school you have tests that you have to take. With six classes a day it is unlikely to go a day without a test. Some days you have not tests, but others you have two or three to take. The people you choose to hang out with at school have a huge impact on you, especially through your high school years. Although many people believe your friends are there for you to lean on and to help you with problems, they also cause much stress through peer pressure. Many students don't realize all the events involved in causing stress in everyday life. Homework, tests, and friends are all major causes of stress in school. Students learn to deal with stress in different ways, and everyone reacts differently.—Jenelle, Melbourne, FL

⁓

What causes stress at school? A lot of things cause stress in a school environment. Some can be positive stress and some can be negative. Most is negative but basically all stress is. Getting to class on time is something that causes stress. Remembering if you did your homework and just the pressures of class are some too. A really bad stress making machine in school could none other be the people you talk with and call friends. Friends could be the most stressful thing in school. They cause peer pressure and sometimes make you do things you don't want to do. Or they could be stressful by getting you involved in their life or them getting involved in yours. So school can be very stressful in many different ways and even in some ways that in wouldn't expect it to be.—Matthew, Melbourne, FL

∿

What I really think about school is that it is too stressful. At this point in my life, having gone through almost 14 years of school, I feel that I need some relaxation before embarking on another four years. My senior year I wish that I could finally relax and not have to worry so much about maintaining my 3.8 grade point average. I am so tired from trying to sleep at night and not being able to because thoughts of what homework I may not have done or what tests I may have forgotten about are racing through my mind. Since school work cannot just disappear altogether from my senior year, I have one idea of how to keep students from stressing not only about their grades and performance in high school but also, which college they will be attending next summer or fall. My idea is to have a mandatory period given to students in the upper grade levels where relaxation techniques are taught, possibly through yoga. This would be a period for students to unwind and forget about everything and anything on their minds. This would be a very easy and beneficial thing to do to help students deal with stress.—Mercedes, Merritt Island, FL

∿

Stress, a horrible factor of life, although sometimes good and bad, it is more often than the usual the latter. School is encompassed by stress, you can't see it dancing right in front of you, but peer at any unsuspecting pupil bustling down the corridor and the panicked expression is a dead giveaway. Also note the severe twitch of the left eyebrow, gritting of the teeth, occasional self-inflicted smacking of one's own self, white knuckles upon a book, and dark circles shadowing those bright and not so cheery eyes. Yes, stress is a monster and it can take over when you least expect it—or slack off. It seems the worst stress for persons age thirteen to eighteen is school. Why would anyone like to put sweet, innocent children through this traumatic event? Well, supposedly, it helps us learn more and get into another stress-ful school and then off to an equally stressful lifetime career. However, if you look at the situation with a positive eye, you'll see that in the long run, school is a good thing. It promises us a future that without would corrupt our economy. Perhaps then that means that stress is a good thing too—or per-haps not.—Brittany K., Merritt Island, FL

∼

There's a lot of things that cause stress at school. School is stressful already, plus we as student have a lot of different other things on our mind. Other things as in tests, projects, grades, and the major thing that causes stress at school is the "FCAT!" The reason why I said that test, projects, grades, and others things stress out students is because that we have other things to do in school besides worrying about tests and the other things. I mean don't get me wrong about me saying that I don't care about tests and the others, it's just that we have more than 1 class and we also have to study. Now about the "FCAT," it's a really stressful test. You have to make a certain number of points to pass and it's a graduation requirement. The test really doesn't make any sense at all cause it asks you crazy questions and it can hold you back in your grade if you don't pass. So, these are some of the things that can cause stress at school to me personally.—Kaniesha, Talla-hassee, FL

∼

When I was in the 8th grade I remember a day that high school seniors came to visit, and talk about their high school experience. I remember asking a sen-ior, "Is high school fun?" She responded with, "Of course, it's one of the best experiences of your life." Until this day, I am still trying to figure out what she meant by "best experience." In my opinion high school has been a place that marks the word STRESS in capital letters. Everyday of high school affects the college that I enter. If I slack off for one week I start to rush and panic because I realize many things. High school affects the college I go to, the type of ca-reer I will have, how much money I will have in the future, and how success-ful I will be in life. These lines are repeatedly told to me by my parents, teacher, friends, and many others. In the first day of freshman year in my sci-ence class my teacher only talked about the importance of high school. It was stressing to hear that because I already had a big fear of high school inside me.—Kathy, San Jose, CA

⌒

What causes stress for me is when I don't get along with administration. For example, during schedule changing my guidance counselor had a nasty attitude towards everybody. I understand that she was going through some rough times, but she decided to be a counselor so she should have put on a smile and ran with the flow of things. The most stressful thing in high school to me is falling behind in an important subject and the teacher doesn't take time to help you with it.

Stress at school can be very hard in a person's everyday life. Stress anywhere follows you everywhere and it tends to stay with a person until the problem is fixed or the brain puts it in the back of the head. I haven't been stressed out much this year, but I'm a senior and there is something bound to come up to push my buttons. But in the meantime I'll just play my cards as they are dealt to me to have a successful future.—Rickeena, Tallahassee, FL

⌒

What causes stress at school are homework, teachers, school things that happen in your home, boyfriends, friends, etc. Homework will cause a lot of stress cause you work and come home and do a lot of work and teacher don't care about other teachers giving you work and things that happen in your household. Stress will be caused by boyfriends and friends that a lot of stress it's first a lot of things that are caused by stress.—Shamika, Tallahassee, FL

⌒

From preschool to my senior year, there's so much to write about. As I grew older each year and went to the next grade by stress level increased with each year. In elementary, it wasn't bad, a few pieces of homework every other night and maybe an easy test to show the teacher what we learned. But in middle school it began to get a little hard, but there wasn't that much pressure to have to do my best. Then in high school things changed completely. It was the first time that I had to work real hard because I knew it depended on my future. From ninth grade to now, I've had to make sure my classes were caught up and make good grades. Each year, taking honors/AP courses, and finding scholarships got worse. This year there's getting a good score on my ACT and SAT and knowing what I need to get in order to get into my future college. This year will probably be the worst, because of the added pressure of getting accepted into a university and getting scholarships to help pay for college. Most importantly, graduating with honors and not failing trigonometry this year tops off the stress I have to deal with in school. Basically, stress is worse in high school than in elementary and middle.—Sierra, Tallahassee, FL

⁓

Many kids during school feel as if they are carrying a luggage of stress on their shoulders. They really have no extra time fit into their schedule. School is a *very big* part of the day, but for me it's sometimes is more overstressing then helping me out. There's the grades, fitting in, passing, failing, catching up, and many more obstacles. The biggest stress burden in school would have to be the FCAT.

During school everyone is preparing for this FCAT. It depends whether you go on to the next level or stay back for one more trip. It also depends if you graduate. This stresses many kids out because the teachers keep pressuring us to pass something you can't even study for. Another cause for stress at school is fitting in. There are many people in schools everywhere who stress themselves out trying to be someone they aren't. There are also ones, the anorexic ones, the geeks, the gothics, everyone trying to "belong" somewhere.

You stay up late trying to please your parents. As for me I study extremely hard to get straight A's. I stress myself out a lot. In order to achieve good grades and get all the homework done in school that all teachers . . . in is very stress causing.—Tanya, Melbourne, FL

⁓

School is like a maze that takes critical thinking in order to get out of and we the students are the mouse. Many student like to learn and discover things but they don't like the stress that comes along with the effort to enhance knowledge. Some of the main stressors are parents and peers.

Parents always want the best and more for their children. Sometimes they just want a little to much. No matter how much we may try not to let them down we do it anyway. Often students might do something no to better themselves but for their parents. That includes everything from school work, sports, and a career. Another stressor is peers.

Peers can be friends, associates, or anybody. There is always some one that a student wants to be like. In school everyone has their picks and chooses with who they want to be friends with. Most students want to be with the so-called in crowd, it is just natural. That is how peers can be a stressor.

The causes of stress will never end in a person's life. There will always be something on your mind that will stress you when you are in a school system. You will always be in demand of something. Students will have more stress than a normal person.—Tiffany, Melbourne, FL

〜

The key to success is no stress. In school there are many causes of stress, one being students. Students, or peers, make a stressful environment when they force you to make a difficult decision in little or no time. These decisions good or bad make it more difficult to do school work. Most of the time it is not purposely given. Another type of stress is teachers. There is always a teacher you just cannot stand and having that teacher early in the day can cause a lot of stress as well as put you in a bad mood which makes other people stressed out.

Another cause of stress is too much homework. This is not an issue for some people but for others it can make you totally stressed out. Too much homework can cause a panic which leads to stress. I guess most of the stress from homework is caused by trying to complete it on time and doing it the right way. Either way stress is going to be in school and in our lives.—Tony, Melbourne, FL

〜

Well being a senior in high school its very stressful. Why, really is the process of passing huge tests, making sure you have your credits in required classes plus staying on top of your books as well. To be honest most students are not very good test takers due to nervousness on passing or failing the exams. Then you have payment plans to meet too, yes those senior fees kick in as soon as school starts.

Besides the students' problems you have the teachers. Really you have teachers who'll break their back trying to help you and teach you, then you have those who don't care nothing about you. It's like as long as the come to work, making sure they do what ever that he/she has to do and leave. Oh and don't let the concern ask about extra help, it a big mess, a with attitude and all. But then it kind of falls back on the students meaning we have to do our job as well. But you have those who has it worster than other students at school and at home. Trust me I know. I've been there, my junior year explains it all. It's like you have to look at the situation from both sides from a student and a teacher perspective.—Victoria, Tallahassee, FL

～

My opinion on school is that it's very stressful. There are a lot of times it seems unbearable. I know that it's not impossible because my parents graduated but times have changed. They expect a lot more from you today than back then. Now we have to pass MCAs just so that we can graduate. Thank goodness I've made it by a few points but I worry for others. There are a lot of kids like me who don't test well but know a lot. They big senior research project is very stressful as well. I know it's standard procedure but it's hard. Especially in our school . . . it's never warm and difficult to learn in. I feel like I'm not prepared for the real world. I have not learned anything that will help me survive out there. The requirements to graduate from A___ High is to pass MCAS, to pass senior research, we must complete 75 hours of community service and have enough credits. I think that is asking a lot because it all seems impossible. I think they should ease up because I've got all this stuff for college to do too. It's too much for me. There should also be days off every once in a while to just get a break from it all. That's the reason why kids skip . . . they all just need a break every once in a while.—Anonymous, Amesbury, MA

～

High school is the fastest four years of your life filled with everything from art to physics to that boy you have a crush on. The average day of a high school student (keep in mind that teenagers want to wake up at 11:30) starts at 5:45, and is a rush to get out the door. And once at school there is a rush to finish homework. Then, after school there are activities, whether they are sports or musicals, they keep high school students out late. And by the time we get home we are tired but keep going out of desire to achieve.

Most people believe that high school students don't care about, this is untrue. There is so much pressure on high school students today. The competition to get into a college is harder every year. This causes stress for high school students today. But stress is a daily thing in high school. Stress from parents, teachers, and even coaches can make day to day life less fun. I believe that this is a problem, too much stress is unnecessary because high school students stress themselves out enough.

High school is like a roller coaster, every day is different. Some days you have algebra and some days it's okay. But for most high school students, there is one constant, they hate homework. Homework can be necessary but not always. There are some teachers who seem to give homework just to make our busy lives harder.

Furthermore, high school is like no other time in your life. It is a mix of all aspects of life filled with so many memories. Everything from your favorite teacher you hate, to the tests and all the stress. But there are so many fun parts of high school: dances, sporting events, parties, hanging with friends.

In conclusion, high school is real training. High school is learning how to deal with life before college. The high school experience can't be determined by a certain event, but all the events. High school is a time of hard work, heavy emotions and great times. The trick of high school is to balance everything. The "real" high school is fast pace mix of life.—Megan H., San Jose, CA

⌒

There are a lot of things that cause stress in my school. Most adults would think, "probably drug, sex, and friends!" that's only the beginning! There's stress with homework, popularity, peer pressure, boyfriend/girlfriend, and THEN drugs, and sex.

Homework always collides with after school activities. If you don't do homework you could fail, but most teens in eighth grade, like me, don't want to just sit around and work all the time, we want to have fun! Also there is the problem with asking for help with homework. I have had many experiences with that. I don't like asking anyone for help. Sometimes it feel like the tutors at your school are your age and are bugging you and not being patient with you. My parents try to help me, but it just gets me more confused. Those commercials about the Sylvan learning program look like they would help but also look like a load of baloney. Who goes to these places? Every teacher teaches different so if the tutor or your parents or the people at Sylvan teach it different than the teachers its harder to under stand what the teacher is talking about in class.

DRUGS. Always a conversation stopper, but not and S___ HS. In my school it's part of the routine. Going home on the bus and driving past a student smoking a cigarette, or during lunch hearing about some one your age going to jail for smoking weed. No one really stops and says: oh-mi-gosh . . . you smoke? I can probably sit in my class right now and point out two or three students that smoke or do drugs. If your best friend smokes does that mean you do? No! I have a lot of friends that smoke or do drugs, not my very best friends, but it still doesn't mean I do drugs. I'm s___ c___ its cool to do drugs, I guess I'm not cool then!

What makes you popular or cool? What makes you a nerd? That's two questions I have and always will wonder about. The definition of popular is: Liked by acquaintances; have many friends or admirers. The definition of a nerd is: A person regarded as stupid or inept, especially a person who is proficient at science, but social inept. The question now is, would you rather be liked by many or smart? I wish there was something called nerd-ular: a person liked by many, but smart.

What are the one-thing parents don't understand the most? Peer pressure! It's not always other peers pressuring you; some times it's your conscience pushing you to be better. In eighth grade the pressure to look better is escalading more than ever. One of my best friends almost dies after sta[r]ving herself thinking that everyone was making fun of her stomach, which wasn't that, big at all! She got help and is much better now. The girls and boys in grade school are very harsh. Peer pressure will never go away fully, but to make it so it doesn't always hurt so bad, my advise, is to ignore everyone and there comments, move on and get over it!

Talking to your parents can sometimes help, but other times it just makes matters worst. When I get home from school my mother always asked what happened at school and I always say nothing. Because telling her what happened doesn't help. You can see it in there eyes sometime that they think you are lying. My mother has her opinions on everything. She says what she wants to say what she thinks on everything, my friends, drugs, sex, and what she thinks goes on around S___ C___. Sometimes it gets annoying!

Some people at my school say if they didn't have a boyfriend they wouldn't go to school. I would come either way. Friendships of mine have ended because of a boyfriend. At S___ HS there is an un-written timeline of what your supposed to do with a boy or girl. First it's getting to see them out of school then there is kissing and for-play and then sex. I'm a virgin and hope to be for a long time. I don't use the un-written time line because of the consequences. You always have to pick the right boyfriend or girlfriend. One that wont pressure you to have sex or play around if your don't want to. Plus, if you do have sex you don't want some one who will spread stuff about you around the school.

If you haven't noticed there are a lot of things that cause stress. There are more issues on homework, how you are labeled, the deans, parents on school related topic, and there will always be drugs, sex and friends. Most people wouldn't know how stressful a teen's life could be!—Amanda, Cocoa, FL, 8th grade

〜

Do I have to go to school today? Why do I have to go? These are the questions that us students ask our parents about going to school. No matter what the problem is there will always be reasons why to hate school. This will all stop if school becomes a more exciting place, just like second home on even an adventure theme park.

One of the reasons why students hate school is "stress". Stress from all the minimal things like waking up early and all the homework. Who likes to do homework? Nobody does. It's just a waste of time when you could be doing something more exciting. Being in school for more then six hours is a torture. Why do we have to spend three more studying at home, and to top it off, studying even more during the weekends? Not only is that stressful but also having to study about boring topics that won't help us in the future is another waste of time. Now the most annoying thing is we have study about things we learned two or three years ago. School will just always be another problem in our lives. This could change if school became a more enjoyable place.

Even thought school may be horrific, it is an experience that turns your life around for good. School is the place where you learn about the life you will have in the future. Simply, it prepares you for a career that will lead to a job. Us students won't realize this until we are over 25, have a fantastic job with the "big bucks in our pockets", but even if that's true we will still hate school for all those years we have to study.—Adilene Escobar, Aptos, CA

〜

At school you go through many different things. Stress, bullying, popularity contests, and the list go on. You go under a lot of pressure, and just in one day, your life can be totally ruined. People talk about other kids in their social groups, and if you do something embarrassing the news travels fast. School and the people in it, are dramatically changing every single year. If you mess up in a school like ours, you are basically finished with.

One of the problems everybody has at school is stress. There are many things that can cause a teen stress. For example, the other day when I was in science class, we were learning some new material, and everyone seemed to understand what the teacher was talking about, except for me! I finally got so frustrated that I just gave up. I tuned out my teacher completely. Some of the other factors that cause stress receiving too much homework, and mean and boring teachers. If it is a dry subject, you know that the class will be excruciating, long and miserable. Take math for example, it is a dull subject, and the answer is right or wrong, no questions about it! Too make class a little it more exciting for the student, it would help to have a crazy, or a funny teacher, so that the students won't be falling asleep in the class. But, instead, most of them choose to be dull, precise, and boring, which can cause students to have a frustrating and stressful day.

One subject that has been going on for decades is bullying. Usually this is a bigger problem with the boys. They always have to show who is the top dog, and always seem to solve the problem in a fight. I have seen some of the fights that go on at my school, and they are a lot more different from what you usually see on the television. The fights are actually real. It is not acting, and can creep you out for a little while.

This is the biggest thing at our school, popularity. I hate it when people have to always be judging other people. We have so many different popularity groups, and we just keep on adding more of them. For example some of them are: jocks, preps, cheerleaders, skaters, surfers, . . . etc. My best friend ___ said, "Aren't we all just people?" I fully support her in that statement. Who cares if you have the most expensive clothes, or if you are rich? I thought that if you went to school, it was for an education, and to learn how to make a living in life. Instead of doing that, lots of people go out trying to beat other people at doing something, and end up going to school for the wrong reason. Why does it matter if you have something that other people don't? We are the future brains of tomorrow, and we are all worried about being popular and beautiful. What is it supposed to prove? I have a major problem with this, and I don't think that it is going to stop anytime soon.
—Melissa, Cocoa, FL, 8th grade

⌣

Halls lined with classrooms, classrooms packed with students, students piled high with books and binders, and books and binders filled with notes and homework; this is the common sight at schools across our nation. Oh yes, with the lack of sleep, amounts of homework, and the daily drama of a teenage life, many students travel through the winding hallways in a sleepy-eyed daze. Does this seem very productive?

Although studies show that students are not any busier than they were thirty years ago, I beg to differ. Being a teenager myself I often times bring homework home to my mother who did the same class work I am doing when she was in college, and math was beyond her comprehension by the time I was in eighth grade. My poor brother is only seven and in the first grade and already learning basic multiplication, I remember not doing that until third grade. If all this x equals z, Newton's law, battle of this and that all in the same year, and writing paper after paper about dead authors and uninteresting topics isn't enough to put some students in a daze then I don't know what is.

Yes I know, kids used to work twenty years ago, and trust me I have heard all the stories of "how we had to walk two miles up a hill in the snow, " but have you seen the amount of students that work in today's times. No, most of us don't need the money we just want stuff, a new pair of pants, that dress from last month's magazine, the new CD that everyone has, and the shoes from that hot store at the mall. Although that may make us seem spoiled it is our way of trying to be responsible and buy our own items. Now I am not saying there isn't the exception where students don't have to save up for their car or need the money to pay the monthly cell phone bills (who can live without a cell phone in this day and age), but either way it doesn't take away from the fact that students are trying to be responsible. Many jobs are very demanding from their employers making students work until midnight which leaves them with piles of homework and little to no sleep. Yes there are child labor laws but if your boss asks you to work late are you really going to argue? Many teachers get annoyed with kids who fall asleep in class but my heart goes out to most of them because they have busy lives and often times don't fall asleep until two in the morning and have to wake up three or four hours later.

It seems like many adults forget what it was like to be our age when they hit their twenties. We are still children trying to play grown ups, its just like when we were five and dressing up in mommy and daddy's clothes, but now our games are more sophisticated. We still need our sleep and maybe even a nap or two, we still want to "play" with our friends, and we still want the understanding of our elders, hey warm cookies and cold milk wouldn't be a bad treat either. No we are not hooligans, and yes we are trying to grow up; sometimes too fast. Many of us are not even eighteen and who is to say that eighteen is grown up. I know when I'm eighteen and heading off to college, I will still be calling my mommy every night and crying because I miss home and want to be in my own bed with my teddy bear.

Remember although we act grownup we still need support. Many of us deal with things that no teenager should be put through. We see our friends falling prey to drugs and alcohol, while we watch other friends die, or those that entered the army and are now in battle, and other friends are having sex and becoming pregnant. We as teens must not let the pimply faced, screw-up stereotype of us take hold. We must stand strong and stay on the right path. All should remember, we are the future leaders, doctors, scientists, firemen, police officers, bankers, actors, singers, etc. of the world. Live your life now and you should have fun, but don't screw up. Mistakes made now can and will affect the rest of your life. Your future is in the palm of your hand, make it magical, fill it with dreams, and stop walking around in a daze. Open your eyes and look at the world around you and imagine how you can change it and make a difference. Oh and about all that x equals z, Newton's law, battle of this and that all in the same year, and writing paper after paper about dead authors and uninteresting topics, who knows, it may become helpful if you are ever on a game show like *Who Wants to Be a Millionaire.*—Amber Lynn, Clover, SC

⁓

Why?
Why?

Why do thoughts run through my mind like a faucet?
I want to stop it
Questions boggling me
Assumptions deceiving me
Everyone here seems to be a different person
So much jealousy, anguish, distress happens
A friend doesn't seem to be a friend to another person in the end
Why? Why do people show their true colors only in high school?
Or is it just that they are putting a false image?
They are getting watercolor, painting over their stupid face to make themselves a "better" being
While others use charcoal, scribble over and over
Practice over and over until they achieve the sketched diagram of what they want their life to be like
Why?
Why everytime I walk past a person . . .
All he/she English language consists of "He said this, she said that . . ."
Do they come from a country that is name Hesaidthis shesaidthat?
If so, I don't know my geography
Why?
Why don't I know my geography?
It's because I'm distracted by close-minded, distraught minds like theirs
They're being taught that the correct way to handle their agitated ways
Was to create violence
Why?
Why do people hold grudges?
It's just "high school"

High school that everyone sees in the movies
But I guess everyone makes an ass out of themselves once in a while
Isn't drama supposed to be a class?
—Kim, South San Francisco, CA, 10th grade

～

If you are late for class you get in trouble. If you are early people think you
are weird. People bother you. You plan to much for homeroom. There are
teachers you don't like. You have to practically be silent all day. At the end
of the day you want to EXPLODE!
BOOM!!!
—Katie, Vestavia Hills, AL, 6th grade

Photo by Angeliese Weeks

CHAPTER SEVEN

~

What I've Learned So Far

I think school is just a time waster sometimes, a way to keep kids off the streets and out of their parents' hair.—Jessica, Merritt Island, FL

Some of the students who submitted writings made reference to the phrase "high school is the best years of your life." They mentioned that this notion often came from their parents and, frankly, the students thought that their parents did not know what it was like to go to school, especially high school, in the 21st century. I know that my high school days, as "good" as they were, come nothing close to the best years of my life. Those involved in education—parents, administrators, teachers, staff members, and politicians—must ask themselves what impressions about schooling students are taking with them into the rest of their lives.

My original intention with this chapter was to present students' stories regarding what they remembered about going to school. However, what I received was that and more. This chapter became a collection of remembrances, hopes, and advice for students from students. After reviewing these accounts, one question emerged: What is the American school experience doing to children and what are the effects?

~

I really think that school is just an prison or a holding cell to keep kids confined while their parents are away from home. Teachers, well most of them, except Mrs. ___, don't really want to be at school, and they'd rather be wild animal trainers, or astronauts, or anything else than being stuck with teenagers for seven hours a day.

Really, in the thirteen years of school, I've learned that everything is a popularity contest, and no matter how hard you try to succeed, the ditzy blond-haired girl, with lots of friends and no common sense always seems to succeed. I've learned through school that politics are the same way. I ran for vice-president of the fifth grade class, and to no surprise to me, the queen of popularity won, although she had no idea about anything, let alone how to fulfill the make-believe campaign promises she made. All this girl did was raise the obesity bar to another level by offering mounds of candy to attract the undecided voters and to over-joy her numerous friends. Congratulations to her . . . she won, and where did it get us?

So I have learned that school is a prison, people are fake, the blond girl always wins, and candy buys votes in make-believe elections. I have come to find that school is not as enjoyable as it once was. I still remember the days of learning the alphabet and coloring pictures with crayons. Oh, it seems like just yesterday . . . then twelve years of school slipped through my fingers, and here I am, a senior in high school. Looking back on all the years, and long hours spent at school, the first things that come to mind are what I consider to be bad things. Now, I do not consider myself to be pessimistic, so after sitting along in my room and pondering my past and wondering about my future, the good things about school flood my mind, even though they only last for a few minutes, until I recall another one of the stresses that plagued my day.—Alison, Merritt Island, FL

~

School. There is never nothing to say about it. When I first started school I really didn't like is even thought I only went for half the day. I hated being away from home. I really never new why (and still don't). I never really made friends, I was a very unsocial little girl. First grade was crazy. I think I cried for the first half of the year in it. I remember crying for about a hour or more after my mom had dropped me off. The school would call her at work and tell her she had to come pick me up, they didn't think I was ready for first grade. Pretty soon I realized my mom was going to make me go no matter what so I gave up and started to get used to it. That year I didn't make any friends because of the whole crying thing. I seemed to be the only one that did it and everyone thought I was weird or had problems. I passed even though my teacher and principal said I should have been held back, but mom said no (thank god she didn't).

I went on to second grade and I made a lot of new friends. I loved it. I wanted to go to school. My teacher was the best. I loved that teacher, to this day she is still my favorite teacher. The one thing that sucked about this year at school was the spelling. I hated it and there was no one at home to help me so I never studied for my test. I really never even looked at the words. Now I realize that was the stupidest thing I probably have done. Well because of it I got held back. I lost all my friends that I had made, and to this day I have never talked to them since then, even though I see them all the time. The only thing that made being held back a little better I got to have my favorite teacher again. I hated being older than everyone else. I mean I was already older because my birthday is at the end of the year. I was now behind a grade level and I could never return to my right grade again. The second time around I did my spelling and I think I passed almost every test with an A.—Amber, Jackson, MI

⌢

Fifth grade was my first school year in America. I must say, now that I look back, it wasn't such a great year. Most memories I receive are of the time students made me cry because of my Indian race. Yes, during my first year here, I had a heavy accent. There were 3 kids that really enjoyed teasing and laughing at me. First, I just never noticed nor understood why they laughed but couple of my friends went & told on them and ever since then it was repeated.—Ewlin, San Jose, CA

⌢

One of my best memories of school is in third grade when my teacher made a deal with our class. If we could be quiet the whole day he would take us outside for the last period. Our class was on its best behavior the whole day. When he finally took us outside, we decided to play football. We asked him if he would play with us, and to our surprise he said he would. There he was with dress shoes, pants, dress shirt, and a tie, out on the field. I had the time of my life. This made me realize that teachers are people too, and they also can have fun. I'll never forget it.—Peter, Merritt Island, FL

⌢

Out of all the years of school I've had, I remember few good things. In fourth grade, I had the best time at recess. I either played soccer or swing. They were my favorite things to do. All the guys would actually let the girls play soccer with them, too. It's not like in high school when guys think all girls suck at all sports. That is my favorite memory of school.—Rachel, Merritt Island, FL

⌒

I do not particularly enjoy school. This being my final year of high school has let me appreciate it more so than I had before. This final year has been my best, but does not make me nostalgic for past years. Of course, I am not the only one who would feel this way, not many children would be saddened if there were a few more snow days or if a meteor were to have it's way with the school. In my younger years I was surely the most vocal in my apprehension against school.

In a piece very similar to this, I had written out the injustices of school. I had no personal vendettas against any teacher or student (although I was very cynical about the administration) but just a general dislike of the idea of school. Looking back, I can narrow my dislike to a more specific feeling—nothing made me feel good about myself. I do not see it as the school's responsibility to make me feel good, but it would have helped. I have always made great grades, fantastic grades, but I found early on that grades are devoid of significance. What does it really say about me as a person when I ace a project? Have I progressed as a person? Have I accomplished anything outside of the system itself? I would say "No" to these rhetorical questions—I really don't see how there is any major influence on my real life when I accomplish something in school.—James, Clover, SC

⌒

My favorite year of school was kindergarten. Those were the days when my biggest problem was a crayon breaking. My teacher was Mrs. ___ and she was the greatest. She was always patient, I think it was mainly because the loved children. I liked her the best because the showed she cared and did things like give me a hug whenever I needed one. This was also my best year of school because there were so many crafts that we could do. I remember one that I did around Thanksgiving. We made a baby out of paper and put it into a paper papoose that actually tied to my back. I wore that thing for weeks. I learned all the fundamentals that year and they are the basis for my entire career as a student.—Tansy, Merritt Island, FL

~

According to what I learned in sociology, school has made me the person I am today and that is a good thing, at least I think so. Without school, I wouldn't have grasped the concept of sharing, and "staying within the lines." School has made me responsible and honest, mainly be learning from the faults of others. I mean, I am not saying that I haven't had faults of my own, because, believe me, I have had my fair share, but what I am saying is that school gives you the opportunity to interact and relate to others, and consequently you should learn from them . . . unless you want to relive the mistakes of others.

I think that the best thing about school is that it has opened me up to new friendships and given me the chance to believe in myself and excel at the things that I do best. School has been that common ground that let me open up and meet people that I may have accidentally passed along the way . . . good people . . . great people, my friends.—Alison, Merritt Island, FL

~

High school is a place of joy. Some may always say that high school is a waste, but school makes life. Without school, there would be no teachers to teach the lawyers and doctors that serve our community. I am very lucky to go to a school like mine. Our school is six years old and is the nicest in the county. Although our school is the Hilton of schools, our population is growing rapidly. We have traveling teachers to meet the students' needs and are running out of classrooms surely and quickly. Starting this school year, four classrooms are being built on each side of our school. We are receiving eight new classrooms, but since my school is growing so rapidly, our school will remain overcrowded.

A teenager's life would be boring without high school. Even though high school may sometimes be rough, it definitely pays in the long run. High school is filled with features that may change you for the rest of your life. This time period is to enjoy everything. When you graduate high school, you will no longer be handed everything on a silver platter, but you will enter the real world.—Amy, Inwood, WV

~

After thirteen years of school, I seriously wonder how much actual time I spent learning, how much time I wasted sitting in a nonproductive class, and the people I have missed meeting because of scheduling errors and inaccurate social stereotypes. These are very interesting topics of discussion, don't you think?

There have been plentiful times, since I entered the public schooling system, that I've wondered as I sat in classes, why am I here? Am I actually learning or being forced to waste a precious second of my grand life for the sake of a single class credit? Seriously, how much do you need to know about tennis or what shade of gray compliments green? I think school would be better spent teaching and learning life skills, things that apply to everyday living rather than a fifty minute waste of my time.

One thing has always bothered me at school. The introduction to making friends and keeping them according to our typical social standards. Unfortunately, then we get into cliques and school groups who form judgment and labels upon other people. These people who I could have established a relationship or friendship with earlier in my youthful years. People who eventually made me better, see the whole picture? But it is because of these school-caused groups I had to wait to see them.—Brittany, Merritt Island, FL

⌢

Some of what we have learned really has helped in my life but honestly most of it hasn't. What is photosynthesis or intergovernmental revenues, yeah that's really important. To boot tests are total cramming sessions and for what really something I'll use once and never again. It's all a waste of time. The fact of the matter is in retrospect, the only classes I ever needed should have been directly in the field I want.

Teachers on the other hand tell us that everything will be used in our life at some time. I just really want to ask one if they have needed to know what the migratory pattern for a swallow is or what the speed of sound is. They live in a little perfect world because in their fields what they did learn in high school they still use, because they are still here. Most kids getting out of school try and get out as quickly as possible, why would they stay, unless to torment kids. I won't ever come back to this school or another high school.—Casey, Merritt Island, FL

⌢

What do kids think about school you ask? Well some kids love school some kids hate it. Well for me anyways I love to come to school and do work and have fun activities like movies, games, parties, dances and just school. I like school but a lot of kids here hate it but hey what can I say. Kids are mean these days yelling at teachers and just plain roud (*sic*). It's wrong. Kids should think about school for learning and when they learn they should respect the teacher that teaches them not yell at them because they can't have their way or because the teacher that is here is not the teacher they want. They want to help you do what you don't want to do. They are here to hope you successed not for it to be hard and some times they like to do fun things with you like field trips and things like that. And kids think of school like I bad thing and it's horrible but they don't care. There trying to make a point by the way they act and dress and look but some of us don't know why I can't figer out why. But hey what can I say, I am just a kid and I know me likes school and wants it to be fun and hard when we need it.

But I think school is fun and every kid can do what they want to do if they try hard enough because I can do it. If I try and any other kids could to so what do kids think about school today you ask. Well I think you an idea now but now you know what I and also other kids think about school.—Donna, Hudson, FL, middle school

⁓

To speak truthfully, I think that 13 years in school is a little long. I would have to say about the last two to three years in high school was review for the year before. I believe students don't learn anything in their last years because if you haven't learned the basics by now, there's a good possibility you won't comprehend now.—LaKendra, Tallahassee, FL

⁓

I don't think school is for everyone, and it's a pain to deal with unmotivated people. I think only the willing should qualify. It's pointless to go through something when it won't make a difference in the long run.—Erika, Merritt Island, FL

⁓

I come to school every day and wonder how all our minds work. Why does everyone think so differently? Some are mean, nice, liars, scared, shy, crazy and things that people have no idea even exist. I wonder this because everyone is so different at my school. It's not like any other school. Half of my school are into drama and dress crazy and different while the other half are punk and thuggish.

At my school everyone is really judgemental. So many people have thought I was a rude, stuck-up cheerleader because I'm really shy and I don't talk to people unless they talk to me. Once people would get to know me, they thought different. No one likes to be judged into something their not. Like someone once said "don't judge a book by its cover." At my school if you're not in drama your considered weird and materialistic. They look at you with an evil eye, like you're an alien who tried to hurt them.

Last year I hung out with a lot of the seniors and only one of my friends was the same age as me. When I first started hanging out with them (seniors) people called me stuck-up and a slut just because I hung out with old people, little did they know I never even kissed a guy. People would make comments toward me about me being air headed, and blond in the head just because I'm a cheerleader. Ha, I'm not blonde, in fact, I'm Mexican. People thought I didn't care about school because I was/am a cheerleader.

Me becoming a cheerleader actually got me into caring about my grades. I met someone who inspired me to get good grades on cheer. Now I have a's and b's. I would like to get into a good college but my test taking skills are really bad and since most college goes off SAT scores I don't think I'll get into any. Not to mention my parents can't afford housing for me and I know it's complicated and hard to get a grant and financial aid. I want to do an outside league of cheer-leading because then I could get a scholarship but it's hard to keep up with my grades and friends. I just want to be a normal teen who goes out with her friends.

In my opinion everyone had always been made fun of in some way or an-other. Why are kids so cruel these days? I have got called many names when I was little and it's still continuing. I've also been made fun of the fact that I'm Mexican, a cheerleader. I care about my grades and dress a certain way. They call me white wash. I think it's really stupid and mean. Why do people talk about other people? We all know everyone has feelings.

High school is way more than just getting some education. It's about how you handle yourself with working with other people. You may or may not like or vice versa. You learn also how to juggle things all at the same time. From what my elders have told me about how it was in high school when they were in it, I think it's different from then to now.—Anonymous, San Jose, CA

～

In the beginning—for about as long as I was in elementary school—education was presented to me as something fun. What lies!! As soon as I hit middle school I quickly realized that school would never be the same. No more recess or snack time. No more duck duck goose or dodgeball . . . all of those things were simply a tease. Things we did because we were too young for essays and pop quizzes. Now, in high school—my attitude is completely opposite of what it was in 2nd grade. I hate coming here, I don't enjoy classes, and I don't feel a desire to be involved at school. Senior year has been my best one at this school—I must admit. I had a crappy sophomore/junior year because I felt like I worked my butt off and got nowhere. Obviously, I DID accomplish SOMETHING with all my hard work, because I'm still here, and almost done. That's a lot these days, considering the enormous percentage of my peers who already dropped out, failed, or were expelled. I try to view my 13 year education as a good thing—despite all the stupid, annoying, grueling, monotonous, pain in the neck stuff we all had to struggle through. My mom has always told me, "that which does not kill us makes us stronger," . . . so coming to the end of it all, I think I'm pretty strong. I think I was one of the lucky ones who figured the whole school thing out pretty early on. I got it, and now I'm moving on to another chapter I'll have to get through. I'm not sure *school* is what got me ready for the "real" world, rather, the experience of being surrounded by a variety of different people and settings and learning what *not* to do.—Becky, Merritt Island, FL

∼

High school is an interesting time. Parents tell you it is one of the most trying, difficult times of one's life; other kids will tend to tell you it's a snap, and half the time you just consider it a morbidly wasteful period of time. At L___ High School, the school which I go to, I have found myself at a much more comfortable position than I imagined in school. Coming from a private school, where I knew much of the same people for nearly five years and being thrust into a seemingly gigantic public school credited for its diversity and openness. I do like L___ for those reasons, and its magnificent drama programs and music classes are of top quality. I go from class to class, knowing I am receiving a great education at a seemingly benevolent school. However, something still feels empty. I miss being able to feel a childhood connection with old friends. I miss feeling a common bond that started from an early age. Friends come and go, so I never feel constant. I feel like time slips away from me, and I can never slow it to stay in a relationship. This lost feeling haunts me day in and day out. High school teaches you how to prepare for college and get a good job with various subjects, but I think it's overall experience has taught me to be more than I will ever learn in its classes.

High school has taught me to be more active with people in life, not worrying about the past, and concentrating on possible futures ahead. However it has also taught me that no friendship in that possible future is always permanent and will withstand time.—Brian, San Jose, CA

∽

When many people think of high school they think of the next step for furthering their education. People also think of high school as a preparation for college. Not only does the three to four years of hard work prepare you for the real world, but the social aspect plays a big role in your future, or maybe even in the rest of your life.

The teenagers at school are very judgmental. Everyone is going through a lot of changes physically and mentally. A lot of them tear others down because their so insecure of themselves, that it makes them feel better by putting there fellow classmates down. Many teens are unhappy with the changes there going through in there lives, that teasing, harassing, and fighting are the extremes they go to. As silly as this sounds the harsh comments and dirty looks kids give can really scar someone for life.

Although a lot of students don't realize this, there are two different types of people they attend school with. There are the motivated people and there are the people that go to school because they feel forced. The crowd you choose to associate with can defiantly increase or decrease your motivation to succeed in school. Most teens are so busy trying to impress others, they immediately crush there dreams to attend college. What most young adults in high school don't know is right after you graduate popularity doesn't mean a thing, all your really left with is a plastic crown and a sash. At the time you think winning prom queen or being the star quarterback is the most important thing in life, but imagine writing that on a job application or a resume you would get laughed at. Don't waste your time impressing others do things that are beneficial to your future.

I know as you read this you might be thinking I'm very stereotypical. Not everything I'm saying applies to everyone. There are people that do go to school just to learn. I give them a lot of credit for not getting themselves sucked into the crazy high school experience. There is also a bunch that manage being popular and social and having great grades, there are the people that have the motivation and drive to do anything they set their minds to. Being in high school is a lot more difficult than most people think.

There are a lot of fun learning experiences you leave high school with. You can make indescribable bonds with teachers that have changed your life.

There are life long friendships you leave with. You will have met people that find happiness in helping you succeed. I think the most rewarding experience in high school is the long journey to self discovery you set out on, and it all coming down to the very moment you shake the principal's hand while receiving your diploma. While you look out into the audience and see your family from afar, you look at your mom while tears pour down her face. That's when you know your journey is halfway over. That's what I think high school is really about.—Brittany, San Jose, CA

〜

School is like white-water rafting down a treacherous river fraught with sharp rocks and danger, but is also one of the most gratifying experiences ever imagined. Those times when the wind and sun are running their fingers through your hair, or when you are flying so fast that you feel free; those are the times in school when you are doing well, everything is going smoothly, and your life could not be better. As with everything good, however, there come the sharp rocks and perilous times. That is when you are barraged with what seems like an endless flow of assignments and projects, you are not doing so well in several classes, and life could not be more stress-filled or worrisome. Fortunately, you can learn something from the bumps and even capsizing of your boat. With a little hard work and diligence those tidbits can be applied to your work, and the rocks grow smaller as your abilities carry you further along the river.—Eric, Moreno Valley, CA

〜

During the time I used to live in India, I always thought of American schools as very different in terms of teachers. I knew I was going to study in America one day. I guess the only fact I was excited was that teachers here in America don't hit their students. I personally had a hard time dealing with the beatings in India. There were times when I would come home with bruises on my hand from the long stick teachers carried to hit the students. Teachers are allowed to hit their students, if they didn't do their homework or did bad on a test. These beatings are not looked upon as bad because everyone believes this is for the better. But me being a scardy cat, I always feared the teachers. I was never able to connect with, nor did I ever speak to my teachers alone on what I need help with.

Once I came to America, things were much different. There was not more hittings and I felt completely okay asking teachers for help. There wasn't anything for me to fear. I must say that all the teachers I've had here in America were super nice and caring. Every one of them always kept me noticed about my grade and what I needed to improve on. This gave me a chance to always get good grades. When I studied in Kuwait (I lived in both India & Kuwait), the teachers were worse than the teachers in India. There was no way I could have a one on one conversations with my teachers, unless in class. This is exactly why I prefer a school here. If students all over the world had a choice in where they wanted to attend, then I'm sure America will be their first choice.—Ewlin, San Jose, CA

～

Why would a student go to school for thirteen years, when they really do not learn much their last year? For me, senior year has been easy going and not much work. There is so much more to do in a day, than sitting in school for six hours, bored to death. I think it is a waste of time to have thirteen years of school. If I would add up all the hours of wasteful time in classes over the thirteen years, a couple years could be subtracted. The requirement of school hours and days is ridiculous. I plan to get my degree in Dance, nothing academically related. And I ask myself, why did I stress out and try to achieve in academics when I should have had my main focus on my dance training. It would have really helped to have an extra couple of hours to dance, instead of sitting in school doing nothing half the time. I understand that a good education is important, but when I have easy classes that teach me nothing, I should not have to be there.

The reason for attending school is to, hopefully, retain some knowledge and comprehension from what we call "education." It is below social standards, nowadays, to go on living uneducated lives. Expectations are placed too heavily on grades, which are merely alphabet letters used in the everyday language. Working for over two hours on the same homework assignment would be considered ridiculous. But, nonetheless, teachers assign worthless matter to be expected complete by the following morning. The homework these days is an outrageous amount. And where does this work go by the end of the year? Into the garbage, as usual. Tests are also a concern among students of all grade levels. Tell me, why must a fourth grader take anti-depressants to relieve stress-influenced medical problems? When a problem rises to that extreme, teachers need to stop and think about how their ways of teaching are positively and negatively affecting their students. It has also occurred to me that the teaching environment has a great influence on students' learning ability. How can one be expected to learn when the teacher crushes their self-esteem by a form of humiliation? The emphasis on school has reached unrealism. It is understandable for school to be a major part of a child's life, but when is enough too much? Not enough teachers are honestly asking themselves that question. Stressing students out at such a young age isn't what I'd call efficient, especially when they're too burned out before reaching high school. Yes, I can honestly state that all the homework, tests, and hours of studying have paid off. But, it was a tough road and a long, hard fight to get there. —Laura, Merritt Island, FL

⌇

These are my thoughts about high school. Please read carefully. I have much to say. . . . First, high school does not mean a thing unless you are popular, athletic, have good grades, and have plenty of good friends to keep you grounded. But, unfortunately, high school for me is just a place with long classes and boring teachers who do not know how to teach. Honestly, what can I say about high school, except that I dread going there. Everyday for the past three years that I have been attending there, I have felt very uncomfortable, and out of place. . . . So, you ask, what makes me dread going to my high school every day?

Indeed, people can be so complex in high school. And so can the teachers. In high school, you usually have two kinds of students—you have kids who care if they pass their classes, and kids who just plain do not care. Teachers should worry about both these kinds of students—and not just covering their lesson plans. Sadly, most do not.

I know high school is supposed to be pretty tough—courses, teachers, grades—and I know that these are just obstacles in life that everyone faces. I also know that to succeed, I must learn to "play the game"—as my parents always say to me. Learning to be responsible—both as an adult and as a student—all starts, I believe, in the home.—Lauren Kaplan, Orlando, FL (Originally published in *Florida Educational Leadership*, 4(1), Fall 2003, pp. 40–41)

⌇

Starting high school wasn't a terrifying experience for me, since I was familiar with the majority of people at L___ [High School]. I've learned that school is more than learning academically, it also teaches us to socialize, and to develop ourselves as independent individuals. One of the most important aspects of high school is the people you make friends with.

When I started high school I was relieved my best friend, ___, would be able to attend L___ along with me (she lived out of district). We became very close friends in middle school because we had so much in common, and we had a lot of fun being around each other. After a year of high school I thought it wasn't anything complicated like people described it to be. However, my opinion of high school changed at the beginning of sophomore year when I noticed how ___ changed dramatically.

Outside of school, she started hanging out with older people with low goals, and those who didn't have a bright future. That year ___ wasn't focused on her schooling anymore, and her grades started slipping severely. When we had lunch together she'd be very tired from staying out late, and she'd spend her lunches scrambling to finish homework. I tried to help her any way I could, but I stopped when I saw she just wasn't trying anymore. Soon she started missing school a couple days a month, then it turned into weeks, then months. She had missed two and a half months all together, and was finally kicked out of L___ for her poor attendance and grades. She told me she was "sick" during that time, but I knew she started doing drugs too. Her belongings were still in my locker, a sign of hope she would come back to school and get on track again. I tried calling her repeatedly to find out what was going on with her, but she was never home. I remember the disappointment I felt the day I went to my locker and finally found her belongings gone. I didn't feel like I was sad enough for losing her as my friend, but I guess every day she was absent from school contributed to my realization that we wouldn't be friends for very long anymore. I couldn't continue to be around someone that would succumb to others that easily down the wrong path.

I've learned tremendously from this experience about high school and about myself. I didn't anticipate how much people would change from middle school to high school. I never realized how much we are guided in middle school, versus the amount of freedom we receive in high school. From this I've learned the importance of making friends with those who care about succeeding in life. The most important decision someone makes is who he or she chooses to be. Friends influence each other greatly, and they have the power to pressure others to act like them to fit in. What makes high school a difficult experience for many teenagers is the numerous temptations that lead down the wrong path. I've noticed that this is the time where students try to figure out who they are and where they fit in. The best advice I have about surviving high school is sticking to your principles, since the future is affected by every decision.—Olivia, San Jose, CA

〜

I think that school has taught me a lot about people. Unfortunately, it's not always the best experience. People are the reason I'm in a bad mood most [of]

the time. School has taught me about life in general, how it's not fair. Ever. Even though it's sad to say, I don't think I've actually "learned" that much. I memorize things for tests but then I just forget it after. I think we lose touch of who we are by the time we leave high school. We're always trying to "fit in" or conform to be accepted or we change to be cooler. But once in college, it won't matter. I think maybe, just maybe, I'm ready for "real life" to begin.—Shannon, Merritt Island, FL

⌒

I am currently a junior in high school right now, and nothing has changed. Maybe I might sound like a typical "nerd", but I care a lot about my future. The stereotypical term for "nerd" is very rarely used because it has so many personal definitions by everybody. However, for some it might be a completely different story. I remember a day in middle school when a student was filed (*sic*) for using drugs. There was another student in my class who also had drugs and he asked to hide it in my backpack. That was the first time I saw what people called "crack". I was horrified by the scene of an illegal drug in school. My friend agreed to help him because she wanted to be part of the "cool" group. Fortunately, my friend didn't get caught and the guy didn't either. Now looking back, I realized that I am glad of being called a "nerd" back then. Why? Because the boy who asked to put crack into my backpack is no longer in the United States. He is now in jail somewhere in Mexico, where he might be kept for the rest of his life. I'm very glad that I'm a "nerd", which in my definition is just someone who is cautious for what lies ahead in the future.

Sometimes I feel really degraded for being Asian. Ever since middle school I was picked on for being Asian. Now that I'm in high school I don't get picked on as much anymore. The only time that I was discriminated for my ethnic background is my sophomore year. I was walking past a group of freshman guys and they blatantly told me to go back to China. It did hurt a lot to hear that from students who are given an education, and I thought they benefited from it. It saddened me that none of my friends who heard it did anything about it except for me. I went ahead and told the principal, but in return he didn't do much of anything. In the end, I felt bad because my friends said I seem like a "snitch". Maybe I just feel that sometimes people need to be punished for their actions, and I guess it's wrong that I thought that way. I noticed that the guys who are now sophomores show a lot more maturity than before. One of them is in my science class and he talks to me very often. People do mature at some points in their lives, then they look back and regret. I forgive him for everything he had done, and now we act as if nothing happened the year before.

Although many people look at these experiences as saddening, but in my case I don't. I'm very glad that I have these experiences because it helps me mature. These incidents can be added on to my long list of experiences that I can save for future reference. Maybe someday, I can tell these stories to my children and make them understand.—Kathy, San Jose, CA

⌢

For most people, the four years of high school are the mot exciting, dramatic, eventful, and emotion filled years of their lives. For some, a daily soap opera revolving around them occurs daily and the only salvation comes from the feeding off of the sympathy of others. There are a select few who are able to see past the drama, not many. Friends and lovers come and go, for some more than others. Some kids are always at the wrong end of a practical joke while others always seem to be on top. In the end, high school doesn't reflect the person you are or who you will become, that is, unless you let it dictate you. The playing field evens out in the future and whether you were seen as the creepy outcast or the homecoming queen bears no weight on your success. Life is what you make it, save the drama.—Ryan, Amesbury, MA

⌢

I don't want to graduate. I want to go back, start over, keep in touch with all of my friends. When I think of things that have happened over the 13 years that I have been in the school system, there are only a few things I would change. There are times in my life when I wish I would have thought more or put more effort in to it. But when I look at how it turned out, I don't mind how it is now.

One thing that I wish I could change is the way I did my homework, or rather did not do my homework. School would have been so much easier if I had just done the homework. Instead it was always, "I'll do it later," or "I don't really feel like doing it." Now I realize that life would be easier with better grades and I wouldn't have had so much stress. I am definitely telling my kids to just do the homework so that they pass their classes.

The one thing that I definitely would not change would be my choice to take auto shop in high school. The reason that I wouldn't change this is that has developed into my future. If I had not taken this class in high school, I probably would not have picked it for my career. I don't really know where I would be without the class, my whole day revolves around it and it's kind of what I am going to do with the rest of my life.—Tyler, Hartford, WI

$\sim$

The Future: Improving Themselves and Schools

I just hope at schools everyone will be treated equally. That's what I would like to see improved.

—Ewlin, San Jose, CA

If one were to judge students and schools by the evening news, the picture might be bleak. With tragedies like the shootings at Columbine or the violence among girls during "powder puff" football, it would seem as if students don't care or are ambivalent about the world. "Kids these days [fill in the blank]" is a common sentence starter, and the ending is mostly negative. However, what I learned from listening to students is that they have definite, positive goals for the future. In particular, they view school as a means to reach their goals. However, some observed their schools' shortcomings and realized that unless improved, all students will be negatively impacted. They have clear and logical (and humorous and satirical) ideas for improving schools. Frankly, I'm impressed.

Future Goals

According to a recent survey, half of all high school students indicate that they hope to pursue a career based upon their own experiences, rather than other influences such as families, friends, and the media. In addition, 40% believe that going to college is critical to future success; 84% of high school seniors plan on going to a community, 2-year, and/or 4-year college after graduation (Horatio Alger Association, 2002). If the student voices that follow are an indication of the types of leaders we will have, then adults have little to worry about.

～

My goals for the future are becoming a sergeant in the Navy and become a nurse in the Navy because my granddad is a nurse in the Navy and he says that they make a lot of money doing what he does. The reason I want to go to the Navy is that I want to fight for my country and become something I know I can be. The Navy shows me that no matter what I do with my life there is always a brighter start in the army (Navy). I want to become a sergeant because that is my rank as of now and because I don't want to go through basic training again. I believe that if I believe it I can achieve making my goals come true.—Dontay, Melbourne, FL

～

I have a lot of goals for the future like I would want to live in Texas. Or I could be a karate fighter maybe even publish a book. I would also like to travel around the world and own my own shoe store. Maybe I would be an elementary teacher. I would like to be a salesman like my sister or even an artist. I could travel around the world painting pictures for people. I would like to get married and have kids with the one I truly love. I would want to be in a band so I can play the guitar. I would like to travel to Death Valley. Maybe I could even be on a talk show with my parents. Or I could have a huge boat and sail away.—Kayla, Hurley, SD, 4th grade

～

So many people love to think I am a person who always thinks about my future. I know what I want to do, how I want to do it, where I want to do it, when I want to do it, and who I'd like to be with while achieving it. I know when I graduate high school I want to go to UCF in Orlando, FL. There I want to major in pre-med (4 yrs.). After that I want to move to Houston, Texas to go to medical school to become a neonatologist. I would love it if while I was going through this I had my boyfriend ABE with me. Hopefully some day we'll get married and have 1 or 2 children. But for now I'm just focused on high school.—Kasey, Melbourne, FL

～

My goal for the future is becoming a kindergarten teacher. I have wanted to be a teacher since I was 10 years old. I think teachers have such a positive impact on students. Teachers help to mold a child's mind. That is one of my goals for the future. Becoming a teacher.—Kelly, Melbourne, FL

⌒

I want to be able to go to a nice college and graduate from it, but I'm not sure when I want to be yet. Hopefully, I will get a nice job and have my dream home and family.—Ashlee, Inwood, WV

⌒

I have several goals for the future, but my main one is to be involved with politics to help my community and my country. Graduate from high school and have a diploma. Go to college and major in political science or something in the T.V. field. Have a girlfriend I can see and call every day, filling my time. Travel around this world, seeing the amazing sites and sounds plus meeting new people and their diverse backgrounds.—LaDarius, Melbourne, FL

⌒

My goals for the future are to study space and the stars. I also want to be a singer or a dancer because it looks like fun. I want to go to college and then try to be the first president to be a woman. It would be cool to get rich, live in a mansion.—Jill, Hurley, SD, 4th grade

⌒

I plan to go to a University or at least and Community College to study maybe Engineering, TV Production, I am not sure yet. I have changed my mind over time. First came paleontology, then came teaching students, and after that there was law. I am still not sure yet but I do plan to get a scholarship in my senior year if I play my cards right about my credits. Some day I plan to write a book of my own.—Briaunna, Longwood, FL

⌒

I have a lot of goals for the future. They are to graduate, be a massage therapist, and help children who get abused. I am trying my best to get those goals passed, but a lot of things that I have done have messed them up to where I don't believe I will make it. I am scared I will not fulfill my dream, goals or fantasies.—Chelsea, Inwood, WV

⌒

After I finish high school with a GPA of 3.5 hopefully I would like to attend Brevard Community College. Once I get my Associate Degree, and a Networking Degree I'll be going to a Artitectural School, and have a good job paying at least 40,000 a year. After I get my Bache Degree I'll have at least three more years to master my profession. Which would be an architect.—Chris, Melbourne, FL

⌒

My goals for the future are simple really. Go to college spending as little money as possible. Graduate as debt free as possible and start my life. I don't know what I want to be, I have no idea. I assume by my second or third year of college I'll have an idea of what I would like to choose for my career. Maybe I will join some branch of the military like my father and brother (my mom wouldn't like that). I really don't know what the future beholds for me but I am ready for it.—Jason, Tallahassee, FL

⌒

I, as a person, has set goals for the future. My goals for the future consists of me graduating from high school. I also want to go to college to be either a nurse or a business owner. I would like to have my associate's, bachelor's, and master's in either field. I would like to be able to someday tell my mother that she doesn't have to work anymore. I would like to go to college either in Florida or Georgia. I just want the best for me and my mother, plus the rest of my family. So, this is my goal for the future of my life.—Kaniesha, Tallahassee, FL

⌒

My goal in life is to become a successful man. I would wear dark cool sunglasses and walking around real cool. I would love to become a business owner, or a doctor. If I own a com. (company) in the future. I would help people in need. I would find cures for deadly deceases. I would also love to become a pro soccer player and to play for the US (United States) soccer team. I would also like to give part of my paycheck to a homeless shelter to pay for food and housing. Not many people contribute to the homeless shelters, but I will. That means in the future I will dedicate myself to helping people.—Matthew, Newnan, GA, 6th grade

~

My goal for the future is to master in computer tech. My first thing I want to do is graduate from high school with a gpa on 3.0. Then go to Florida State college and master in computer tech. I want to fix computers and sooner or later design my own computer. My last goal of all is to become a multi-millionaire.—Kerron, Tallahassee, FL

~

By successfully graduating college and starting a career in pharmaceuticals, I would like to give my gratitude to my family, most especially to my parents. I would like to repay them financially, considering all the money they will spend for me, and for giving me encouragement. Although, they don't usually verbally push me to succeed, they are whom I get my strength. I know that, before they both go to sleep, they pray for me. They pray for me to do well in school, to make the right decisions, and to always have faith in the Lord. For me, they've done so much, and maybe too much in fact, all the arguments we've had between us and the stubbornness I've shown them seems pointless. It would be a pleasure to give something in return for what they've given me.—Karen, South San Francisco, CA, 10th grade

~

I have many goals for the future. One of my goals are me being able to graduate high school with at least a 3.0 G.P.A. I would also like to achieve going to college to become an administrator in the medical field. Once I get that done, I'm able to have a job where I'm not being told by someone else of what to do. I'll be able to support my family, and be able to make one of my own. Basically, I hope to have a future where I'm nonstressful and happy. —LaShaune, Melbourne, FL

~

The goals for the future is finishing high school, go to TCC or FAMU to major in theatre and move to California to become an actress so I can play in the movies. After I pursue my goals I would like to raise a family of my own. So see how I would be a good mom trying to run a family and to get married.—Shamika, Tallahassee, FL

⌒

I want to be an animal police when I grow up. I what to help animals and take care of them. I know animal police don't get paid a lot of money but I don't care that much. Animals can be a person's best friend; they love on you and can go some places with you. They can teach a person responsibility. I love animals because the are there for you. If you are an only child they can be like a sister or brother.—Cassi, Newnan, GA, 6th grade

⌒

My goals for the future would be to finish high school, go to college, and try to become someone. I like to read the daily news out of the newspaper. I would like to learn more, also stop the violence.—Shenedria, Tallahassee, FL

⌒

I only have a few goals for my future. I really want to get really good at surfing and maybe become a professional. Another might be that I want to get into the Air Force and fly planes. I would also like to meet the "right" girl and have a family of my own. Probably the one goal that I want to come true the most would be to go on a surfing trip to everywhere in the world that has waves and has warm climates. These are my goals for the future.—Steven, Melbourne, FL

⌒

My goal for in the future is to become a police officer. My reasons for wanting to become a cop are I would like to help people especially teenagers. I would also like to be the cool and understanding cop. Through my teen years I have messed up my life majorly. I use to always get into trouble with the law and always get stuck with the mean cops who don't listen and think because you're a teen you are terrible. I don't want to be a cop who judges you because you're a teen, adult, male, female, black or white. I want to sit down and understand the problems. I want to help make a difference in someone's life. So yes, this is my goal for when I graduate high school and get on my own.—Yvonne, Melbourne, FL

There are my goals that I would like to accomplish in my life. My number one goals is to graduate from high school, with a diploma. I'd like to pass my ACT and SAT classes, and be accepted into a four year college. The school I would like to attend would be Tennessee State. If I'm not able to attend Tennessee, I would love to attend Florida State, the University of Miami, or Florida A&M. I would be full of jubilation if I was accepted into college on a academic, volleyball, or triple-jump (track & field) scholarship. My life long goal is to major in computer engineering/technology or business. —Takira, Melbourne, FL

My goals for the future are finish high school and go to college. Then when I'm in college I would like to study architecture for major. I would like to get a scholarship for basketball or football but if not I would like to do something with art. I like to go on and have a family like my father had, and have a nice wife like him but not his career. I want to become rich enough so I could take care of my whole family especially my mom and my grandmothers.—Uriah, Melbourne, FL

One of my goals in life is to go to the University of Georgia (UGA), then join their law firm. I think I would enjoy being a lawyer, because I am argumentive (most of the time), and I like money, and I know that lawyers make pretty good money! I also like the "classy" look that they have it is like, -I-am-good-and-I-know-it-look-. They also are very smart, and to "get by" these days you have got to be intelligent! You also have to make good grades in school, and to do that you have to pay a load of attention in school! And if you do that you can be/do whatever you want in life, like become a lawyer like me, and probably accomplish your goal/goals like me!—Haley, Newnan, GA, 6th grade

My goal in life is to be a zookeeper, zoologist, or a crypto zoologist. I want to be any of these so I can go around the world and see animals that I've never seen before. I can try to discover the legends of the Loch ness or Slimy Slim.

I've loved animals ever since I was 2 or 3. When I was 5 or 6 I got this certificate from my cousin to get free zoo books in the mail. Ever since then I've been getting zoo books and reading the amazing facts about animals. Like frogs can be frozen in an ice cube and when the ice cube melts they are still alive. I love going to the zoo. Seeing all the animals at different zoos is awesome. My favorite zoo is the North Carolina zoo. So all this started me thinking about being a zoologist or a zookeeper.

Then I read this book on the Loch ness or Slimy Slim and all these other strange animals people have seen. So that got me in the idea of being a crypto zoologist. Crypto zoologists are were you go and look for legendary monsters. Yes, I would love to be any of those three.—Jimmy, Newnan, GA, 6th grade

～

When I get older I want to live in Montana. I love the outdoors. I think reading the Gary Paulsen book has inspired my dreams of adventure and help me to enjoy and appreciate nature.—Daniel, Vestavia Hills, AL, 6th grade

～

My goal in life would have to become a doctor. So a school education would be necessary. The subjects that would be involved with me becoming a doctor would have to be chemistry, math, language arts, and health. These are all important because they have to do with what all a doctor needs to know. I want to become a doctor for a whole lot of reasons. One I love to help people. Second I have always wanted to become a doctor. Third a doctor has helped someone really special in my life to stay alive. When I sit down with my mom and watch doctor shows I become more and more interested in becoming a doctor because they help someone really special to stay alive maybe not to you but to at least one person. Like my mom and dad still say to me "Never Give Up What You Really Want To Be."—Chelsea, Newnan, GA, 6th grade

～

I have many goals set for the future. I believe the higher you set your goals, the farther you will go and the better you will do. Since I was eight, I had wanted to be an astronomer. My highest goal is to become part of Mission Control at NASA. In the end I think no matter how much of a hassle school can sometimes be, it all helps us to reach our goals faster and better.—Kate, Vestavia Hills, AL, 6th grade

⌒

If I had independence I would be happy but if I had the respect of someone I will feel fulfilled. I could have all the possessions in the world but I really want the respect. I will be remembered for my contributions to this world and I want to be admired by others. This is a fast paced and cruel world and we tend to forget the wealthy when they are gone but the true heroes can be remembered for their actions. I just want someone to pass me in the hall and think, "where would I be without that guy."—Franklin, South San Francisco, CA, 10th grade

How to Improve Schools

A school's culture has a tremendous impact on students' attitudes and achievement (DeWit, McKee, Fjeld, & Karioja, 2003). School culture can be defined as the transmitted patterns of meaning that include the norms, values, beliefs, ceremonies, rituals, traditions, and myths understood, maybe in varying degrees, by members of the school community (Stolp & Smith 1994, as cited in Stolp, 1994). What a school values, then, may be outdated, or not appreciated by today's students. Thus the phrase, "you don't understand," may have more meaning than originally thought.

A school's culture can also be affected by its environment, and the quality of its buildings and facilities. According to the AFL-CIO (2004), "of the existing 80,000 schools at least one-third are in need of extensive repair or replacement. At least two-thirds have troublesome environmental conditions. Many schools can't support the infrastructure needed for advanced technology, including computers and access to the Internet." As a former high school teacher, I can attest to the direct link between a school's state of repair and how its students act, react, and learn. Although some students wrote to me, particularly the younger ones, with outlandish wishes about how to improve their schools, others had clear and mature desires.

⌒

The school dress code is one of the most aggravating issues of school. I'm sure that many students agree with me on this issue. I feel that our freedom of expression is being taken away from us. I think it is completely unfair that a school board can tell you what you can and cannot wear. Just because a students wants to wear a bandana we are automatically considered gang-related. Some of us just have bad hair days. Does wearing a baseball cap in class disrupt the learning process? We as students are being oppressed and can no longer express ourselves.—Aaron, Tallahassee, FL

～

I think we should have longer recesses because we work hard. We need to rest our brains.—Daniel, Key West, FL, Elementary

～

R___ High School needs a lot of improvement. If I gave a list of things that need improvement at R___, then the paper will be filled from front to back. A couple of the things that I would like to see improved at R___ is the administration. For example, the first two weeks of school was a disaster. Many students were missing classes and some students had no schedule at all. Many parents had to come out because their child's school records had been transferred to other schools. The administration and teachers had been back two weeks prior to us coming back and it seemed like nothing was being done while they were there.

Another improvement that I would like to see taken care of is our restrooms. They are very unsanitary. I thought that the custodian's job after school is to clean the restrooms. There is never any tissue or paper towels in the restroom. Most of all, the soap containers are always empty. Who wants to use the restroom and not have anything to wash up with? I feel that a public school should also have seat covers for the students to use also. If these things can be improved, please do so.—Brittany, Tallahassee, FL

～

In order to make the very most of American ideals, where all children are guaranteed twelve years of free education, public schools deserve more governmental funding and more support from the community.—Carolyn, San Jose, CA

～

At my school I would like to see better help from the teachers and booster clubs to help fund sports, clubs, and activities.—Bintu, Tallahassee, FL

⌒

Here's some stuff I'd like to see improved in my school. We need new books and better chairs. We need more equipment and desks that don't wobble. If this was improved I'd be as happy as a millionaire.—Gabe, Reno, NV, 4th grade

⌒

Many things could be changed at schools to make them better. First of all, more discipline should be taken on kids who disobey the rules or laws. This would cut down on wasted time from teachers having to write referrals. Also, schools like P___ B___ High School should hire more teachers. Smaller classes would be possible with more teachers. Finally, schools should serve better food and snacks. If food was improved, students would be able to eat healthier and maybe learn quicker and better.—Garrett, Melbourne, FL

⌒

If we had no homework and not as much school work then I would be fine because I like my teachers and especially my homeroom teacher. I want to have more recess time and no English.—Jack, Tallahassee, FL, 4th grade

⌒

The key to me is if you pay attention and do your work, you will be just fine. When you step in the high school doors it's all about your future. You have to start thinking about what you want to be and the colleges you would like to apply for. My future goals are to graduate from high school, go to college, and become successful in some way.

There's really not a true way to improve school. People make days good in different ways. You just have to make it the best for yourself as much as you can. If you keep your head high and your grades up, you have it down pat. The days and the years are only good as long as you make them out to be that way. Make goals and look at all the options so that you look forward to the future.—Jennifer, Inwood, WV

⌒

What I would like to see improved at R___ High is some of the students and teacher attitudes. Some students and teachers wake up with a bad attitude. I say school is a place to learn and not a social group. Teachers can have an I don't care attitude and others have a do what you can attitude.—Kizzy, Tallahassee, FL

⌢

First of all I think we should have at least a couple of books to read in free time. I'm one that gets finished fast, so I need something to do when I'm finished. Second of all I think we need more pencils. I can go through one in a month! I brought a full bag of pencils at the beginning of the year. It had about fifty pencils. Now I have about twenty pencils left.

That was my first category. Now I'm going to tell you what I think we should change about special areas. I think we should have art more. I mean it does express our feelings and it can calm us down. With art it doesn't matter how you do the art because art is almost anything. Next I will tell you about how we should have less P.E. A lot of people get plenty of exercise in recess and we have fun.

Now I will tell you about my third topic. It is about homework. I think we should have lighter book. Book bags with all your books in them make your backs and shoulders hurt. Also we almost never have holiday related homework.

Now I will tell you about subjects. I think we should have more reading and less English. We know plenty of English but we need to read faster. I have plenty of reasons, these are just a few.—Merina, Tallahassee, FL, 4th grade

⌢

If I had school my way, everything would be totally different. Health class would be field trip class. School needs to have excitement waiting around every corner. Kids would pay attention if school had some pizzazz to it. Children would be begging to go to school, and if they misbehaved then they weren't allowed to go to school. There should be snack bars in every classroom. No more homework or test, you're only tested on how much fun you've had that day.

In the end, maybe school will never be the way I want it to be, but I'll be all right. Someday I'll build a school that has nothing but fun waiting inside its doors for you. That will be the day, when all children enjoy their days and have one hundred and one fun things to tell their parents. It might happen, and even if it doesn't, there's always going to be college. —Paul, Inwood, WV

⌒

I would like to improve the way we learn. For example, there are many teachers who give assignments and don't explain to their students anything. On the other hand there are teachers who take it seriously. How would students benefit from these type of teachers. So, we need better teachers that actually help us learn better and better.—Ranya, Melbourne, FL

⌒

If I could change something it would be starting school a little bit later. I take classes that are pretty hard, then I have an after school sport with 3–4 games a week, a part-time job and 2 extracurricular activities. After I finish all of these and get to my homework, there isn't much time for sleep left. I think students would come to school more willingly and ready to learn if it started at 9:30–10:00 am.—Anonymous, Amesbury, MA

⌒

I'm a 17 year old senior at R___ High School. From my experiences there, I can name plenty that should be improved. I think the guidance counselors should be much more helpful. When I asked about scholarships in my junior year, the counselor pointed to a stack of unorganized papers and said to find what I needed. When I asked about information my teacher said had to be sent in your junior year, again, the guidance counselor told me to just find what I needed. I've also had a bad experience with the lady who runs scheduling. Being this is my senior year and I wanted to know I had the classes I needed I went to school the Friday before school started. When I inquired about my schedule, she treated the situation as if it were some kind of difficult task, the worst part was that its her job! She then proceeded to down talk me and tell me it was sad that I would pick classes based on teachers. Now I hate to be rude, but some teachers can teach good, others just need to find a different job. In my opinion, it's staff members like that that can make school experiences stressful and bad. If a staff member has a problem with helping and doing their job, then they need to quit.—Reba, Tallahassee, FL

⌒

I think our school can be improved by making the cafeteria with better food and water fountains that work. The bathrooms can be improved by cleaning a lot better, and teaching can be more fun and entergetic.—Shana, Vestavia Hills, AL, 6th grade

～

What I would like to see improved in my school? I would like to see the discipline in the class changes. They need to crack down on that problem. Not much more needs to be improved other than discipline in class and in school. The classes and the school discipline needs to be fixed before something bad happens.—Richard, Melbourne, FL

～

I think school is a place to learn, but teachers should make efforts to make learning fun. No students want to come to school to hear the teacher go "blah, blah, blah!" And, I think if we're going to read, let's read something interesting. It should be something that can relate to teenagers. Who wants to read about things that happened in the 1700s and 1800s?

School is a great place to learn. But why teach us useless things? If you're going to teach us, teach us things that are going to help us later in life. Teach us something that will help us get a good job. And I think we should let the "old teachers" go! Teenagers listen to the younger teachers. I think it is because of the age range. Old teachers like to use the words "back in my day." They need to realize that times have changed; the world is not like it was when they were young.—Shawna, Tallahassee, FL

～

Schools can be improve by teaching the teachers how to relate to the newer generation. Most of the teachers aren't up to date with this generation. Teachers should be down to earth and easy to talk to about anything. They should be able to relate to our daily situations.—Tiffany, Melbourne, FL

～

One of the grievances would be the fact that I have to wake up quite early to get to school on time. School starts awfully early and I have to wake up at a quarter past six to get there on time, I don't particularly enjoy this. I think myself and a lot of other people would be willing to stay in school two hours later in order to start school two hours later.—Patrick, Vero Beach, FL

⌣

My experiences in school were not that bad until I started high school. I was a freshman, and I am that kind of person that likes to dress in black and to wear all kinds of chains and spikes. My first two periods were good, and then I got to third period, my English class. I entered and sat down, the teacher was totally staring at me, and I was like, "what?" later during the period, that teacher told me to go outside (this happened like the second week of school). I was all confused and wondering, what did I do wrong? I was outside, and she came out of the classroom, and she said, "those chains and spikes have to go." I was like, "what?" She said, "you heard me," and I asked why and she said, "because of the school dress code, you can't have dangerous weapons in school." I started to laugh, and she asked me what I was laughing about. I told her, "because you think chains and spikes are dangerous weapons and they aren't." Every day was the same thing with that teacher, but I didn't listen to her. What I think the school should do is to have special contracts with students that wear these things so it could make the school a better place to be.—Juan Medina, Aptos, CA

⌣

"A Dialogue Between Friends" by Sergio Nunez, Aptos, CA
One beautiful morning two boys are walking to school. The boys, Alex and Luis, are talking about the problems and the good things about school.
Alex: So why do you think things aren't right in your situation in school? Why don't you feel comfortable?
Luis: Well I don't know, I guess it's because the teachers are not too helpful, some of them are, some of them aren't. And to be honest some of them are racist, too.
Alex: That really bothers me because they don't really help you that much, just because you are from another country, doesn't that bother you?
Luis: Of course it does, but what can we do? We just have to take the little help they give us. Which is not that much. We cannot talk back to them, or else they will give us something worse than help.
Alex: Yeah, you're right, we can't do nothing about it. But hopefully someone will do something about it and make this situation change.

⌣

I would [want] my teacher to be very nice. I would want my teacher to be very funny because I don't like boring teachers because they never do anything fun they don't ever try to make you laugh. And I don't like teachers who give you a lot of homework like on the weekends. I would want my teacher to give us prizes like if every one does good on a test or if our class does really good on a test or she could give us homework pass so we wouldn't have to do homework. And maybe if their was a substitute and we did really good she would give us a surprise or candy. I don't like teachers who give you a lot of work and don't explain it like my fourth grade teacher gave us a lot of work and never explained it.—Adam, Newnan, GA, 6th grade

〜

I think that our school should have a vending machine. Because the teachers get a teachers lounge where they can snack on food. So why can't we have a vending machine at least.

There are a lot of days when kids don't eat lunch, so they have to go all day without eating. At least with a vending machine they can have a snack. The things in the vending machine may not be the best thing to snack on, but they're better than not having anything to snack on at all.

A vending machine would also be a benefit to our school. It would bring money in whether the kids went to lunch or note, because during the day they may want something to snack on. Teachers say that you need to eat so you can stay focused. But if you don't eat you're thinking about eating all day. So if we were to get a vending machine in our school it would help us to focus a lot better. Just think vending machines would benefit our school and also help the students who don't eat lunch focus a lot more.—Nikki, Max, ND

〜

Every student has his or her own idea of how school needs to change to improve; but I have my own opinion. In order for school to improve, the school needs to find a way to raise enough money so books, supplies, and even the latest technology could be given to classrooms in various schools. Also teachers should make it a mission to find out what kids/teenagers like now-a-days, and they should try to make school fun (because we do spend the majority of our lives at school).—Brian, Woodland Hills, CA

〜

If I could change one thing about school it would be how much homework we have. Kids do not like doing homework every day. When we get home we would rather play video games, play with friends, or get on the computer. I would rather play with my little sister than do homework. Homework is like being in jail getting out doing more work then going back in every day.

Since kids would rather work on computers more than paper the teachers might be able to make a program. A program where you could do your homework any day of the week since doing it every day is stressful. As long as you did how many pages your teacher told you to in a week. That way homework will not kill us as fast as smoking or being Freddy Krougers next target.

The teachers would not waste trees for paper or pencils. They would not have to check it all week and sit with red eyes, shaking hands, and a big cup of coffee all night. The computer would check it for us. There would also be no more lost homework.

Some of the problems would be not all kids have computers. Plus it would take up enough energy to make three extra suns. This would make tax go way up. Then if a virus gets in it will destroy the program like the nuclear bomb on Japan.—Alex, Newnan, GA, 6th grade

⌣

The number one problem that I would like to see improved in school is the regularity and tediousness of it. Each day, students around the world do the same thing; our lives are regulated by the bell schedule. Students can not stand the dullness of a regular day. The routine day for me is as follows: I wake up and get ready for school. Then there is 1st period History, after that is 2nd period Biology, then nutrition, 3rd period English, 4th period Geometry, Lunch, 5th period P.E., and then finally 6th period Health. Every day of the week is the same exact schedule; that is why students enjoy it here when there are special events at school such as when fast food restaurants come and serve our school, not just because we like the food but because it is a break from the ordinary and everyone enjoys a change in scenery once in a while. Some of the ways that the school can revolutionize the schedule is by creating a block schedule. In this new schedule kids could have only two classes a day; where they are still as long as a regular school day. This schedule would change things up, where you wouldn't have the same thing every day. There would be various subjects taught during the week, and it wouldn't be simpler, yet more exhilarating.—Ari, Woodland Hills, CA

⌣

There are three things I would like to see be improved in schools. I believe that these changes would help the students have a less stressful environment.

These changes can also improve test scores. First, school should start and end later. This will allow students to do their homework and study for tests without becoming tired when they wake up in the morning. Secondly, schools should learn how to prioritize their funding or try to gain more money from families. Schools waste their money on things like parades and dances many people do not even attend. They can use that money to buy better books and more paper and ink. Lastly, schools should make more free extracurricular activities and sports teams. Making more of these organizations will keep kids of the streets and motivated to do their school work. This will make the school more enjoyable and will give more school spirit to the students. —Anonymous, Woodland Hills, CA

～

If I could change one thing about school it would be the homework. Kids have a problem with homework every time they do it comes and bites them in the butt. Talk about a world of pain. We need a break because every time it hurts more and more. Plus homework is so dull I rather listen to cheesy music.—Thomas, Newnan, GA, 6th grade

～

A major improvement I'd like made would be prior to the learning experience. Learning should be fun, not boring. Students should not hate going to school. They should at least be a little excited. They should be happy to learn something new. Because rite now learning to us is memorizing and reading boring books. Fun learning might even make us want to go to school.—Amy, Vestavia Hills, AL, 6th grade

～

If I could change one thing about school, it would be to have DVD players on every bus. That way it wouldn't be as boring as usual. It would be a DVD player and a flat screen T.V. on every seat. That way no one would argue about watching anything. You could even bring movies from home, buy some, or use the ones that are already on the bus. You might not want to bring any because we'd probably already have it on the bus. It would have 2 DVD holders on the seat with 15 DVDs in each one. There would be drama, action, and all kinds of other movies. Everyone would have a remote that way you wouldn't have to wait for anyone else to get finish using there remote, you could just have your own. That's what I want for change.—Malcom, Newnan, GA, 6th grade

⌢

I would be happy if the government shortens the school year so we could have more fun in life . . . there is a world out there and we really can see it if they make school shorter.—Joseph, Vestavia Hills, AL, 6th grade

Photo by Jessyka Orala

CHAPTER NINE

~

Good Experiences
and Missed Opportunities

While the education system is far from perfect, I am not ungrateful for the opportunities it has given me. The hard work many people have contributed to make those opportunities possible does not go unappreciated. (That means you too, Mrs. W!)

—Anna, Merritt Island, FL

For countless students school was viewed as one entity, and it could not be separated into specific areas such as teachers, tests, sports, and so forth. As such, student writings could not be grouped or assigned to a particular chapter, nor could they be omitted. After reading and rereading the submissions a theme emerged—the good experiences and missed opportunities that come with 13 years of school.

~

To many students, school is dull, boring and a waste of time. At times I must admit to having those feelings, but I know that what I'm doing now will be extremely helpful to my future. I try to take advantage of the opportunities that I have been given.—Cassondra, Moreno Valley, CA

~

As time goes on I am sure that adults forget that actual hardships of school life. Though it is widely known as a place of learning, many adults to not know what kinds of learning. Of course a student learns English, math, science, and other various subjects. As students, we also learn profanity, racial slurs, how to obtain and use drugs, how to fight, and many learn how to be a complete jerk to others.

The positive effects of school greatly outweigh the negative, though the negative effects are still quite noticeable. I heard my first f-word used in first grade, along with seeing the middle finger raised. Both of these obscenities were toward my teacher at the time. I had seen fighting on television plenty of times, but when I witnessed by first real fight, I was horrified. I was in second grade when I saw the first fight that was actually a real battle. The winner proceeded to kick his defenseless opponent in the face and stomach while the poor kid tried to crawl away. It was quite shocking for a second grade student.

When someone is in such a sociable environment, they are bound to be exposed to many different lifestyles. Sometimes these different lifestyles are not positive ones. This means that children are exposed to negative events at an early age, which make high school life the same way. Once we reach high school, we have already been exposed to so much negative stuff that while in the school atmosphere, we are different people. In school I hear more swearing and see more aggressive behavior than out of school.

Many consider school to be a place of learning only positive things, while in reality it is also a breeding ground for hate and negative thoughts towards others. High school creates monsters backed into corners and ready to lash out at the world. In such a competitive atmosphere, many are consumed with fear and anxiety. Though I am not one of those people, I have felt a certain degree of competitiveness and stress. This leads me to conclude that school is a place of knowledge of all sorts, good and bad.—Grey, Clover, SC

〜

School is a terrible place. The education kids get from schools is accessible at libraries placed strategically throughout our country. Kids are lazy these days. The education kids get from school they only get because someone is making them. If it were up to kids there would be no libraries or schools. This world would be a terrible place without education but if everyone was dumb then we'd have no wiseasses.—Anonymous, Amesbury, MA

〜

After second grade school was not as eventful, I mean there was nothing as memorable as the first few. I don't know why. The one thing I remember was that up till around 7th or 8th grade, well around the time everyone got to junior high in my case P___ Middle School, we all had changed. I don't know how but we did. The people I hung out with in elementary school didn't really want to hang with me anymore. They had other friends there own color to hang out with. I still don't understand it. I remember that the color of your skin didn't matter and racial slurs weren't around. We all knew of them but never thought we would ever use them. I had so many black friends in elementary now I only can count about one or two but I don't really talk to them outside of school. The thing is I wasn't the one who decided to stop hanging out with them; they just stopped talking to me. In middle school we still said hi once in a great while.

I really miss the days when racism wasn't a issue but I guess it always has been. The thing that gets me is how people think it's gone and it's not. The first day I stepped into my new high school (J___ High) the first thing that happened was a group of black girls were walking by and one pushed me or ran into me. It really doesn't matter but she turned to me and said watch out you white bitch. From that day on I had many more encounters with people like that, and I am not a fighter so I just bit my tongue and walked away. I never was the slightest bit of a racial person but now I am. I know I shouldn't say that.

J___ High School has probably the highest percentages of racism in and around [here]. I have wanted to drop out so many times that I can't believe I haven't. I guess my big thing was that I wasn't going to let anyone win. After the first week of school I decided to stay to myself and just be pushed around cause there's no point in fighting back cause you'll never win. There is always something like the main one. No one can just fight one on one anymore. If you fight with one person you end up getting jumped by their friends. You can also get suspended and if you win the fight or hurt the person you can probably guarantee that you be getting in another fight. If you're a senior which I am if you get into a fight in your last year you won't be able to walk so you get into way more trouble at home. I think this year I have had more people wanting to fight me than any other year. I am nineteen years old and I have these little freshmen that are 4 or 5 years younger than me trying to fight me so on top of getting suspended and not walking I also get sent to jail and who knows what else, maybe even sued. The thing that I don't understand is everyone I know says I look like a total bitch and they say I even look a little psycho, when someone pisses me off. I don't say anything but squint my eyes and get really pissed off but don't do anything but people usually leave me alone after that but not the black kids. They insist on messing with me for no reason. I admit not all black people are bad, I even talk to a lot of the nice ones at school. I'm not the only one in my school that thinks this way, none of us talk about it to anyone but ourselves.

Really I hate school. I keep wondering if I had gone to a different school would it be better. Would I be a lot happier person? Would I like going to school? Would I have tried out for a sport or even cheerleading (I always wanted to be one)? I know it's too late to find out. I know I won't be sending my children to a public school. Last year I had visited my old elementary school and it was horrible. The kids are so bad. I can't imagine what they are going to be like when they get to high school. There was even a girl that was pregnant. When I was that age I didn't even think about that. —Amber, Jackson, MI

⌒

School is like most things in society, a well intentioned but grossly flawed convention. The American education system, in particular, has taken an intrinsically wonderful idea—to have the government pay for its young people to be smarter—and made it into an inefficient and generally ineffective process. How has this unfortunate degeneration come to be? There are several culprits. The motivation for prospective professionals to enter the teaching field has traditionally been lacking in American culture. Consequently, our schools are overrun with unmotivated and incompetent teachers and administrators. (That is not to imply that there aren't talented exceptions to the rule.)

Additionally, the grading and accountability system is hopelessly outdated and archaic. It seems designed to increase student stress load to almost incomprehensible extremes, while fostering a "learning environment" that encourages cheating and memorization as alternatives to learning—and indeed the only way for many students to achieve success.

My involvement with U.S. First robotics has been more than a positive experience for me. It's been a life-changing one. Direct mentoring from NASA engineers has, in the true spirit of the organization, been as inspirational as it has been educational. Ostensibly, FIRST is merely an extracurricular club which, during a 6-week season each spring faces the daunting challenge of building a functional robot to complete certain announced tasks. But it becomes more than that for the students who take it seriously. In FIRST, students learn lessons about teamwork and determination of such immeasurable value I have not the power to articulate their importance in this brief ditty.—Anna, Merritt Island, FL

～

These are things I like about school. We get to learn something new each day like math or reading. My class does lots of science and social studies, wich are my favorite subjects. We have different activities each day. On Monday and Wednesday we have music class where we sing songs, play games and play insterments. On Tuesdays Elk Club learns about the elks habitat and we learn the elk call. Thursday morning we have computers and on Thursday afternoon we have P.E. Often times elementary school is as fun as going on a water slide.

These are reasons why I dislike school. Our lunch for hot lunch tastes horrible. I think we need better food. A girl got sick from the schools popcorn. The Gatorade you can buy is warm. The toy on our playground is so small. We need more equipment and more teather ball poles. The toy should be different colors like yellow and bright green, instead of red and blue. Sometime school is as bad as eating a cockroach.—Andi, Reno, NV, 4th grade

～

Do you really want to know what a typical high school student thinks about school? I honestly think the information is way too overwhelming. Well, according to how I feel, school is crucial. With the teachers now, you learn nothing. I hate the dress code and the way school is perceived. Now in time, school is basically a waste of time. The majority of the teachers come to school to play around with the students. In others words, they get paid for teaching "nothing." The staff is also getting carried away on dress code. It's ridiculous. It's like when the school tries to make too many rules, it drives the kids away from school. I know from experience because I hate school. I'm an average student who makes decent grades, but school don't have nothing to do with my profession.—Ashley, Tallahassee, FL

～

What I like and dislike about school. First to start off with I feel as of school should be over at 2:00. School is too long. I also dislike that you can't wear a head band at school. Also school is a trap, the reason why I say that is because we have to go to school for 12 or 13 years and it don't even matter, because we have to pass the FCAT. If you don't pass the FCAT you don't graduate.

The things I like about school is that it's something to do. I also like my teachers because they are trying to help me get out of the school's trap. My favorite classes are physical education and math. I also like school because you meet new people and those people could make someone's day. But overall school is just something for me to do, so I can have a wealthy and pleasant future.—Bernard, Tallahassee, FL

～

You know that I'm in 5th grade. I am leaving B___ Elementary School this year to go to middle school for 6th grade. B___ has been a great elementary school for me and I know I will miss all of the teachers that I had in the past. It is going to be hard to get used to middle school. I will have to get used to new teachers, new books, new classrooms, switching classes, and who could resist the new lockers. Yay! I know that I will make new friends. Guess what! In every class it's different subjects like homeroom, social studies, science, language arts literacy, math, reading, English, Spanish well you could pick from Spanish, German, or French, and maybe health for a subject. There are different kids in each classroom for each subject. I can't wait until I get my own locker! I wonder if we go on any field trips? We have gym every day of the week except for Friday. Oh man! It will be so cool. I can't wait to make new friends! How many teachers am I going to have? How much homework are they going to give? How many classes am I going to have? Mrs. ___ was my 5th grade teacher in B___ Elementary School and I'm especially going to miss her!—Danielle, Turnersville, NJ, 5th grade

～

What I think of school is many things. School is like an elevator; it has ups and downs. Middle school and grades below are easy levels for some. Subjects weren't that hard for me and homework didn't take up your whole night. When you reach the high school level, it's a whole different story. Subjects get harder and there are more tests than you can ever imagine.

High school, to me, isn't all that scary like people make it sound. The making memories and meeting new people is the best! You meet a lot of different types of people and learn a lot more by getting involved in other groups, clubs, and even sports. I met a lot of new friends when I made the varsity cheerleading squad. We are all pretty close and get along well. They can make school more easy at times too.—Jennifer, Inwood, WV

～

School is great but I have some things that I don't like. Here's two of my complaints. One, the homework is terrible because I think it cuts into time when you're supposed to be spending time with my family and play. Number two, the schedule. I think there should be a time where there will be three subjects. For example, P.E., drama, and science. You pick which one you want to go to. So everyday for an hour go to a different subject or activity.

Here are two things that I think most people, including me, like. Teachers are so fun, happy, and encourageable this year. Last year was the worst year of my life. My teacher is fantastic. I learn so much from her and there are the friends. I have many friends that are nice, happy, and funny. Last year I had about three friends. Now I've got about 8. My mom told me that "if you could count at least one friend that's never gotten in a fight with you then you are lucky."—Lauren, Tallahassee, FL, 4th grade

⌒

School has its ups and downs. I love the fact of being surrounded by my friends, but at the same time I despise not being at home by myself. I enjoy being presented with a challenge. But after a while of working on them, you get pretty bored.

One of the nicer things at school is, like I said earlier, being surrounded by funny kids at your own age. Sometimes, if you complete an out of the ordinary task, you are rewarded with either bonus points or candy. And lunch is the best part of the day, unless you want to include after school activities.

On the other hand, school has many boring qualities. Such as tests that are given just to see if teachers can flunk you. Homework is the pits. It takes up almost all of my free time, and makes me look like I'm lugging around a turtle shell on my back. You get in tons of trouble is you don't do it. How fair is that?—Paul, Inwood, WV

⌒

For me, school is a place that I enjoy. I enjoy school due to the fact that it is somewhere I gain knowledge while being educated. School lets us know about the real world, and how we must work hard to achieve things. The best thing about school is that it prepares us for our future. Our future is the most important thing that we need to work up to so that it can be bright. Everyone wants to be successful in life, but without an education in today's society it is very hard to do. I enjoy learning because you can learn something new every day to help you in life, and school gives you this.—Roshaunda, Tallahassee, FL

⁓

I, myself, like school. I love being able to see my friends all day long. I couldn't get through the day without them. I will admit it is tough at times. When I have a big test or project due I tend to wait till the last minute to get it done. I have learned over the years that I cannot do that any more. I am now prepared when something like that comes up in one of my classes.

I like being able to interact with people and learn at the same time. I can understand why people don't like getting up in the morning, because I don't like getting up early either. My strategy is to go to bed early. Sometimes I have a difficult time with that, because there is usually something on television at night that I want to watch.

I know that it takes hard work to get good grades. So when people don't come to school that often, it seems like they really don't care if they pass or fail their classes. Don't get me wrong I know people get sick, but if people don't come to school because they don't want to they don't deserve to pass in my book.

I like going to school events also. They are a chance to hang out with your friends and just have fun. We usually go to the football and basketball games but not always; it we have homework to do we have to get it done first before anything. Most of my friends work hard at their grades and still find time to hang out and have fun. I'm like that too. Learning is very important to me and I want to have a good education. I try and surround myself with good people who will try and help me the best they can if I need help on something.

My favorite subject is science because it comes easy to me, and my teacher helps me with anything I need explained. My least favorite subject is math. I'm in algebra one and it seems really hard to me. My favorite teacher is my language teacher. She makes us laugh non-stop. So really my normal day in school is fun. I get to see all my friends and learn at the same time.—Tara, Inwood, WV

⁓

Going through school is something that every child has to go through according to the law. Once you are 17, you can drop out and it's no big deal. Up until that day, unless your parents just don't care about your education, you have to learn the same curriculum as every other teenager. Even though some form of schooling is inevitable, we always find something to complain about. Whether it be the food in the cafeteria, the rules, the teachers, or just school period, there is *always* something to complain about.

Students always seem to complain about how hard school work is. Have they ever tried to work a 9 to 5 job and complete the *really* hard tasks? No. It is against the law for teenagers under the age of 16 to work more than 30 some odd hours a week. Kids my age don't understand how good they have it during high school. If we don't turn in an assignment or if it's a couple of days late, all we get is a few points off. We don't get fired and have to go out and find new jobs to support families. At my school, C___ High, our schedules are separated into 2 semesters. One semester takes place from August to winter break, and second semester is from the end of winter break until sometime in May. We get 3 months to do nothing. Do adults get this luxury? No. they're lucky if they get Saturdays and Sundays off. We have four classes a day at an hour and a half a piece, with a 10 minute interval between classes. At a job, you only get one break for lunch. And teenagers think that's easier . . .

As I am thinking about ideas on what to write in this paper, I decide to ask some friends what they hate the most about coming to school. My boyfriend is one of those guys who loves hats. He'd wear it to sleep in if he could keep it on his head. One of the dress code rules at school is NO HATS. He continues to wear his hat to school even though he knows it's wrong. Then when a teacher tells him to take it off and give it to them, he gets mad. I tell him, "If you'd just leave it at home, we wouldn't have this problem." He has gotten detention slips so much about his hat that he has used up all of his after school detentions and in school suspensions. Now, if he gets written up it's an automatic out of school suspension. He finally got written up for the hat, and now he gels his hair. So if he could change one rule, it would be that one.

A rule I find absurd is our new smoking policy. Personally, I do not smoke, however some of my friends do. Our new policy on smoking goes something like this: the first time you get caught, you have to attend four classes with your parents. In these classes, you learn about the harmful effects smoking has on your body and they try to help you come up with other alternatives than smoking. If you get caught a second time, you have to complete ten hours of community service. If you are stubborn enough to get caught a third time, you have out of school suspension. And yet, there is a fourth offense and you will get suspended from school for a week. Most of my friends have gotten caught smoking at school and have to attend these smoking classes. What's the point? Do teachers honestly think that showing smokers photographs of a blackened lung oozing with emphysema is going to make them

stop smoking? I really hope not, because if they do then they are more ignorant than I thought. Smokers usually know the harmful effects it has on your
body before they even think about smoking a cigarette. Teachers have to
come back to school and teach yet another class and work overtime for something that is going to have no effect whatsoever. These classes put the school
out of money for much needed supplies as well as waste a lot of people's time.
Why can't we just have a designated smoking area for students like they did
back when our parents went to school? It's not that much to ask.

Now that I have ranted on and on about what students don't like at
school, I will now discuss what we enjoy. Nothing makes me feel a bigger
feeling of accomplishment than getting back a paper with a big red A on it.
Knowing I worked hard studying and trying to do my best and succeeding at
what I have worked so hard on gives me a feeling of pride. Even though
some of the work is challenging and difficult it's good to try it anyway. You
may surprise yourself at how well you do. School isn't supposed to be easy. If
it was easy, everyone would do it. Socializing is another big reason kids like
school. We enjoy sharing mindless gossip. It's what teenagers do. We all
have friends we would never had met if it weren't for school.

I am *not* a nerd. I like school. If we didn't have to go to school, we would
be fat and lazy and dumb. One of the main reasons I enjoy it is because I get
fulfillment by doing well on something. At a job, it's not the same if your boss
simply tells you, "Good job." You do your school work for you, not for anyone else. Teachers don't care if you fail or not. Of course they'll help you out
on things if you don't understand them, but it's not going to get them in trouble if you fail their class. When we do get jobs, our work will reflect on our
bosses, so you must do well even if it's not something that's important to you,
because if you don't, you'll make your company look bad and possibly get
fired. Even though some kids don't appreciate the whole learning experience
right now, they will when they graduate. Nothing will feel greater than receiving your high school diploma. It's the thing that takes the longest part of
your life to achieve. A whole 12 years of your life. I can't wait . . .
—Meghann, Clover, SC

～

"Life is like a box of chocolates; you never know what you're going to get"
(Forrest Gump). Life is especially "like a box of chocolates" for teenagers attempting to learn in high school. Each student has different likes and dislikes
when it comes to classes, assignments, and especially teachers. Sometimes
learning is like picking out a coconut candy from the box and taking a bite.

For me, the coconut chocolate is completely disgusting, and so are some of the things a student is required to do in school. However, learning is sometimes being lucky enough to pick out a caramel-filled chocolate. There may be a bunch of coconut candy, but when a student applies herself and learns there will always be the caramel candies to look forward to at the end. The reward may simply be a skill that is picked up along the way, like the dark and milk chocolate candies. Fortunately, the good grades, the immediate congratulations for the hard work and self-discipline poured into learning are also preparation for the future. . . . "Whoso neglects learning in his youth, loses the past and is dead for the future." The statement from Euripides is an excellent example of how the things that we do and learn today will affect the things that we are to learn and do tomorrow.—Brittany, Moreno Valley, CA

⌒

In my personal opinion there is nothing wrong with the academic aspect of school. I don't mind the teachers or the homework and I don't mind getting up early. I realize the opportunities that good education brings you and I appreciate the fact that I am able to attend a good school. You won't hear the typical "school sucks" complaint from me.

The one thing that really gets my goat about school is my fellow students—all of the prissy girls in their too short skirts worrying about their hair and clothes, all of the jocks cheating on quizzes and tests just because they think that no one will tell on them and all of the bullies pushing people around. Then there's always those groups of people that deem themselves so important that they creep slowly down the hall, not let anyone get past them and talk as loudly as they wish. It is annoying to me that my quest for knowledge is so interrupted by these miscreants that plague the halls of my school.

I suppose the point I'm getting at is that I can't stand everyone's lack of interest in learning. They focus their efforts on impressing their friends and cutting others down. All I'm trying to say is that I want to learn enough in high school to get by in college and make something of myself, and that it bothers me that I spend my days surrounded by people who don't care about their education at all.—Esther, Clover, SC

⌒

I hate school. I hate when kids label other kids just because they are not the same race and they think they're cool. I hate some teachers at this school, too. I hate when we raise our hands and teachers look the other way, leaving us looking like fools. I hate how easily we can get lunch detention. All because of a lousy second that we were not paying attention.

I hate school and so do you. So why don't you stop to deny the fact that you do too?—Ricky, Aptos, CA

It was once said that "the early bird catches the worm", but try telling this to one of the many high school students across the nation that wake up a little groggier in between Monday and Friday mornings. Hundreds of thousands of teens that attend a public or private high school know that, after awakening, they'll spend the next five to eight hours listening to an underpaid educator drone on about such topics as parabolas or enzymes. This may sound, thus far, like a prison camp would, but this is not always the case. Depending on the viewpoint of the student, school seemingly has its advantages and disadvantages. Gaining powerful friendships as well as higher a learning to help one in their career orientated future, school can be viewed as a great opportunity to the eager student. On the other hand, school can be looked at as a prison in which no one can escape until their four year sentence is up.—Ronny, Vero Beach, FL

First, I believe the one thing school does for you that most teenagers fail to realize is that it makes you successful. We, and when I say we I mean society as a whole, don't understand the value of a free education. Why is it that so many kids claim school is a waste of their time when children in poverty stricken countries are fighting for their lives? Never have we once wondered where our next meal is coming from and yet when a teacher assigns 10 pages of reading for homework there are sighs and moans. Someone tell these "students" that it is quite the contrary. They are wasting *our* time. To learn is live and the purpose of life is not to just exist but to live. I love learning and studying and although it takes a certain level of dedication at times, I do so fully because it means success for the future. No one except God is all knowing, so why should we stop making an effort to learn? Also, I like learning because it provides me with a sense of accomplishment with which I take on larger journeys through life. We all need to learn, yes, but what about the fun stuff you might ask. . . . Then there are the school spirit and extracurricular activities. What this means is that you have so much fun during school that you want to be there after hours hanging out with the administration right? Wrong. Students want to socialize and most of just let loose for a few hours. Barring that you have you school work in check, extra activities are tremendous and exciting. You may be involved in clubs or the band; perhaps a sport or competitive academic team. Life after school is a fun and exciting time and one where I can honestly be myself at. We've all been there: cheering at a football game, attending a math competition, clapping at a x-country meet. Good times are had by all, but what happens when your perspective is altered? CHANGES take place.

Lastly, school is roughly 13 years long and by the time you hit that 10th year or so, you'd think it would get boring. Wrong again. Things are just getting good and the atmosphere not to mention your mind and body are all going through considerable changes. Some may shy away from this topic but I think it contributes immensely to your high school experience. The rest of your life is largely dependent upon how things go these next few years and never again will you claim that 8 hrs. of sleep a night is enough. Problem is, with school's stresses and pressures for your future all coming about in your mind, 8 hours is going to have to cut it, for now anyways. The advice I give aspiring students is to deal with it now and as it comes so that you may be happy and live comfortable in the future. I once read an advertisement referring to peer pressure. It said this, "no one can make you feel inferior without your consent." What I got from this quote was that we all have the ability to succeed but it has to come from your heart, not somebody else with misguided intentions. It's fine and normal to feel pressured and to perhaps place some on yourself because success is dependent upon motivation and that comes mostly from pressure. More than anything, we must accept and understand the seemingly bad because if you altar your perspective ever so slightly, it may turn into quite an amazing and enriching experience. That's the way I see it anyways.—Robert, Vero Beach, FL

⌒

Kids these days are not like they used to be, they were more respectful and hard working, but neither is the education system in Florida. It is pretty hard to find a reason to enjoy school for anyone around really, but there are many more reasons to despise it. It's great for socializing and sports, and so on, but what I really dislike is all the busy work we receive instead of being taught. School is a boring, grinding experience every day for half of a year with the same material everyday.

I do enjoy school for the social and athletic opportunities and other extracurricular activities, like football and baseball, or Spanish and Key club and so on. It's the only decent part about going to school otherwise many more people would not go. Participating in sports is one of my most favorite activities to do during school.

One of my biggest annoyances with school is busy work. All teachers give it but I am not sure why at all. Most students, though, would agree it's a waste of time. I guess teachers assign busy work because a class has so much time to fill. My only class that I learn much in, without busy work, is my AP American History class. We have no busy work and we learn by just going through the material and not doing worksheets.

Maybe one of the reasons for all the busy work is because the classes are too long. An hour and a half is pretty long to be sitting in one place, hearing one person speak. The school year extends into every month of the year except July. If we had less time in school or an extra class to take up time it would take out busy work and more interaction.

Overall school is OK for most people otherwise most do not enjoy it. The school system here is not very good. Back in the day kids just did what they were told what to do without question, they were also more respectful and conformists than our generation is today. I know I am ready to be out of there and I am pretty sure college will be better than this place. I am also hoping that my teachers have done enough to prepare me for it.—Chris, Vero Beach, FL

⁓

While preparing to complete my eleventh year of schooling in the public education system and as I begin to look towards the future of college and beyond, I reflect on my likes and dislikes of school over the years. Gone are the first days of kindergarten, allowing you to familiarize yourself with being away from home for some of the day. Here are the days of long hours at school and seemingly longer hours of work at home. To come is the day when I pack my bags and begin a new chapter in my educational career with classes of higher education.

An average school day is nearly impossible to define the farther along I get in school. With the myriad of extracurricular choices in sports, clubs, and activities, and the never-ending responsibilities with schoolwork outside of the classroom, one's day begins earlier and most likely ends later than anticipated. Every Monday morning brings with it mixed emotions of yet another week in the thirty-eight cycles until summer. Dreaded are math and science subjects, but even more the teachers whom you just don't understand. Anticipated is literature, even more if there was more nonfiction literature involved, and more so history, eager to expand knowledge in your favorite subject.

But for whichever class you prepare, a level of stress always overcomes you in an attempt to attain a respectful grade point average. No longer does school have an easy-going, low-maintenance atmosphere. I enter my school day every morning worried any question on any quiz or any response on any assignment may drastically affect the outcome of my grades in high school. I think the leverage grades hold in your entrance to college and the pressure applied by teacher, parents, and competitive peers alike are enough to turn any teenager's hair gray.

Sometimes I wonder if it's all worth it, the long nights, the sports and the extra stuff that looks good on a college application but has no value in and out of itself. The new numerical average system gives even more importance to the already overrated tests that continue to choke the educational system. Aside from all of this, I feel that school, especially my time in high school, has adequately prepared me for my life beyond the halls of a lower education facility.

Speaking of facility, even though plans are finally underway to renovate my seventy-year-old school building, in which my grandfather attended classes as a young student, the situation of school facilities, quality, or lack thereof, is deplorable. With the funds American taxpayers continue to throw at their local, state and federal governments, the fact that schools are literally crumbling, textbooks are missing entire chapters, desks face annihilation if someone dares to sit in them, and teachers run out of ink cartridges and printing rights before the first progress reports come out is deplorable. It is the responsibility of representatives in statehouses across the county and authorities in Washington, DC, to ensure that America's schools are the best built and America's teachers are the best equipped, best trained, and best prepared in the world. No longer should American citizens accept a second-class education system, or furthermore, two education systems; one for the privileged and powerful, and one for everybody else.

With the immense challenges facing our public education system, I have often wondered a lifetime in that system, rather than my present interest in politics, would result in the most being done to further my cause. But I'll have plenty of time to make that decision between now and my completion of my undergraduate work. One thing, however, is certain. I will strive, no matter what my occupation, to ensure that America's schools continue to grow and make strides to ensure that every student is educated, is prepared for the rapidly-changing world ahead, and succeeds. An education system which does not meet those goals is not one at all, and has failed at its primary responsibility. Those are the thoughts of a high school sophomore.—Matt, Atlanta, GA

⌢

School is the best way to get an education, and I greatly value my education. Not enough teenagers in my generation value school, they see it as a type of "prison" that they are forced to attend; I do not see it this way. I also do not appreciate my peers viewing their high school this way, this is the most important and influential time of our lives, and we will learn the most in these short years than in the rest of our lives, it is extremely important to learn, and to cherish what high school has to offer. I am often disappointed that I cannot attend high school a little longer, so I can take more secondary courses. There are always things that get me down about school though, so it is with mixed emotions that I go.—Patrick, Vero Beach, FL

⌢

My theory on teenage life is simple. I am the Milky Way galaxy. The sun represents my education. Just as without the sun, all life on Earth would not exist; without my education, I will never prosper in life. All of the other planets represent my additional values and activities. Without education and only enjoying life and never working hard one will never progress, without enjoying life and always working one will never enjoy life. Both working hard and enjoyment are like Yin and Yang; both are needed for balance.

To me stars represent chance. When we wish upon a start we think there is a chance for our dreams to come true. Yes, anything is possible, but even though we have many dreams, we must think realistically. A star in my galaxy of life may represent a dream of quitting school and becoming a basketball player. Our chances of teaching the closest star are one in a million. My chances of making it to the NBA no matter how good I am are one in a million. Just remember, what you accomplish now when it comes to school is what will decide how you spend the rest of your life. Would you rather study now and make a good living or would you instead fool around now and suffer the consequences when you grow up?—Vedant, Woodland Hills, CA

⌢

Walking down the crowded halls of my high school, full of bustling papers and slamming locker doors, I feel like one-thousandth of a large school of silver sardines. Everyone has the same expression: tired. Everyone I see looks the same as everybody else, no matter how hard they strive to be different. It's as if everyone has caught a "high school plague." As easy as it is to catch this "high school plague", it is also easy to prevent catching it.

Depriving yourself of sleep and time to study can greatly affect your grades and experience in high school. Try to adapt to reliable study-habits and get enough sleep to keep you awake and for all of your classes. When you give yourself these things, you have more time to focus on yourself and to find out the person you are. Many people tend to devote their time to partying and watching TV, so they never get a chance to figure out who they are, and end up acting like everyone else.

If I could tell an incoming high-schooler a piece of advice that I think is most important, I would tell him/her to remain the person they are and to re-sist falling into a trap of fads and trends, which can corrupt imagination. The most important thing to remember as a high-school student is to be your-self.—Bonnie, Woodland Hills, CA

⌒

I will tell you about bullies, a big problem in schools today. My best friend was labeled as a *NERD*. She went to a school in M___ I___. [She] was bullied by two girls (___ and ___) at first it was only name calling and of course she did not say anything to anybody but me. She told me how they would push her down in the halls and one time ___ pushed her so hard she fell down and hit her head. That night I got a call on my cell phone from her mom telling me that [she] was in the hospital with a broken arm and the she was in a C-O-M-A. I still hear that word in my head like it was yesterday. About a month later she was back in school and still got bullied but this time ___ was not there. ___ was in jail instead and was convicted of attempted murder for pushing her. ___ still continued to pick on her. I think ___ bullied her because she was prettier than her. "Nothing got bet-ter it just keeps on getting worse" she said "I think I will just end my life and the pain will stop" I really hated hearing her talk like that so I decided to help. ___ had gone to the movies that Friday, so [my best friend] and I had decided to go to. I though I could help but I only made things worse. ___ started to pick on me. She pushed me and I got mad and hit her in the middle of the face. That was the end of ___ picking on me but not the end of my best friend. She did what she said and took a lot of her mom's prescription pills. She did not live from this. It was hard not only on her family but also on ___. She was at the funeral and said she did not know that this little stunt would lead to someone dieing. She told me she was sorry and that she would miss her almost as much as I missed her but nothing she said made me forgive her for what she has put me and my friend's family through.—Kendell, Cocoa, FL, 8th grade

~

The regular school day isn't much bright of sunshine, but I do feel proud staying in school, no matter how much I can say that I do hate it. I'm proud that I've accomplished the eleven years I've been in school. Although the regular schedule of mine is very repetitive form waking up in the morning to classes, I will miss this normal life of high school, once I graduate to leave to college. Every student does have their own way of dealing with school. Even though school may be a big bore, it's one of those things where you've hated it when you were young, but once you grow old, you begin to think how great it was.—Alexa, South San Francisco, CA, 10th grade

~

When I told my dad that I had signs on the outside of my locker, he was surprised. Now I was surprised and didn't know why this would astound him so much. Then he told me that when he went to school, if anyone put any pictures or signs on their lockers, other kids would just tear them down. I started thinking about that and came to the conclusion that kids use to have certain freedoms that kids of today do not have.

You see, I think that when a younger kid gets out of line, and older kid should be able to put them back in line. Simply put. It's called seniority. It is defined as precedence of position, especially precedence over others of the same rank by reason of a longer span of service.

In my school seniority is virtually dead. Kids have very little respect for the upperclassman. I'm not saying kids do not respect anyone anymore, but the problem seems to be getting worse. More and more kids now days show little respect for their elders, and do not abide by seniority at all. And if you do try and put these kids in their places, you get ISS (In School Suspension).

Call me old fashioned, but when I was little, in elementary, almost all kids accepted seniority and listened to it. It was like an unwritten rule. I think the days of seniority are past us, and I'm kind of sad about that, but that's life. —Jacob, Max, ND, 11th grade

~

In 6th grade I learned for myself that schools could be corrupt. For me middle school sucked I hate it and couldn't wait to be done with it. Middle school was the hardest part of my schooling out of the thirteen years. If I could have dropped out I probably would have then.—Codey, Hartford, WI

〜

Now with most people high school is going to be one of the best times in your life but that never quite happened with me. It was actually one of the most boring and drawn out times so far in my life. Don't get me wrong the school itself is nice it's a lot better then the other schools I have been to. The school has money and good programs for its students but I personally have been treated like shit by most of the faculty in the school.

Now I'm not saying I am the best student and I am not going to say I am the worst students just an average students with average friends. We all have different goals in life but are still a lot alike. Now when I came into the high school my freshman year I was just a little freshman but I did have a positive attitude and I wanted to be here and graduate. By the end of the year I didn't want to come back to the school. Sure some of the problems I had were brought on by myself, but none the less I was having problems with some teachers and my A.P. The year started off good and then at semester I just stopped caring I'm still not sure why but I just did. I didn't give a f___ about anything. So I started missing school a lot and then they took my work permit and that just pissed me off more. So I started working a job that I didn't need a permit for and just said f___ it and I think I showed up to school 5 days in the forth quarter. I passed some of my classes but it wasn't a good start.

My sophomore year was coming up and I was thinking to myself I don't want to f___ around like I did the year before. I wanted to go to school and get back on track. . . . I lasted the first day then I started feeling like shit and stayed home the next day . . . went to the doctor the next day to find out I have mono. . . . I was out of school until mid October. Then I was still out of school off and on for the next month because I caught any little cold or flu that came past me. . . . I came back to school and tried as hard as I could only to find out that my A.P. thought that I was working the entire time I was out . . . he has to "talk to me" about something. I walk in and he starts giving me this bull___ that I was working during school hours for the past two months and I wasn't really sick. I f___ hate this guy, I really do . . . I try to stay calm . . . he says that he is think[ing] about taking my work permit again "to help me out." I made it real clear and simply said "you better not f___ think about taking my work permit." Then he tried acting tough . . . by the end of this little meeting I didn't have a work permit again. . . . I had a choice. Either I get to go to court about my truancy or I go see a psychologist because _____ and the school social worker think I need to talk to someone because I don't like school and I have missed so much. . . . The psychologist made it real simple. There is nothing wrong with me, and that I need a change in A.P.'s.

I went back to school and everything was working out. . . . I finished up that year . . . it was the best year so far. This was it this is my senior year and I'm going to get out of this b___. I started the year with this problem in my back that no one knew what it was. . . . I went from doctor to doctor . . . missing school left and right but still trying to keep up. I finally found out I had a herniated disk in my back, I needed surgery. I wasn't liking that at all. I need to pass every class to graduate on time and now I am going to miss all these weeks of school. . . . I had my surgery and missed 7 weeks of school . . . this right here is where I am right now. Me graduating on time is on the line . . . everything is up to me. There are a few teachers that are helping me get everything in and pass there class but then there are some that just don't give a f___. This is the story of the 4 best years of my life. What a great time high school has been for me. I just hope I can graduate on time so I can prove every one of those f___ wrong.—Rick, Hartford, WI

～

School is out, the teacher's gone,
All kids play from noon to dawn.
School is in, the children shout,
But most of all, the teachers pout!

For me, it's very difficult to label school good or bad. School, like many other subjects with as much controversy, is a mixed bag of so many ups and downs, one wonders if it is a building or a roller coaster. Some may think of school as a red brick building with a golden bell perched on top of it, but it is much more than that. School is the place where you learn jokes, whisper secrets, and make friends. School is where you learn life's lessons, deal with bullies, and learn the rules of popularity. School is the cause for joy, sorrow, and crying yourself to sleep at night. School is where you learn to make decisions, work hard, and be the best person you can be. Nobody can call *that* a schoolhouse.—Peter, Vestavia Hills, AL, 6th grade

CHAPTER TEN

∽

Stories That Must Be Told

Four Years

A place where I feel wretched,
but at the same time, overwhelmed.
So much takes place here.
My future controlled by my retention of the acquired facts.
An easy-going personality struggles to survive.
Educators try to enlighten your questions of who you really are, and what you may want to endeavor.
It all depends on your own condition of mind.
Your future really does depend on you.
Count on yourself, independence is important.
Stay strong.
Don't expect others to be there for you, or help during the truly tough times.
Your high school years are tough, it's the truth.
But the strives you encounter now will
enhance your ability to handle worse things to come.
—Hayley, Knoxville, TN

Finally, I end this book with what might be the most important chapter of all— stories that must be told. After reading through over 800 submissions, these emerged and made such an impact on me that I decided to include them as a separate chapter. For critics who proclaim that schools are not doing their jobs and that students "these days" are less competent than those that came before, they obviously have not met these interesting, smart, intuitive, and capable scholars. It is the perfect way to end this book.

〜

My experience of school are mixed, at best. With my outlook of life, one must take the good with the bad in order to be content. I have achieved contentment now, but it hasn't been easy. It seems to be against human nature itself to be happy and content. In a society where there are so many problems with today's world, so many things we don't have and want, so many people who sit on their cushy couches and sip beer, thinking about how badly life has served them, it's hard to know what to strive for. If life is an obstacle course and pleasure is the goal, then one must force oneself to enjoy the exercise.

School hasn't always been easy for me. Doctors and teachers named me a "gifted" child (what better way to inflate a seven-year old's ego than to tell them they really ARE better than everybody else?) but that didn't help me to fit in. Due to my habit of harsh self-criticism, others found me unpleasant to be around, and so most of the time through my elementary and middle school years, I was alone. Somehow, I got it into my head that friends are more important than grades; which is why I started to fail. My parents couldn't understand it; one day, I just stopped trying. They yelled at me, sent me to tutors, and after countless counselors and psychologists, divulged that I had stopped trying because I was unhappy. To a child, working hard isn't quite as important as it is when we are adults; money is always supplied by our parents, and we never have to worry about things like paying for toys or having a place to live. Naturally, a child's social life is everything to them, because that is the world they live in at the time. However, failing at school did not make me more friends, nor did it make me a happier child. In fact, I became more depressed, because now I was being berated constantly by my parents, and because of it, felt truly worthless. Sometimes I would wonder if anyone would miss me if I died.

Things changed; time went on. Once in high school, my grades got better. Suddenly, you're a teenager, and you realize that what you need NOW is material things: stereos, games, and whatever clothing is in style at the time. The importance of money suddenly becomes a very clearly defined concept. At that point, my focus changes; friends were what you had when you had the right STUFF to make them appreciate you. I felt better now that I was secure, and my grades improved because of it.

Then, one day, my dad told me that we would be moving. I was upset at first, but eager to try something new. I had no idea what was in store for me. . . . The new school I went to was called M___ High School, located right in the middle of rural West Virginia. It was as if stepping off the plane from

Colorado, I had entered an alien world. Styles and attitudes were different; what was in style in Colorado wasn't heard of here. The astonishing ignorance of the local populace was unbelievable. High schoolers behaved like little children, making plenty of fart jokes, while girls giggled over stories of who they had sex with last. Racism and homophobia were witnessed frequently, issues I had thought were no longer existent in today's average society.

Rather than adapting to this new environment, as I had done before in my teenage years, I pulled back, working myself into a style that best suited me. It mattered no longer to me what other people thought; if immaturity and stupidity were the accepted norm of this place, then I would have no part of it. Eventually, I became more accepting of the culture of West Virginia, but for a period of a few months, I was in shock. Fortunately, there were others in my same position who became my friends. No longer feeling insecure, my grades improved greatly, and more importantly, I am being myself. Society is always influenced by other people; whether we realize it or not, everyone follows another person in some way. We just need to find the most positive influence, the one that feels true to us. Only then can you achieve happiness.—Caroline, Inwood, WV

⌒

As a high school junior having grown up in America, with a free enterprise society and free public education, I feel spoiled, with so much potential power and freedom at my fingertips. It's hard to realize that if I was instead born in a less developed country somewhere else in the world, I would not even have a fraction of as many options as I do right now. I sometimes feel so overwhelmed by this complete lack of limitations. How do I deal with the ideal that I can do anything I want, within the nearly boundless limits of the Constitution?

The fact that America supports free public education is important in every aspect of our society. The United States' literacy rates are 97%, whereas countries without as many developed resources such as Niger (14%) and Nepal (28%) have significantly lower rates. Our country's insistence that all children under the age of eighteen must attend school is one of the contributing factors in making our country as influential as it is. With this in mind, I fully support that a generous portion of a state's tax dollars should be directed to the enrichment of public education.

I've spent eight and a half [years] of my student career in public schools. These years have been for the most part enjoyable and I have learned a lot, but the one grievance I have about public education is the lack of resources and the dismal pay that the teachers receive. Today's youth are the leaders of the future, and unless today's politicians plan on fixing all the world's problems permanently before the next generation comes to power, we need to be putting a considerable amount of our time and money into feeding today's students with knowledge and confidence.

One thing that opened my eyes to the downsides of public education was my middle school experience. Instead of having me attend the neighborhood junior high school, my parents sent me to The G___ Middle School (no, I'm not kidding about the name . . . but that's a different story), a private girls' school in Mountain View. They were a brand new organization and my class was the inaugural year. We became known as the "Pioneer Class."

The approach to learning at GMS came as a pleasant surprise. On my first day of sixth grade we made three-dimensional cubes with drinking straws as an introduction to graphing in algebra. In engineering, we built bridges out of popsicle sticks and string and experimented with how much weight each type of bridge (arch, suspension, beam, cable) could hold. The classes I took over the three years I attended GMS ranged from photography to self-defense, JAVA and HTML, to yoga, and creative writing to drumming. I even took a two-week course in which I learned to fly an airplane, and the weekend after, I put my knowledge to the test and flew a private jet around San Francisco Bay. But the amazing part was not the broad variety of electives, but the multitude of hands-on activities that we did on a daily basis. Each new class was an exciting adventure; I was really looking forward to attending class for the first time since I was about six years old.

In my eighth grade year at GMS, after three years of intense Spanish immersion classes, the entire eighth grade class (consisting of about 35 girls) packed our duffel bags and flew down to Michoacan, Mexico. We attended a small camp, kind of like the Science Camp I did with my class in fifth grade. But it was much different in many ways. Nobody besides our classmates spoke much English. For seven days, we attended workshops, ate, played soccer, and took showers alongside the native Mexican girls and boys. We made friends with many of them in the process, and I learned more in that weeklong trip than I could have in a whole year of any Spanish class.

I enjoyed my three years at GMS for many reasons. First of all, there were smaller classes, which make it a lot easier to learn, and each student got more personalized attention from the teacher. The teachers were able to change their teaching style slightly to help each student or group of students. It really motivated me, knowing that my teachers had a vested interest in my success. It would be great if the public school districts could receive more money from the state for salaries for teachers. With just a few more teachers per school, the class sizes could be diminished and the individual attention for each student would increase, making the chances for success higher.

Also, when I went to GMS, the level of parent participation was high. Whether it was driving for field trips or sports games, coming in to speak about their occupations, or even volunteering in the library or office, the girls' parents were a common sight around the school. I got to know all my friends' parents quickly, and their presence gave the school a much safer, community-like feeling. I was really sad to graduate, because I felt like I was moving away from a great big family. It would be nice to try and get more parents involved with the public schools.

I also enjoyed the amount of field trips we went on during middle school. The school did a large program for Take Your Daughter to Work Day, in which they matched up every girl with a profession that suited her interests and sent them all to the office of someone in that field for the day. Every girl participates and we all enjoyed ourselves and learned about the profession. Increasing the amount of field trips would be a tougher chore to tackle in public schools because it would be harder to get the kind of funding they would need, but this attribute would greatly increase the quality of learning.

I know that it is harder for public schools to receive generous enough funding to support these kind of programs. But it is really frustrating to hear about budget cuts in education that force schools to cut back really valuable programs like music, sports, art, and electives. These classes are a very important factor in a student's education. In order to become a well-rounded and educated student, it is valuable to take a variety of classes and hone many different skills. The well-rounded students will become well-rounded citizens, and these are the people that are truly going to make a difference.
—Carolyn, San Jose, CA

⌒

Every now and then, there are certain questions relating to the present or the future ahead. And the most frequently asked question that ties to the present or future is often a statement regarding "school." At most, one of the main questions asked would likely be how is school? Even though this is a relatively simple question, I often find myself struggling to respond. It's awkward that such a simple question could possibly be difficult. However, every time the word school is mentioned in a conversation I end up having difficult decision choosing the best answer. I realized that school can not be defined because it's such a broad subject. School in many ways is similar to a menu at a local restaurant. We've all been to a restaurant and have seen the outrageously long list of foods. And when I'm at a restaurant I end up taking forever to choose a meal because every item is very scrumptious and delicious. Unfortunately, school isn't delicious, but we are able to choose a schedule. It sounds like a simple task but it's quite hard to pick classes because everything sounds great. For example, at my school there is a wide range of classes such as music, dance, art, and many more. It's majorly important that schools nationwide provide performing art classes because it's proven that children who are enrolled in these classes are above average. Also, with a wide range of classes children today are introduced to diversity.

Diversity is considered to be one of the main issues in the eyes of many. Diversity is everywhere ranging from the color of our skin, the music we listen to, or even the foods we eat. Most importantly, we should all accept diversity rather than harassing one another because we see diversity everywhere. In school, we all are introduced to many heritage because every one of the students is different. Unlike any other country, America is made up of people from every part of the world. It makes it interesting to be in school and learn about all these different cultures or even make friends with kids who are different. I enjoy making new friends and experiencing new things because it helps me learn that it's okay to be different. Not everyone's family is perfect or resembles a sitcom family because we are all special in our own ways. But over the years, I recognized that there are still people who are incapable of accepting others because of their gender, religion, race, or any other factor. Having witnessed harassment, I strongly disapprove of stereotypes and prejudiced remarks. I believe every single person should be treated equally no matter what background they may a part of. People like Martin Luther King, Jr. fought hard to create equality among us all. It was his dream and his speech that made the difference, but I feel that his dreams have become my dreams as well.

Thinking about equality over the century has been stressful for all. I'm very fortunate to live in a world where many civil leaders have taken a stand and created a path for us all. Today, the only thing that I find distressing are the finals taken twice a year. These finals create stress and pressure on me because the only thing that crosses my mind is the fact that colleges will see my grades when I apply. It puts pressure on me to do well because I want to get into a great school and pursue a career in the medical field. And in order to achieve this goal I need to maintain good grades. As I write this now, it may sound scary and horrifying but each student will be able to adapt to school at their own pace.

As a child, I remember hearing how hard middle school and high school would be. I was very scared to go to school and meet all these mean and bad-tempered teachers who were rumored to eat other children. But once I reached middle school I realized that school isn't bad at all. It's actually fun to challenge yourself and meet new people. And as for teachers, they're not as bad as you think. Once in a while you'll meet a crazy or stern teacher but put in consideration that they want you to do well. In fact, some teachers end up making a difference in your life and even help you realize something that you were never aware of. The best advice for students who are afraid of school is to try it before you judge it. But mainly challenge yourself to do well by setting goals and standards.—Connie, San Jose, CA

⌒

It is said that you can tell a lot about a person by what they wear. At V___ HS you can distinguish between the good, the bad, and they ugly at any given time of day. Imagine briskly walking through a long, crowded hallway and discreetly giggling about the days gossip when suddenly presented before you is a plumber's crack. Yes, we're talking about a dimply, hot pink thong coverage, gone horribly past PG rated. This scenario cannot be avoided when a little trip to your locker is in need. A suggestion would be to close your eyes and run home, but anyone would be better off just trying to picture little pink bunnies instead.

Sadly it has come to my attention that wandering eyes are all around and no homework is safe. It's a different kind of jealousy, the kind where you remember why your arm hardly has the strength to slap the kid with wandering eyes because of the eight hours of sleep you didn't get because you, the wonderful student that are, stayed up all night studying for that test. They may be green, or maybe even purple but remember those wandering eyes are all around you and can be found at a school near you.—Tara, Vero Beach, FL

⌒

I was sinking further into the emptiness, drowning, gasping for answers. A wavering light twinkled high above my head; a final sense of hope slowly blinking out with the foreboding darkness. I flailed in the surrounding thickness. It engulfed me, consumed me. Pressure hit me from all sides, cutting short my breath, and crushing my weary mind. All hope lost; faith devoured in expectation.

Tiny hands seemed to pull me under, dragging me farther and farther away from familiarity and deeper into oblivion. I desperately sought for something to hold onto, anything to aid me in my peril. Yet, I was alone, and for the final time in my fatal uncertainty, I cried for help, silently, into the darkness. The words caught in my throat, and I choked on my screams. I could feel the unbearable chill of helplessness flood through me as I gave in, allowing my mind to shut down.

Suddenly, something crashed into the abyss beside me. I reached out blindly, not knowing what I sought. An illusion, I was sure of it; the last of my glimmering faith dying. Yet as I grabbed out with my exhausted mind, I brushed against my saving grade: a rope, one of golden fibers woven with the magical ideas of wise persons. I fought to keep the final beads of air down in my lungs as I held onto it, determined not to let go of my miracle.

I surfaced, drained of the energy to do anything but breathe. It was enough. With exhaustion pounding in my head and sleep waiting impatiently on my doorstep, I welcomed rest, closing my eyes and listening to the lasting words of my rescuer. "Intelligence is not always knowing the answer. It is always asking the question." So a wise woman saved my fading confidence. Maya Angelou's inspirational idea fed my recovering courage in the pounding seas of knowledge, just when I had let go of all hope.

Renewing my once dwindling security, I knew I would no longer hide myself in dark corners, wishing to go unnoticed. On the contrary, I would seat myself front and center; notebook open, hand ready to acknowledge a questioning thought before the idea got too far from my grasp. With amounting pride, I would observe my insecurities wither and die before me. And perhaps one day, I would return to the same sea for a final glance at the death I escaped, only to realize that I hadn't been alone, lost in the equations, theorems and rhetorical devices. There had been others lost, floundering, trying to reach above the surface of suffocating information; gasping for a breath of something, anything, that made the utmost sense to them.

I would kneel on the deck just above their heads, crying and smiling at the same time. Their pain was, once, once that I shared. Carefully, I would retrieve a golden rope from my coat pocket, and cast it into the sea in front of me, expecting a bite. And as I would feel the tug on my end of wisdom, I would hold my smile, and pull another from the depths of despair, relaying to them, an all too familiar speech. . . . "Intelligence is not always knowing the answer. It is always asking the question."—Jackie, Merritt Island, FL

~

Firstly, I like to talk about my first day at a high school in United States of America. It was one of the formidableness day in my life. When I came to this country I did not know good English. At first, I thought American students are really good, and they will help me. Unfortunately, I was totally wrong. Most American students don't care about other students. I am from India and I don't know good English. Therefore, they don't like to talk with me. It hurts me a lot. At that movement I felt like I am in hell. Also, I felt go back to India. American students are not only avoiding me but also say very bad word at me like f___ you, mother f___, bitch, etc. At first, I did not understand the meaning of these words. Then, when I know the meaning of these words I felt very uncomfortable because the behaving of an American student is very bad. From that day, I started to hate Americans. These days I was totally alone. After a few days my English teacher started to understand my situation. Then, she helped me a lot. She became a good teacher. She tried to say everything about schools and American students.—Jose, San Jose, CA

⌣

129 Days

Do you really want to know what school is really like?! Wow what a question. Well all teachers look at the kids and think wow, look how good they behave. Now with the kids point of view is "Come on come on can the fire bell just ring and evacuate the entire school." Then I glance at the clock ten seconds. 5, 4, 3, 2, 1. I leap out of my seat. But the strange thing was I am the only one celebrating. I felt like a new student from Russia who couldn't speak English. Oh but then I notice it's only 10:40, language arts. Then I mumble under my breath "Why do you torture me?" My head is racing, my underwear is slipping, . . . I mean my heart is pumping. I have a staring contest with the clock. 30 seconds 25 . . . 20 . . . 15 . . . 10 . . . 5, then the whole class gets together and screams "5, 4, 3, 2, 1." I open my desk, sprinkle my homework on the floor. I hear my teacher yelling. The class doesn't listen. I scream, "Only 129 days 'till summer."—Luke, Turnersville, NJ, 5th grade

⌣

My name is Kokob. I came from far away. When I first arrived in the USA, I scared a lot. The reason why I scared were first, I never been out side my country before. Second, the language is new for me. When I was in my country I used to speak a language that is completely different from English. That means, when I came to the USA I have to learn a new language from the beginning. Third, the culture was completely different from my culture. The way people are dressing is different from the people in my country. Most of the foods are different. Also, when I came I didn't know any body except my family. Therefore, I feel lonely. After I stayed one month in California, I started school in September 22, 2002.

At my first day of school every thing was new for me. The students were from different country. It was very interesting to me because in my country the students were from the same country that means all of us are from our country. The first class that I stepping in was an English class. My heart beats a lot. The teacher was very nice. After saying hi he introduced my name to the class. Also he gave me the first sit in the class. All the students said in one voice well come to America Kokob. At that time I felt boring and lonely. The time was to long for me. After I staid one week and a half I got new friends. All my teachers tried to help me especially my English teacher. After all this I started to feel comfortable with every thing. Also I started to know a lot of new friends and new places. I really enjoyed school in the USA. June came very fast and school closed. In that next September I started my school in more confidence and preparation than last year. I already started to communicate English with out any problems that were very simple to me to get friends, to do shopping and other things that helped me to enjoy life in America.

Education is much easier in USA than in my country. In my country most teachers asked you to do math with out calculator. Also the tests are very hard over there. In addition they don't give you enough time to finish your tests. You also have to show all your works step by step. 90% of the tests are reasoning questions. Some times they bring some questions out side of the book. Also we don't have enough libraries. That's why education is much easier in the U.S. than in my country.

In conclusion I want to see myself pass through all this processes and be a computer engineer. The reasons why I want to an engineer are first, I want to make good money. Second I love to work with computers. In addition it's very interesting job for me and my family.—Kokob, San Jose, CA

⁓

School Is . . .

Stress is ongoing
Homework never stops
Time consuming, day in day out
Redundant, redundant, redundant
Repetitive, repeat, repeat it
Cause and consequence

Trial for the new
Error for the old
Finals for the young
Tests for the old
Extremes and
In-betweens
Lockers hold your life
Friends stay with you less than
4 years. Old.
Wouldn't change it for the world.
—Anonymous, Amesbury, MA

⌣

When I imagine my future, I think of how I will remember the times I am currently living, my high school years, these four years of my life, which are supposed to be so influential, and memorable. Overall, how will they affect me? Will they make an impact on my life, or merely be just another phase of my adolescence? The life I am living at this moment is everything I have; it contains everything I do and feel, and most of all everyone I know. But years from now will any of this matter?

My day consists of going to school, eating and sleeping, and that is truly the extent of it. At school I struggle through my academics in which I find myself having little to no interest in, and desperately trying to grab every piece of knowledge I can out of my performing classes. Performing is what is important to me, and as of now is what I want to do with the rest of my life. If I don't make it as a performer I see my future as a failure, and I am very unaware if the training I am receiving at the present moment is enough to help me achieve my goals later in life. My life revolves around the show I am in at any given time or any current project I happen to be working on. At the moment these things are a big deal to me. But will that ever change, and if so, will that make these past years in which this has been my priority pointless? I don't know.

Obviously a huge part of my life is the people I share it with, without them I am not who I am today. For good and bad they make me, and I thank them for that. In my mind however there are two categories of people, the ones I know well, and the ones I don't. The ones I don't confuse me, because its hard for me to comprehend how I can have something so huge as high school in common with them, and still not even know their first name. My friends, on the other hand, do something more than confuse, they depress me. Although at the

190 ~ Chapter Ten

present time they make me very happy and bring me lots of fun and joy, in such a short amount of time they will be taking that away so quickly with their departure. Graduating and going off to college is seen as a triumph and time of happiness, but to me it has such sadness to it. One is leaving their entire high school career, not to mention childhood, friends, and family behind. And I'm supposed to be okay with this? Well, I'm not. There are so many people who I am close to currently that I can't imagine never seeing again, and it drives me crazy that this will most likely be a reality. It's the way life works, the way things happen. But why? I don't know.

In the end we all end up in different places, and my question is does high school really matter? I mean, what's the point? If I don't care that much about my classes now, lord knows I won't care about them later, and if I don't accomplish my goals as a performer, what's the point of trying so hard now, and if I end up losing all contact with the people I know now and maybe even forget them, what's the point of even having their acquaintance? Does any of this really matter? Does high school matter, or is it something you just happen to do? I'm scared because I don't know how things will turn out. I don't know what my future will be like, and I don't know if I will be happy. And, most of all, I don't know if the life I am living right now at this very moment is pointless. I just don't know.—Megan, San Jose, CA

~

I figured a lot of people would be writing you happy fun stories about what high school is like, but I knew you needed to read another account of the dangers that students can so easily get themselves into. My teacher told our class to be very candid and tell it really how it is, since that is the only way improvements and knowledge can be gained from our experiences. Well here is a copy of my short story titled "running with the wrong crowd."

At a high school reunion 20 years from now, you won't remember what shoes you wore, the jeans you had or who had a date to prom; rather at that time you will remember and reflect on the decisions you made which have turned you into the person you became. Priorities do change but hopefully the results of the things you did will not. It has been described as the "butterfly effect"—a small single action has a rippling effect on later events. If only we could be aware when we are creating little butterflies of our own.

High school is a difficult and trying time for all students, and many pupils will find themselves looking for a crutch to lean on to relieve the stress, pain or just confusion many students feel. Some kids turn to drugs, some entrench themselves in academics but most kids just rely on their friends. I did a combination of the three.

I came from a wealthy primarily white middle school where I was very popular, one of the "cool kids" I was a skater and played in the band; not really doing much besides being cool was my forte. Middle school was a breeze for me I got A's in all the classes with the hard teachers while fooling my friends that I was an idiot which for some reason is "cool" in middle school. My friends all split up following our middle school "graduation" and the process of making friends and connections was about to begin again.

High school was a drastic change for me; having classes w/ real big kids was much different then joking around w/ prepubescent 6th graders back in middle school. I needed to quickly latch on to some friends to protect me from the big kids, and I happened to be a "starter" on the football team so I could go talk to anyone and they would listen. Only certain kids will stick around and talk to a little freshman for long, and a specific crowd is always willing to do so: the druggies. Now I consider there to be many different levels of druggies: the stoners, the tweakers, and the "e-tards". Thank god I didn't get in with the worst of them, but any group of kids known to be involved w/ drugs is not a responsible friend choice. But I needed friends and the stoners were perfect (in my eyes) to fill that void. Now what parents don't realize is the bad stuff their kids can easily get themselves into, or rather how casual activities they could view as atrocious are. Yes, kids smoke pot in the bathroom, but what people don't realize is that good kids get in with them to do it, not just the "druggies" as mentioned before but many regular kids do things they see as rebellious, are really just dangerous to their future.

I'm not going to keep hitting you with poetic statements trying to make myself sound intelligent among proof of my stupidity so I'll just tell it as it happened. I became great "friends" with bad kids. And I use quotation marks because they really weren't friends they were all willing to turn their back on my in a moment to save their own hides, just as I did. Now a major rule of high school is that if you do anything, even if you didn't word will get around and once word started getting around that I was "dealing" with these kids, I was f___. Even though I wasn't actually doing that people talked and offhand comments got twisted into such. I was approached by my coach whom I've known since 4th grade regarding these allegations, I denied them and even this didn't have much of an effect on my behavior. These bad kids, as my mother would like to say had "gotten their clutches into me" and shaking them loose would take a huge event, bigger then losing the respect it takes 5 years to build.

A couple of weeks later I thought I had the luckiest day ever, I was walking through the quad when I looked to the ground and found a bag of pot, worth probably about 20 bux. Sweet, I thought, unbeknownst to me the school principal thought next period would be a "sweet" time to ask me about these drug allegations. I have never been filled with as much fear as I had when he walked into my classroom next period, pointed at me and told me to bring all of my stuff. It was all over for me, that was it. I was about to be caught w/ marijuana in my pocket at school and this was on top of the principal hearing that I was a middle man: someone who knows who has drugs (which I never was) but anyways two very bad things. We walked into the office and I saw several of my teachers and they must have seen the fear and desperation in my face because I remember hearing one of them just mumble that they were sorry; and so was I. The principal and I walked by the campus police's office and he said "come into my office in a minute were going to need you". That was the most intense moment of my life, not a good intense, a very very bad intense. But it was about to get worse. We then made the fun walk into the principal's office where I was to meet my doom, but luckily just for a second the principal looked away and I took the stuff out of my pocket and clenched it in between my butt cheeks. I did that for the next 3 hours.

My bags were searched my pockets, but I had nothing on me because I never did, but if only they would have bent me over and given me the spanking I so deserved, I would have been dead. But through the entire interrogation I was spanking myself, mentally of course. I needed that, now I am totally against parents hitting their children or corporal punishment or any of that bru-ha-ha but I believe there may be a time when a kid needs a swift kick in the behind to get back on track. Thank god that fright got me back on track. The principal asked me if I wasn't engaging in these activities who was? I realized that my "friends" had given my name to him trying to get the heat off of themselves. So fine turn them in for the scums they were.

The end result of the whole incident was that I had to start over at ground zero looking for new friends and respect of my peers and teachers as a distinguished individual. "Friends" 1, 2, 3 and 4 all went down. "Friend" 1 got sent to a drug-rehab/boarding school in Mexico. "Friend" 2 got expelled a week later after the principal found a $300 pipe and hash in his car. "Friends 3 and 4" had a delightful summer in juvenile hall after they were pulled over driving drunk and on shrooms on highway 17 (a notorious road near Santa Cruz, CA) with 1/2 a pound of pot. My result was I cleaned up my act; a good pun since I have become extremly involved with the theater program and do an average of 6 shows a year. Unlike my loser friends my summer was spent in

Edinburgh, Scotland, performing in the world renowned Edinburgh Fringe Festival.

Everything we do has a lasting effect on our lives, and if we look into them we can hopefully pull good out of the bad. I did, I completely turned about by nearly destroying myself. The long-lasting effect that my shenanigans had on my life must of come from a beautiful butterfly.—Thomas, San Jose, CA

∼

The first day of school is always the best, with new hopes of completing the school year with a four point zero grade point average, and staying on task with everything you want to get involved with: drama, chorus and various clubs. I was always an ordinary student who never received the perfect four point zero or been a super high school sports star, but I always felt like I could to better. Having the opportunities to take above average classes gives me confidence, but not too much confidence; as my English teacher would say "Don't brag. You don't need to brag. If you did something good, people will know about it." The classroom varies from teacher to teacher. Some teachers work hard and are dedicated to their students and job. I have grown to admire many of my teachers.

Admirable teachers are encouraging, but constructive. A student cannot learn if he or she doesn't want to learn or even be at school. The real change in education must be that within the student. Knowledge isn't a building nor is it books, nor is it computers; it is an event that occurs daily and when we can use it in an environment it is a powerful tool. People don't take advantage of this. According to my opinion, we have lost our desire for knowledge and our respect for school. Our society has become reliant on the government for providence. We have also lost the effect or work when we can use computers and calculators (which were once simple adding machines for faster, more efficient use), now used as crutches so that we can use less of our brains as possible. I, myself, am guilty of this. Technology is changing and we can't stop it because we like it too much.

Procrastination . . . for as long as I let the thought sink into my mind, I can remember countless nights I have been pulling together a last minute project. I have a belief that this causes the most stress in teenagers. There are three kinds of teenagers: those who don't care, those who care then there is no time to care and those who get the job done as soon as they receive the assignment and even have time for more studying. Should the change be in the teachers: "No more reports, essays, or projects," or in the student: "I must study hard and get my work done to the best of my ability."

School is also a social place. The hierarchy of students begins at the bottom with the freshmen and works its way up to the seniors. As one becomes older, each begins to forget that they were a silly freshman once, but why remember. With the over population of our school and the decreased size of lockers, it has become impossible to even shove a skinny freshman geek inside. The social ladder invented by students at a school won't even exist when you leave, but don't worry there will be a completely different social ladder and you will eventually work for that skinny geek you once stuffed in a locker. Forgive me for such sarcasm. I know I'm a foolish teenager as well. Students shouldn't stress over social needs and appearance at school. School is the amazing place of learning. This being the major topic in my life right now, shows in my comments.—Rebecca, Inwood, WV

⁓

We Are
We are overwhelmed
We are judged
We are immature and loud

We are scared
We are hormonal
We are cautious and proud

We are willing
We are degrading
We are rambunctious and thriving

We are liars
We are cheats
We are scandalous and crying

We are happy
We are difficult
We are fake and dumb

We are secure
We are boastful
We are different, we are one.
—April Hood, Aptos, CA

⌢

Only a few months before I had been a star on the football team. At the end of the season I hung up my cleats and put on a pair of dance shoes. As much as I liked football, I loved theater more and figured that taking a dance class would enable me to get better parts. Besides, much like everyone else I hated regular PE and would much rather take a dance class to fill my football void. What I didn't count on was how the homies would react.

At first I received little if any criticism from my peers for taking on such a "girly" activity. But after awhile, it all changed. Putting on dance pants and a tight shirt was viewed as drastically different from the other guys in the locker room, especially when just weeks earlier we had all been on the field in the mud chasing the pigskin.

High school is probably one of the most common places for ridicule. Those who are different are often made to suffer, but I had no personal experience with such thing since I had never been the kind of kid that was made fun of. I was in for a rude awakening. Take a dance class and you're instantly as weird as Boy George.

The homies in my math class were positive that I had another thing in common with Boy George, and that was that I was gay. I am not gay, so when I heard them making off-hand comments I would brush it off as though they were joshing with me. But little comments add up and become a big hurts if they are not stopped.

Rude comments are commonly referred to as "playground talk" since it's basically the nonsense that boys say to each other outside of the classroom. Teacher often disregard foul language they hear on the "playground" since it is not in the classroom and so much it just part of our society's vernacular. But what are the results when a teacher adopts that attitude in their classroom?

Pain is the result for those of us who are the focus of harassment. I know because I experienced pain revolving around the fact that it seemed no one cared about my feelings; or, thought to stop something that was wrong. The homies in my math class decided that by taking a dance class I was a "fag" in their cruel words. I was made aware of their opinion in a very public way. I would walk into class and pictures of me and the words "ballerina bitch" would be on the chalkboard. The homies would have chalk on their hands and smirk. My teacher would just erase the epitaphs from the board and not say a thing, even though in the state of California we have laws protecting people from harassment of *perceived* sexuality.

I started to not want to go to that class. I was embarrassed and subconsciously put my dead down whenever I saw those kids, avoiding eye contact at all costs for fear they would say something. How ridiculous a situation it was. I wanted to say something to try and make them stop it but at the same time find the right words that would be sensitive to the feelings of my gay friends. And further I wanted to know why my insensitive math teacher wouldn't look up from his algebra book to stop a child from being destroyed. Was he a fundamentalist fanatic who thought gays deserved AIDS and other atrocities, or was he himself simply frightened of the power of the homies?

I got a few of my friends to come with me to confront the main perpetrator. I figured if I beat him up that would show him I wasn't a fairy. It was finally going to be my day, but like most viruses these homies came in numbers. As I approached the homie it seemed like 300 of his friends came and stood behind him; all taunting me. This was finally enough. I could not take it anymore, and I needed to talk to someone.

Many kids have no idea who to talk to when they have a problem. Thank goodness I have a great teacher who is the advisor of the Gay-Straight Alliance (an on-campus club) who I figured would be very understanding and compassionate. She went to our school's principal who happened to be very sensitive to such an issue, and he put an immediate stop to the students inappropriate comments, and assured me this would never happen again.

In retrospect, it wasn't a huge terrible ordeal in my life, rather a difficult time that I went through that taught me a good lesson. Much like racial bigotry that infested our country until 40 years ago, sexual prejudice is the current form of intolerance our country must fact. Throughout all of history, some social group has been the subject of being treated inferior—it's been the Jews, Christians, Irish, Japanese, Chinese, Blacks, and not it's the gays. Finally our society has realized that it's wrong to be prejudice towards all of those groups, except it seems, against the gays. African American people were not even fully recognized as people until about 100 years ago. How much longer is it going to take for our country to realize that all people, no matter what their physical or mental attributes are should be treated the same. Hopefully soon, because I know I am not an isolated case and am sure all over our country students of all races, sexes, and ages have similar stories. With a little education in 100 years maybe this dark age of acceptance will be history as well.—Thomas, San Jose, CA

⁓

When one spends nearly seven hours a day within a single institution, biology deems that nature shall inevitably call. Assuming this basic fundamental, it would be safe to state that the very facial apparition of any form of toiletry facility is of the utmost import—indeed, such a place should be held as sacred. Humanity seems to draw nearer and hold close those apparitions that are kept in cleanly regard; thus, the restrooms inherent within the educational system should, aesthetically, be endeared to its users. This would be the way of things in a perfect world—unfortunately, however, this world is far from perfect . . .

Taking such to heart, one might spend hours ranting about the horrors of restroom-sanctuaries within the educational asylum. However, such would be a gross waste of time, and utterly unnerving to the stomach—thus I will spare you, o' enlightened reader, the monstrosities which run rampant amongst the stalls and urinals. I shall simplify such a task, though: the subject of "potty art" comes to rise. This new, visually "enthralling" work happens to consist of various articles of toilet paper, paper towels, a package of Planter's peanuts, and an orange peel. This lovely spectacle, in all its glory, is displayed quite commonly (upon an every day basis, sincerely) and happens to be a massy obstacle to any intent upon using the toiletries in either of two fashions. Such would lead to the question, "Why?" An inquiry to that nature shall boggle the world for years to come. One must also wonder, is it an art? Or, is it just filth? Such must be answered, and soon.

Am I bitter on the subject? Hardly. As wretched as such an expertly crafted statuette truly is, I have seen worse and (and again, I shall spare you the details). Let it be said, however, that it would be a much more regal cause to attempt methodizing a means of policing these "holy grounds." Though, perhaps merely hiring an excavator whose inclination to the restroom arts happens to peak my own, or that of the current incarnation of the janitorial spectrum. At any rate, one must conclude. Thus, I leave you on this note: Art should be displayed on walls, not strewn about stalls. Remember: only *you* can prevent potty art.—Russell, Merritt Island, FL

~

Both of my parents are teachers. I suppose this had made it so school is different for me than most kids. I practically live at school. My dad teaches at my high school, while my mother teaches at a middle school. She worked as a custodian at my elementary school, however, while getting her degree. I've had my parents at my school, breathing down my neck, for most of my career.

One of the upsides to this is the fact that I don't have to ride the "cheese wagon." But I do have to get up quite a bit earlier than most of my peers. On top of that, dad has to be at school by seven o'clock. We leave by six thirty. (I live outside the district, so it's a bit of a ride to get to school.) I get up at five thirty. It's killer! I get a lot of one-on-one time with my father, though. I know enough people to understand how nice that is.

When we get to school I have a half hour before classes start while my dad runs around going mysterious teacher stuff. Sometimes I go to the cafeteria and discuss the finer points of politics. *Lord of the Rings*, and string cheese with my friends. More often than not, though, I stay in my dad's room and do homework, study, or take a nap before class.

From there I go to the Most Dreaded of Places—Math class. Now, admittedly, I *chose* to take this math class. I had my required math credits. But I knew that if I didn't take a math class I would forget all my math (By repression of awful memories, most likely) and when I took math in college I'd flounder and drown. So this is a gruesome torture of my own doing. That doesn't mean I have to like it, though my teacher is cool.

The bell rings and I go to a great class. I love AP Psych. It's hard, yes, but interesting. And our class discussions can be great fun. Mr. ___ knows his subject, but he's a cool enough guy that if you ask him a question that he doesn't know, he'll tell you (I've had teachers who wouldn't admit to not knowing the answer). I'm in that class with my best friend (whose name is also Sarah . . . it gets confusing). That always helps.

To biology! (Affectionately termed "blogy"). I adore this class as well. Admittedly, it's often painfully easy, and since I had Zoology last year with the same teacher, I know half the material. Plus, I'm a super-fan of biology. I read Animal Encyclopedias for fun and can spend twenty minutes just watching ants build stuff. I love it. And besides, my career involves biology in the utmost (I want to be a writer for National Geographic and maybe even have my own show on animals one day). I've even made tentative plans on my Ph.D. in biology. It's the best! This is also with Sarah.

Quasimodo's at it again, and the bell tolls. I'm a TA this period for a great teacher. I had her my freshman year in Mythology and my junior year in Creative Writing. I love to write, so I became her TA. I sometimes get to participate in various writing assignments (like this one). Mostly it's pretty boring, though. I grade papers (she teaches ninth grade English, too, but I had Honors then), sort and file essays and stories and poems, and help in the computer lab. It's a handy study period, though.

Then I get to Latin. I practically worship Latin. It's awesome. I took Japanese my freshman year, but then I switched to Latin sophomore. I'm in Latin III now (there are only three of us in the class and I have the best grade). Latin I was the easiest. Last year I had to be in the class by myself because my schedule conflicted with the Latin II class period, so I sat in the back of the Latin I class and translated stories. I also helped tutor some of the Onesies (my term). The beginning of this year was a pain because I missed about four weeks last year due to a chest infection. But I caught up very quickly. I tutor the Latin II kids, now the (the Onesies grew up to be Twosies!), and I even help my other two classmates. They help me just as much, though. I just do my homework.

I go to lunch from Latin. Lunch is the best time of the day. I consider it my Free Though Class (school tries to beat that out of you, but I have persevered!). We get into these fantastical discussions about all sorts of random things, from limp lettuce to the psychological impact of *1984*. It's so much fun! We're all drama students, too, or people who should be drama students, so it can get pretty rowdy. Just the other day we got into the evolutionary roles of men and women and why gender roles are as they are today. Then I threw a walnut at ___ and it all went downhill (he thinks women should be submissive . . . I obviously do not concur).

After lunch I wander down to the bus to take me to driver's ed. I like some aspects of this class, like BTW (Behind The Wheel), but I *hate* driving on the range. I also dislike most of my classmates. Okay, I don't *dis*like them, but they aren't my friends. You know? But there are enough in there that I can comfortably do group activities and have driving partners. I am thankful that it's just a half-credit class and that I'm almost done. Yay! I'm going on OSE (out of school environment, I think), which means I get to leave two periods early. I'm quite pleased.

Then I get to go home (or hang around the school some more while my dad does even MORE incomprehensible teacher stuff). I do homework, get on the Internet, read, talk to friends, and eat. Boring average-Joe (or in this case, Jane) stuff. But then I'll get my hermit crab out to play, or my rat, or watch my mouse do back-flips in his cage (he's too hyper to play with), or go downstairs and let my puppy treat me like a puppy. I might go outside and watch the chickens, or the squirrels, or the birds. I can also walk over to Sarah's house and bother her family.

This all happens if I'm not in a play. As I mentioned before, I'm a drama student. I don't have a class this year, nor did I last year, but I was in both Drama I and III (yes, I mean three . . . I skipped two), and once in you're stuck. I don't do many plays at school anymore, but when I did I could be at school as late as nine o'clock. I also have a night class on Wednesday (I take English 101 and 102 instead of high school English) which goes from six to nine. Like I said before, the school is my home. I'm there quite often.

I like school, mostly. Some of the pure crap we have to put up with is a pain (I.D.'s, dress codes, some of the teachers, Bush's No Child Left Behind policy

. . . Crap). I get to see my friends, though, and this year I actually get to learn (last year I had a lot of classes with people who didn't wan to learn . . . which meant cutting into my learning ability . . . to say the least, I don't speak with those people). I'm quite happy that I can finally see my graduation on the horizon, and I'm actually looking forward to the extra twelve years of schooling it will probably take for me to get my Ph.D.—Sarah, Inwood, WV

⁓

The XIII Haikus of Hell

1
the crowded hallways
cliques brush by me
so this must be hell

2
hurry, hurry, rush
frantic homework at lunch time
ah, to sleep, to dream

3
tiny lake of drool
seeps forth from his tired lips
the teacher drones on

4
I frantically rush
Through the halls past slow moving
Freshmen. I am late

5
the hours drag on
some strange loop time marches on
yet no work gets done

6
she brushes a strand
of hair behind her ears and
gives me empty looks

7
they fight pointlessly
rusty locker hangs from wall
save it for the game

8
ah, my favorite thing
the time all students yearn for
essay time in class

9
what goopy thing is
this science experiment
alas, it is lunch
10
like gladiators
running from lions we face
from PE teachers
11
your idle hands move
under the desk to nether
land and the blob of gum
12
excruciating
are the last moments in hell
so close, yet so far
13
like angels in song
it's blessed note touches you
you have been released
—Anonymous, Amesbury, MA

References

AFL-CIO. (2004). *Building, improving and modernizing school facilities*. Retrieved on April 4, 2004, from http://www.aflcio.org/issuespolitics/education/schoolconstruction.cfm.

Alan Guttmacher Institute (AGI). (1999). *Facts in brief*. Retrieved May 30, 2004, from www.guttmacher.org/pubs.

Anderman, E. M. (2002). School effects on psychological outcomes during adolescence. *Journal of Educational Psychology, 94*(4), 795–809.

Banner, J. M., & Cannon, H. C. (1997). *The elements of teaching*. New Haven, CT: Yale University Press.

Baumeister, R. F., & Leary, M. R. (1995). The need to belong: Desire for interpersonal attachments as a fundamental human motivation. *Psychological Bulletin, 117*, 497–529.

Bluestein, J. (2001). *Creating emotionally safe schools: A guide for educators and parents*. Deerfield Beach, FL: Health Communications.

Brophy, J., & Good, T. (1986). Teacher behavior and student achievement. In M. Wittrock (Ed.), *Handbook of research on teaching* (pp. 328–375). New York: Macmillan.

Bru, E., Stephens, P., & Torsheim, T. (2002). Students' perceptions of class management and reports of their own misbehavior. *Journal of School Psychology, 40*(4), 287–307.

Child Trends. (2002). *Marijuana use*. Child Trends Data Bank. Retrieved June 23, 2004, from http://www.childtrendsdatabank.org/pdf/46_PDF.pdf.

Child Trends. (2004). *Child Trends databank indicator: Adolescents who feel sad or hopeless*. Figure 1. Retrieved June 10, 2004, from http://www.childtrendsdatabank.org/indicators/30FeelSadorHopeless.cfm.

Cochran-Smith, M. (2003). Teaching quality matters. *Journal of Teacher Education*, *54*(2), 95–98.

Corbett, D., & Wilson, B. (2002). What urban students say about good teaching. *Educational Leadership*, *60*(1), 18–22.

Credit, A., & Garcia, M. (1999). *A study of relaxation techniques and coping skills with moderately to highly stressed middle and high school students*. Master's action research project. Saint Xavier University and IRI Skylight. [ERIC Document ED 434 298]

Darling-Hammond, L. (1995). Inequality and access to knowledge. In J. Banks (Ed.), *Handbook of research on multicultural education* (pp. 465–483). New York: Macmillan.

Darling-Hammond, L. (1996). The right to learn and the advancement of teaching: Research, policy, and practice for democratic education. *Educational Researcher*, *25*(6), 5–17.

Darling-Hammond, L. (1997). *The right to learn: A blueprint for creating schools that work*. San Francisco: Jossey-Bass.

Darling-Hammond, L., & Youngs, P. (2002). Defining "highly qualified teachers": What does "scientifically-based research" actually tell us? *Educational Researcher*, *31*(9), 13–25.

DeMoulin, D. F. (2002). Examining the impact of extra-curricular activities on the personal development of 149 high school seniors. *Journal of Instructional Psychology*, *29*(4), 297–304.

DeWit, D., McKee, C., Fjeld, J., & Karioja, K. (2003, December). *The critical role of school culture in student success*. Retrieved on April 4, 2004, from http://www.voices4children.org/report-Dec2003-1.htm.

DiMaggio, P. (1982). Cultural capital and school success: The impact of status culture participation on the grades of U.S. high school students. *American Sociological Review*, *47*, 189–201.

Doyle, K. O. (1977). Development of the student opinion survey. *Educational and Psychological Measurement*, *37*(2), 439–443.

Eisner, E. (1992). Educational reform and the ecology of schooling. *Teachers College Record*, *93*(4), 610–627.

Eisner, E. W. (2003). What does it mean to say that a school is doing well? In A. C. Ornstein, L. S. Behar-Ornstein, & E. F. Pajak (Eds.), *Contemporary issues in curriculum* (3rd ed., pp. 239–247). Boston: Allyn & Bacon.

Ekstrom, R. B., Goertz, M. E., Pollack, J. M., & Rock, D. A. (1986). Who drops out of high school and why? Findings from a national study. *Teachers College Record*, *87*(3), 356–373.

Elkind, D. (1981). *The hurried child*. Reading, MA: Addison-Wesley.

Evans, W., & Bechtel, D. (1997). *Extended school day/year programs: A research synthesis*. Philadelphia: Mid-Atlantic Lab for Student Success.

Fine, M., & Zane, N. (1989). Bein' wrapped too tight: When low-income women drop out of high school. In L. Weis, E. Farrar, & H. G. Petrie (Eds.), *Dropouts from school: Issues, dilemmas, and solutions* (pp. 23–53). Albany, NY: SUNY Press.

Finn, J. D. (1993). *School engagement and students at risk.* Washington, DC: National Center for Education Statistics.

Fraser, B. J., & Fisher, D. L. (1982). Predicting students' outcomes from their perceptions of classroom psychosocial environment. *American Educational Research Journal, 19,* 498–518.

Gazzaniga, M. S. (1992). *Nature's mind: The biological roots of thinking, emotions, sexuality, language, and intelligence.* New York: Basic Books.

Gilman, D. A., & Knoll, S. (1984). Increasing instructional time: What are the priorities and how do they affect the alternatives? *NASSP Bulletin, 68,* 41–44.

Glasser, W. (2003). A new look at school failure and school success. In A. C. Ornstein, L. S. Behar-Ornstein, & E. F. Pajak (Eds.), *Contemporary issues in curriculum* (3rd ed., pp. 231–238). Boston: Allyn & Bacon.

Gross, M. (1999). *The conspiracy of ignorance: The failure of American public schools.* New York: Perennial.

Guzman, L., Lippman, L., Moore, K. A., & O'Hare, W. (2003, July). *How children are doing: The mismatch between public perception and statistical reality.* Research Brief 2003-12. Washington, DC: Child Trends.

Haney, W. (1993). Testing and minorities. In L. Weis & M. Fine (Eds.), *Beyond silenced voices: Class, race, and gender in U.S. schools* (pp. 45–73). Albany, NY: SUNY Press.

Heubert, J. P., & Hauser, R. M. (1999). *High stakes: Testing for tracking, promotion, and graduation.* Washington, DC: National Academy Press.

Horatio Alger Association. (2002). *The state of our nation's youth, 2002–2003.* Washington, DC: Horatio Alger Association. [ERIC Document ED 467 073]

Hudson, L., & Hurst, D. (1999, August). *Students who prepare for college and a vocation.* (Issue Brief NCES 1999-072). Washington, DC: National Center for Education Statistics.

Huitt, W. (1997, April). *The SCANS report revisited.* Paper delivered at the 5th annual Gulf South Business and Vocational Education Conference, Valdosta, GA.

Inman-Crews, D. (2000). Children are cheated by emphasis on testing. *Tallahassee Democrat,* September 20.

Kingston, P. W. (2001). The unfulfilled promise of cultural capital theory. *Sociology of Education,* 88–99.

Kohn, A. (1999). *The schools our children deserve.* Boston: Houghton Mifflin.

Kolstad, A. J., & Owings, J. A. (1986). *High school dropouts who change their minds about school.* Washington, DC: Office of Educational Research and Improvement.

Kunzman, R. (2002). Extracurricular activities: Learning from the margin to rethink the whole. *Knowledge Quest, 30*(5), 22–25.

Lamborn, S. D., Brown, B. B., Mounts, N. S., & Steinberg, L. (1992). Putting school in perspective: The influence of family, peers, extracurricular participation, and part-time work on academic achievement. In F. M. Newmann (Ed.), *Student engagement and achievement in secondary schools* (pp. 153–181). New York: Teachers College Press.

Leonard, L. J. (2001, November). *Erosion of instructional time: Teacher concerns.* Paper presented at the annual meeting of the Mid-South Educational Research Association, Little Rock, AR.

Mann, D. (1987). Can we help dropouts? Thinking about the undoable. *Teachers College Record, 87*(3), 307–333.

Marshall, C. (1988, Spring). Bridging the chasm between policymakers and educators. *Theory Into Practice, 27*(2), 98–105.

Martirano, M. J. (1997, May–June). Changing seasons: Stress in a student's life. *Schools in the Middle, 6*(5), 39–40.

McLaren, P. (2003). *Life in schools: An introduction to critical pedagogy in the foundations of education* (4th ed). Boston: Allyn & Bacon.

McNeil, L. M. (2000). *Contradictions of school reform: Educational costs of standardized testing.* New York: Routledge.

Merrett, F., & Wheldall, K. (1989). *Positive teaching in the secondary school.* London: Paul Chapman Publishing.

Mitchell, D., Wirt, F., & Marshall, C. (1986). *Alternative state policy mechanisms for pursuing educational quality, equity, efficiency, and choice.* Final report to the U.S. Department of Education on Grant No. NIE-G-83-0020. Washington, DC: U.S. Department of Education, Office of Educational Research and Improvement.

Muto, D., & Wilk, J. (1993, July). *Managing stress.* Paper presented by the U.S. Department of Education. Topsham, ME.

National Center for Education Statistics (NCES). (1995, May). *High school students ten years after "A nation at risk."* Washington, DC: U.S. Department of Education.

National Center for Education Statistics (NCES). (1998, March). *Students' reports of school crime: 1989 and 1995.* Washington, DC: U.S. Department of Education.

National Center for Education Statistics (NCES). (2002). *The condition of education.* Washington, DC: U.S. Department of Education.

National Center for Education Statistics (NCES). (2003). *Mini-digest of education statistics, 2002.* Washington, DC: U.S. Department of Education.

National Council for Research on Women. (1991). *Risk, resiliency, and resistance: Current research on adolescent girls.* New York: Author.

National Council for Research on Women. (1998). *The girls report: What we know and need to know about growing up female.* New York: Lynn Phillips.

Nenortas, G. (1986). *Implementation of a program to reduce stress in middle school alternative education students.* A Practicum Report. Nova University.

Nesoff, E. (2003). Sounds of budget ax falling. *Christian Science Monitor.* Retrieved on August 26, 2003, from www.csmonitor.com/2003/0826/p19s01-lepr.html.

Oakes, J. (1985). *Keeping track: How schools structure inequality.* New Haven, CT: Yale University Press.

Oakes, J. (1990). *Multiplying inequalities: The effects of race, social class, and tracking on opportunities to learn mathematics and science.* Santa Monica, CA: The RAND Corporation.

O'Brien, E., & Rollefson, M. (June, 1995). *Extracurricular participation and student engagement*. Education Policy Issues: Statistical Perspectives (NCES 95-741). Washington, DC: NCES.

Ohanian, S. (1999). Is that penguin stuffed or real? In E. Clinchy (Ed.), *Reforming American education from the bottom to the top* (pp. 15–30). Portsmouth, NH: Heienmann.

O'Malley, P. M., Johnston, L. D., & Bachman, J. G. (1998). Alcohol use among adolescents. *Alcohol Health and Research World, 22*(2), 85–93.

Ornstein, A. C. (2003). Critical issues in teaching. In A. C. Ornstein, L. S. Behar-Ornstein, & E. F. Pajak (Eds.), *Contemporary issues in curriculum* (3rd ed., pp. 77–93). Boston: Allyn & Bacon.

Palmer, P. J. (2003). The heart of a teacher. In A. C. Ornstein, L. S. Behar-Ornstein, & E. F. Pajak (Eds.), *Contemporary issues in curriculum* (3rd ed., pp. 66–76). Boston: Allyn & Bacon.

Pope, D. C. (2001). *"Doing school": How we are creating a generation of stressed out, materialistic, and miseducated students.* New Haven, CT: Yale University Press.

Posner, G. (1988). Models of curriculum planning. In L. E. Beyer & M. W. Apple (Eds.), *The curriculum: Problems, politics, and possibilities* (pp. 77–97). Albany, NY: SUNY Press.

President's Council on Physical Fitness and Sports. (1997). *Physical activity and sport in the lives of girls: Physical and mental health dimensions from an interdisciplinary approach.* Minneapolis: Center for Research on Girls and Women in Sport.

Public Agenda. (2002). *Reality check 2002.* Retrieved January 2, 2004, from http://www.publicagenda.org/specials/rcheck2002/reality.htm.

Redd, Z., Brooks, J., & McGarvey, A. M. (2002, August). *Educating America's youth: What makes a difference.* Research Brief. Washington, DC: Child Trends.

Rose, L. C., & Gallup, A. M. (2003). The 35th annual Phi Delta Kappa/Gallup poll of the public's attitudes toward the public schools. *Phi Delta Kappan, 85*(1), 41–52.

Rutter, M., Giller, H., & Hagell, A. (1998). *Antisocial behavior by young people.* Cambridge: Cambridge University Press.

Ryska, T. A. (2002). The effects of athletic identity and motivation goals on global competence perceptions of student-athletes. *Child Study Journal, 32*(2), 109–129.

Sanchez, R. (2004, February 23). More overachieving teens being urged to slow down [online]. *Rocky Mountain News.* Retrieved February 24, 2004, from http://www.rockymountainnews.com/drmn/education/article/0,1299,DRMN_957_2676031,00.html.

Sanders, W., & Horn, S. (1998). Research findings from the Tennessee Value-Added Assessment System (TVAAS) database: Implications for educational evaluation and research. *Journal of Personnel Evaluation in Education, 12*(3), 247–256.

Scherer, M. (2002a). Who cares? And who wants to know? *Educational Leadership, 60*(1), 5.

Scherer, M. (2002b). Do students care about learning? A conversation with Mihaly Csikszentmihalyi. *Educational Leadership, 60*(1), 12–17.

Schmidt, W. H., McKnight, C. C., & Raizen, S. A. (1996). *Splintered vision: An investigation of U.S. science and mathematics education: Executive summary.* Lansing, MI: U.S. National Research Center for the Third International Mathematics and Science Study, Michigan State University.

Schmoker, M. J., & Marzano, R. J. (2003). Realizing the promise of standards-based education. In A. C. Ornstein, L. S. Behar-Ornstein, & E. F. Pajak (Eds.), *Contemporary issues in curriculum* (3rd ed., pp. 262–267). Boston: Allyn & Bacon.

Seeman, M. (1975). Alienation studies. *Annual Review of Sociology, 1,* 91–123.

Senge, P.(2000). The industrial age system of education. In P. Senge, N. Cambron-McCabe, T. Lucas, B. Smith, J. Dutton, & A. Kleiner (Eds.), *Schools that learn: A fifth discipline fieldbook for educators, parents, and everyone who cares about education* (pp. 3–58). New York: Doubleday.

Singh, K., Granville, M., & Dika, S. (2002). Mathematics and science achievement: Effects of motivation, interest, and academic engagement. *Journal of Educational Research, 95(6),* 323–332.

Sizer, T. R., & Sizer, N. F. (1999). *The students are watching.* Boston: Beacon Press.

Sizer, T. R., & Sizer, N. F. (2003). Grappling. In A. C. Ornstein, L. S. Behar-Ornstein, & E. F. Pajak (Eds.), *Contemporary issues in curriculum* (3rd ed., pp. 141–148). Boston: Allyn & Bacon.

Smith, T. M. (1995, May). *High school students ten years after "A nation at risk"* (NCES 95-764). Washington, DC: NCES.

Stiggins, R. J. (2003). Assessment, student confidence, and school success. In A. C. Ornstein, L. S. Behar-Ornstein, & E. F. Pajak (Eds.), *Contemporary issues in curriculum* (3rd ed., pp. 197–209). Boston: Allyn & Bacon.

Stolp, S. (1994). *Leadership for school culture.* (ERIC Digest, 91. ED370198).

Stolp, S., & Smith, S. C. (1994, January). *School culture and climate: The role of the leader.* OSSC Bulletin. Eugene: Oregon School Study Council.

Taylor, K. L. (2003). Through the eyes of students. *Educational Leadership, 60(4),* 72–75.

Texas Commission on Drug and Alcohol Abuse. (n.d). *TCADA online.* Retrieved February 12, 2004, from http://www.tcada.state.tx.us/research/studies.shtml.

Thompson, S. (2001). The authentic standards movement and its evil twin. *Phi Delta Kappan, 82(5),* 358–362.

Tomlinson, C. A. (2002). Invitations to learn. *Educational Leadership, 60(1),* 7–10.

U.S. Department of Education. (1983). *A nation at risk.* Retrieved on July 15, 2003, from http://www.ed.gov/pubs/NatAtRisk/index.html

Weber, D. (2004). 3rd-graders are bracing for FCAT. *Orlando Sentinel.* Retrieved on March 1, 2004, from http://www.ctnow.com/entertainment/orl-asecpassfcat 01030104mar01,0,3959883.story.

Webster, C. (2000). Pitching, dancing, and budget cuts. In L. Weis & M. Fine (Eds.), *Construction sites: Excavating race, class, and gender among urban youth* (pp. 235–248). New York: Teachers College Press.

Weis, L., Farrar, E., & Petrie, H. G. (1989). Introduction. In L. Weis, E. Farrar, & H. G. Petrie (Eds.), *Dropouts from school: Issues, dilemmas, and solutions* (pp. ix–xvi). Albany, NY: SUNY Press.

Wiggins, G. (1993). *Assessing student performance*. San Francisco: Jossey-Bass.

Wilson, V. (2002). *Feeling the strain: An overview of the literature on teachers' stress*. Edinburgh: Scottish Council for Research in Education.

Winne, P. H., & Marx, R. W. (1980). Matching students' cognitive responses to teaching skills. *Journal of Educational Psychology, 72*(2), 257–264.

Wong, H. K., & Wong, R. (1998). *The first days of school*. Mountain View, CA: Harry K. Wong Publications.

Wittrock, M. C. (1986). Students' thought processes. In M. C. Wittrock (Ed.), *Handbook of research on teaching* (3rd ed., pp. 297–314). New York: Macmillan.

Wragg, E. C., Haynes, G. S., Wragg, C. M., & Chamberlin, R. P. (2000). *Failing teachers?* London: Routledge.

Index

~

About the Author

Lisa Scherff is an assistant professor of English education in the College of Education, Health, and Human Sciences at the University of Tennessee, Knoxville, where she teaches methods, research, and educational policy courses. Her research interests include opportunity to learn, the effect of high-stakes tests on the language arts curriculum, methods of teacher preparation, and the mentoring and retention of new teachers.